Journalism and Citizenship

Journalism is in the middle of sweeping changes in its relationships with the communities it serves, and the audiences for news and public affairs it seeks to address. Changes in technology have blurred the lines between professionals and citizens, partisan and objective bystanders, particularly in the emerging public zones of the blogosphere. This volume examines these changes and the new concepts needed to understand them in the days and years ahead.

With contributions from up-and-coming scholars, this collection identifies key issues and paves the way for further research on the role of journalism in today's world. It will appeal to scholars, researchers, and advanced students in journalism, communication, and media studies, and will also be of interest to those in public affairs, political science, and government.

Zizi Papacharissi is Professor and Head of the Communication Department, University of Illinois-Chicago. Her research focuses on the social and political uses of newer media, and has appeared in *New Media & Society, Harvard Journal of International Press & Politics*, and the *Journal of Broadcasting and Electronic Media*, among other journals. She is currently working on *The Networked Self*, an edited volume on online social networks, and *A Private Sphere*, a monograph volume on contemporary and digitally enabled modes of civic engagement.

New Agendas in Communication
Roderick Hart and Stephen Reese, Series Editors
*A Series from Routledge and the College of Communication
at the University of Texas at Austin*

This series brings together groups of emerging scholars to tackle important interdisciplinary themes that demand new scholarly attention and reach broadly across the communication field's existing courses. Each volume stakes out a key area, presents original findings, and considers the long-range implications of its "new agenda."

Interplay of Truth and Deception
Matt McGlone and Mark Knapp

Journalism and Citizenship
Zizi Papacharissi

Understanding Science
LeeAnn Kahlor and Patricia Stout

Political Emotions
Janet Staiger

Media Literacy
Kathleen Tyner

Journalism and Citizenship: New Agendas in Communication

Edited by
Zizi Papacharissi

A Volume in the New Agendas in
Communication Series

Routledge
Taylor & Francis Group

NEW YORK AND LONDON

First published 2009
by Routledge
270 Madison Ave, New York, NY 10016

Simultaneously published in the UK
by Routledge
2 Park Square, Milton Park, Abingdon, Oxon OX14 4RN

Routledge is an imprint of the Taylor & Francis Group, an informa business

© 2009 Taylor & Francis

Typeset in Gill Sans and Goudy
by Swales & Willis Ltd, Exeter, Devon
Printed and bound in the United States of America on acid-free paper by Edwards Brothers, Inc.

Library of Congress Cataloging in Publication Data
Journalism and citizenship: new agendas in communication / edited by Zizi Papacharissi.
    p. cm. — (New agendas in communication series)
    Includes index.
    1. Online journalism. 2. Internet—Social aspects.
    3. Internet—Political aspects. 4. Web publishing.
    5. Media literacy. 6. Convergence (Communication)
    I. Papacharissi, Zizi.
    PN4784.O62J66 2009
    070.4—dc22
    2009004355

ISBN10: 0–415–80499–X (hbk)
ISBN10: 0–415–80498–1 (pbk)
ISBN10: 0–203–87126–X (ebk)

ISBN13: 978–0–415–80499–8 (hbk)
ISBN13: 978–0–415–80498–1 (pbk)
ISBN13: 978–0–203–87126–3 (ebk)

Contents

Preface   vii
Acknowledgments   xiv
Contributors   xv

Introduction: Toward a (New) Media Literacy
  in a Media Saturated World   1
  DAN GILLMOR

PART I
**Journalism's Evolution in the Era of the
  Active Audience**   13

1 Journalism, Citizenship, and Digital Culture   15
  MARK DEUZE

2 The Citizen is the Message: Alternative Modes of Civic
  Engagement   29
  ZIZI PAPACHARISSI

3 Institutional Roadblocks: Assessing Journalism's Response
  to Changing Audiences   44
  WILSON LOWREY

PART II
The Public's Relationship with Digital Content 69

4 Producing Citizen Journalism or Producing Journalism for
Citizens: A New Multimedia Model to Enhance
Understanding of Complex News 71
RONALD A. YAROS

5 Information Surplus in the Digital Age: Impact and
Implications 91
HSIANG IRIS CHYI

6 Blogs, Journalism, and Political Participation 108
HOMERO GIL DE ZÚÑIGA

7 The Many Faced "You" of Social Media 123
SHARON MERAZ

PART III
The Impact of the Citizen as Mass Communicator 149

8 What the Blogger Knows 151
DONALD MATHESON

9 "Searching for My Own Unique Place in the Story": A
Comparison of Journalistic and Citizen-Produced Coverage
of Hurricane Katrina's Anniversary 166
SUE ROBINSON

10 Mapping Citizen Coverage of the Dual City 189
LOU RUTIGLIANO

Index 206

Preface

Zizi Papacharissi

Journalism and Citizenship: An Uneasy Alliance

The relationship between journalism and citizenship is symbiotic, though not always synergetic. Journalism is enabled by the democratic emphasis on freedom of speech, free will, and collective decision-making. Journalism can function within or without democracy; in dictatorships or monarchies, journalists' coverage of abuses of power is typically instrumental in cultivating democratic resistance. Journalism is based on democratic values, but can thrive with or without democracy. The argument can be made that journalism becomes more central to a society, and possibly more potent, the more directly it is connected to serving a democracy, its polity, and its people. On occasion, this may occur in the absence of democracy. *Association*, the coming together of people for a common purpose, presents the opposite of monarchy, and in a democracy, is facilitated by the press.

It is via *association* that citizens are able to perform their democratic duties, and the press has been instrumental in providing citizens with the information, venues, and tools needed to associate freely and for the common good of a democratic state. Journalism is perceived by many as synonymous with democracy (Carey, 1995; de Tocqueville 1835/1840; Dewey, 1927; Lippmann, 1922), although as Schudson (2008) cleverly points out, most philosophical works on democracy tend to leave journalism out of the picture. Even those who engage the press in discussions of democracy are careful to specify the circumstances under which journalism functions optimally for a democracy. Ambivalent about the merits of freedom of the press, de Toqueville had found the American Press too de-centralized, commercial, and editorial to be truly powerful. Lippman (1922) had hoped to task journalists with the democratic charge of creating and relaying a *pseudoenvironment* of events that might be too remote or complex for ordinary citizens to experience and comprehend. Essential as this *pseudoenviroment* was to maintaining an informed public, Lippman (1922) maintained reservations about the ability of the average individual (including journalists) to obtain perfect information, process it impartially, and engage in competent decision-making. Dewey's (1927) model of journalism evolved beyond Lippmann's (1922) transmission oriented approach, to one that specifically outlined the ways in which journalism enabled the audience to become informed and involved citizens. Even though Dewey (1927) was more hopeful than Lippmann about the prospect of a "Great Public," and journalism as communication enabling this "Great Community," he expressed reservation about the role of elites and commercially imposed hegemony interfering with the objectives of public journalism. Carey (1995) channeled this idea of public journalism to a contemporary context, and characterized the concepts of democracy and journalism as overlapping and serving the same end: an intelligent and informed community of citizens. But of course, his argument also paid attention to the role economic and socio-cultural forces, as well as technology, play in adjusting the ways in which journalism connects with citizens.

But scholars are trained to analyze the world around them, and to then sketch out ideal models, and there is an operative difference between the ideal roles assigned in a democracy, and the conditions under which these roles may be optimally performed. In *Six or Seven Things News can do for Democracy*, Michael Schudson (2008) listed the following seven functions journalism has served in democracies: informing the public, investigation, analysis, social empathy, public forum, mobilization, and the latest one, publicizing representative democracy. Complex social, cultural, political, and economic conditions affect the ability of journalists to perform these functions, frequently and sometimes, inadvertently, disconnecting journalists and citizens further. For instance, the "dumbing down" of the public, the tabloidization of news, and the focus on infotainment de-emphasize the democratic function of the press to inform, analyze, and serve as public forum for discussion (e.g., McNair, 2000). The professionalization and subsequent commercialization of the news further distances reporters from the public (e.g., Benson & Neveu, 2005; Bourdieu, 1998). These trends build on growing public cynicism and distrust of the media (Cappella & Jamieson, 1996; Entman, 1989; Fallows, 1996a, b; Patterson, 1996), which compromise the social empathy and informative/investigative functions of the press. Finally, web-related innovation enables direct citizen intervention to the media agenda, reifying citizen journalists, and thus rendering making the democratic space upon which citizens and journalists interact more "porous" (Blumler & Gurevitch, 2001), pluralistic (Bimber, 1998), and directly representative (Coleman, 2005). Online technologies create alternative ways for mobilization, public discussion, and news coverage that frequently leave journalists confused about their own place in a dormant public sphere.

The socio-cultural context that journalists and citizens inhabit outlines and complicates the paths on which journalists and citizens intersect in a contemporary democracy. In July of 2007, a group of scholars from around the world convened at the College of Communication, in the University of Texas at Austin, to participate in a two-day conference titled "Journalism and Citizenship: New Agendas." The goal was to collectively contemplate how technology has changed the role of journalism in society, in the first in a series of academic conferences featuring up-and-coming scholars studying the most important issues in communication. All of the conference participants contributed a chapter to this volume.

The chapters in this volume examine the intersections of journalism and citizenship in the present tense, informed by past practices and with an eye to the future. The contributors to this volume evaluate the confluence and tensions between journalism and citizenship from a variety of perspectives. Dan Gillmor kick-starts this volume by arguing against a model that employs journalism's past in order to predict its future. Placing the emphasis on citizen media, he sketches a media landscape on which citizen and commercial media emerge as complements and not substitutes to each other. In this landscape of the present, the question, per Gillmor, is not "Who is journalist," but rather, "What is journalism." Within this context, Deuze, Papacharissi and Lowrey consider processes of stability and change, as journalism evolves to cater to an audience equipped with the ability to consume and produce media content. Mark Deuze sketches out the theoretical boundaries of newer modes of citizenship and journalism. Accepting that the contemporary citizen is "monitorial," he argues for a "liquid" journalism that best serves this citizen. The basis of this relationship is removed from a perfect information premise; a tradition that conceives informed citizens as the end-goal and journalism as the means to that end within contemporary democracy. Journalism beats to the drum of democracy; albeit a networked democracy, resting on a journalism that becomes enabler and amplifier of conversations of varying content and potency.

Operating from a similar set of assumptions, Zizi Papacharissi focuses on the citizen within this model, who, in this abundance and multitude of information retreats to a private sphere, from which this complex and information-filled democracy may be managed. Stepping back from public spaces, the citizen returns to a (frequently domestic) private sphere of activity, equipped with tools that enable, but do not guarantee engagement. It is from this private sphere that the contemporary citizen scans information, deliberates, lurks in on political conversation, becomes engaged, produces, consumes, or rejects media content, and elects to enter the public sphere again (or not). As the citizen tends to civic duty in solitude, (s)he is alone, but not lonely; isolated, yet connected at the same time. The citizen is fully poised to become active, but whether activity follows depends on socio-cultural structure.

In an environment of ongoing change and instability, attention must be heeded to the processes of stability and stasis. Wilson Lowrey examines the forces at work behind journalism's complicated relationship with the public, explaining both journalistic tendencies to preserve norms and traditions and tensions emanating from human agents both within and outside the media organization. Lowrey argues that change is a function of both socio-cultural structure and human agency, but is best effected through an understanding of its polar opposite, stasis. It is through this understanding of inability to change that the divide between news media and audience may be re-conceptualized, and it is within this framework that the possibility of a decentralized, egalitarian news generation and distribution system presents itself.

So, journalism in the era of the converged audience is set to both change and remain the same. Yaros, Chyi, Gil de Zúñiga, and Meraz explore what it means to be part of a converged audience in an era of evolving stasis for journalists. Certainly, audiences are equipped with the technological equipment, and, in some cases, the technological know-how and literacy to function as both consumers and producers of media content. Possession of the ability to produce content does not guarantee content-producing behaviors. How may scholars incorporate this potentiality to research journalism and citizenship? Ron Yaros specifies that communicating complex issues is not new, but the circumstances under which the challenge presents itself in contemporary democracies are. Within a web based, non-linear environment of information accumulation and dispersion, different patterns of informational hierarchy and sense-making emerge. Through the proposed *PICK* model, Yaros articulates four components around which scholars and practitioners may begin to organize thoughts: Personalization, Involvement, Contiguity, and Kick-Outs. Examining points of engagement (and disengagement) with information online, Yaros maps out the boundaries and methods for citizen and professional journalists to communicate complex issues.

In the same vein of explicating audience activity in the age of convergence in journalism, Iris Chyi turns her attention to the concept of information surplus to explain changes in information seeking behaviors. From this economically-oriented standpoint, information surplus produced in excess under zero-sum assumptions can only flood out the information market. Faced with the prospect of indefinite and infinite amounts of information, the question then becomes: Is there a point at which excess information leads to dysfunction? And, within the schema of deliberative democracy, how does information surplus enable (or disable) informed decision making?

Homero Gil de Zúñiga analyzes general data on blogging uses, and traces relationships between bloggers, journalists, and political engagement, thus mapping out the intersections of citizen and professional journalists with the objectives of contemporary democracy. The data specify distinct patterns for citizen and professional journalists, depicting different ways in which both contribute to the information management routines of a representative democracy. More than anything, citizen journalists cannot only expand and watchdog the information sphere, but can also help reconnect detached citizens to a more robust democracy.

Sharon Meraz picks up on peer-to-peer news sharing in social media news aggregators as an organic response to the need for managing such information surplus. The democratic potential of sites like Newsvine, Digg, and Reddit is located in their ability to host citizen input and allow citizen-determined news agendas to emerge. At the same time, the open structure, as Meraz shows, induces elements of disposability and infotainment to the processes of citizen-based news gathering, which in turn compromises the democratic viability of these sites. Less deliberative and focused more on community-based information management, these sites grant the citizen a negotiating hand at the news agenda-setting table. How this hand will be played, and with what repercussions to the ways in which we practice democracy remains to be seen, and is a question examined by the final chapters to the volume.

Matheson, Robinson, and Rutigliano directly engage the impact of the citizen as mass communicator. Donald Matheson situates blogging within wider socio-cultural values in Western societies, which emphasize immediacy, the subjective, and reward decentralization. Blogs emerge out of, reflect, and reproduce these tendencies. Their power and place in democracy is both granted and compromised by them. And yet, Matheson asks, perhaps we are better off looking for the impact of blogging not in displaced journalism, but rather in the displaced citizen psyche, which via blogging, is offered a path toward self-actualization and group cohesion. Of course, cynics would argue, contemporary democracy is filled with citizens obsessed with themselves and self-referencing, a practice that does not inherently help them tune in to the civic demands of the polity (Lasch, 1979; Sennett, 1978).

In search for this "displaced citizen psyche," Sue Robinson shows how blogging Hurricane Katrina helps society form its collective memory of the tragedy, in a manner that enables identity expression and social cohesion. Robinson documents how online versions of collective memory differ from mainstream recollections of the event. In this case, the individual's self evolves beyond narcissistic self-reflection to the level of authoritative memory writer. Citizens contribute their memories and reflections of the event, which place them in the story, and alongside mainstream journalists as equal and unique contributors to news gathering and recollection. Thus, online storytelling space is claimed and used to re-negotiate the locus of the narrative, and place of the individual within this narrative, putting forward a model of practicing journalism that allocated citizen and journalist unique storytelling duties.

Still, Hurricane Katrina presented a major news story, covered by the mainstream and through blog and alternative news sources. Rutigliano turns to untold stories that escape the news gathering radars of both mainstream and alternative media, or remain in marginal spaces where the possibility of intersection with networked or online spheres of news coverage is minimal. It is these "unknown" stories that expose digital divides of access and literacy that persist in both journalist and citizen-produced news coverage. How do the inequalities of the offline world transfer on to the online sphere of citizen and professional journalists? Evolving beyond enabling citizens, the question then concerns enabling marginal citizens and their invisible stories, an ethical responsibility that Rutigliano argues remains with professional journalists and effectively renders them agents of democracy.

All contributions demonstrate how functions that have, in the past, been associated with journalism are now redistributed across a variety of organizations, some of which involve media professionals and others which develop around involved citizens. Each chapter outlines what we know about the evolving question of journalism and citizenship and ponders what we don't know, coming up with distinct and unique answers: Gillmor's call for a New Literacy, Deuze's Liquid Journalism, Papacharissi's Private Sphere, Lowery's Change and Stasis antithesis, Yaros' PICK model, Chyi's use of Information Surplus, Gil de Zúñiga's parallel paths of citizen and journalist bloggers, Meraz's Many-Faced-You, Matheson's locating of the Displaced Citizen underneath the poignant "what the blogger knows," Robinson's appropriation of citizen and journalist signature matrixes to lead the misplaced "self" back into the story, and Rutigliano's connection of misplaced and unknown stories to the ethical responsibilities of journalisms.

These works reflect the ways in which a representative democracy depends on journalism, in order to be both wholly representative and utterly democratic. Concurrently, the ideal of a vibrant democracy breathes life into journalism, in democratic and non-democratic eras. Converged media environments outline newer directions for scholars, students, and practitioners of journalism and democracy. What constitutes journalism, and what does not? Under what theoretical premise do we judge and evaluate offline and online journalism? What is the ethic of the contemporary, fluid journalism, and does it include a democratic compass? Who is the citizen journalist and how is (s)he different from the citizen? What is fact, and what is story, and who is responsible for providing either, citizen or journalist? Finally, as the boundaries between public, private, political, cultural, social, or economic blur, how do we raise intelligible citizens? Some of these questions will always be with us, as it is part of human history to struggle with the distinctions between fact, story, and ultimately, truth(s). And journalists, both citizen and professional, may always be imperfect agents of bringing us closer to fact, story, truth. Perhaps this is where Schudson's (2008) seventh "thing" that the press may do for democracy becomes relevant, as it outlines an ethically-oriented responsibility for journalists: that of publicizing representative democracy. In an environment of constant fluidity and reflexivity, where stasis and change are equal partners, where literate citizen journalists negotiate a place for themselves and their stories in the news agenda yet unknown stories remain untold, this ethical responsibility is the one constant of the journalistic profession.

If the current times enable everyone to inform, analyze, investigate, then the responsibility of the journalist is to still do all of those things, via publicizing representative democracy. If current technology allows public spaces where empathy, mobilization, and expression may exist outside the formula mainstream media organization, then it is the responsibility of media organizations to continue providing these opportunities because these opportunities are representative democracy. Of course any citizen may choose to publicize representative democracy; it is not a task exclusive to journalists. But for journalists, it is the ethical responsibility that marks and bounds their profession, just like doctors are bound by the ethical responsibility to not refuse care, lawyers by the confidentiality of client information, and academics marked by the obligation to share and pursue ideas. It is this ethical responsibility that does not separate journalists from citizens or citizen journalists, but rather, reconnects journalism and citizenship within the ethos of a democracy.

References

Benson, R., & Neveu, E. (2005) (Eds.). *Bourdieu and the journalistic field*. Cambridge: Polity.

Bimber, B. (1998). The Internet and political transformation: Populism, community, and accelerated pluralism. *Polity, 3*, 133–160.

Blumler, J. G., & Gurevitch, M. (2001). The new media and our political communication discontents: Democratizing cyberspace. *Information, Communication & Society, 4*, 1–14.

Bourdieu, P. (1998). *On Television*. (Trans., Priscilla Parkhurst Ferguson). New York: New Press.

Cappella, J., & Jamieson, K. H. (1996). News frames, political cynicism, and media cynicism. *Annals, AAPSS, 546,* 71–96.

Carey, J. (1995). The press, public opinion, and public discourse. In T. Glasser & C. Salmon (Eds.), *Public opinion and the communication of consent* (pp. 373–402). New York: Guilford.

Coleman, S. (2005). The lonely citizen: Indirect representation in an age of networks. *Political Communication, 22*(2), 197–214

de Tocqueville, A. (1835/1840). *De la démocratie en Amerique (1835/1840)—Democracy in America*. Trans. and Eds., Harvey C. Mansfield and Delba Winthrop (2000). Chicago: University of Chicago Press.

Dewey, J. (1927). *The public and its problems*. New York: Holt, 1927.

Entman, R. (1989). *Democracy without citizens*. New York : Oxford.

Fallows, J. (1996). *Breaking the news*. New York: Pantheon.

Lasch, C. (1979). *The culture of narcissism*. New York: Norton & Co.

Lippmann, W. (1922). *Public opinion*. New York: Free Press.

McNair, B. (2000). *Journalism and democracy: An evaluation of the political public sphere*. London: Routledge.

Patterson, T. (1996). Bad news, bad governance. *Annals, AAPSS, 546*, 71–96.

Schudson, M. (2008). *Why democracies need an unlovable press*. Cambridge, UK: Polity Press.

Sennett, R. (1978). *The fall of public man*. New York: Vintage.

Acknowledgments

This edited volume is the product of the conference on "Journalism and Citizenship: New Agendas," hosted by the College of Communication at the University of Texas at Austin in July 2007. The editor would like to thank Mark Tremayne, Assistant Professor in the School of Journalism, University of Texas at Austin, for his work on organizing and hosting the conference. The conference and this volume would not have been possible without the support of Roderick Hart, Dean and Allan B. Shivers Centennial Chair in Communication, and Steve Reese, Jesse H. Jones Professor and Associate Dean of Academic Affairs at the College of Communication at UT–Austin. The contributors to this volume make it stand out, and I would like to thank them for their inspiration, insight, and diligence.

Contributors

Editor

Zizi Papacharissi is Professor and Head of the Communication Department, University of Illinois-Chicago. Her research focuses on the social and political uses of newer media, and has appeared in *New Media & Society*, *Harvard Journal of International Press & Politics*, and *Journal of Broadcasting and Electronic Media*, among other journals. She is currently working on *The Networked Self*, an edited volume on online social networks, and *A Private Sphere*, a monograph volume on contemporary and digitally enabled modes of civic engagement.

Contributors

Hsiang Iris Chyi is an assistant professor in the School of Journalism at The University of Texas at Austin. Her research interests include the economics of new media, online journalism, and news framing. The goal of her recent research is to demystify the economic nature of online news. Her work has been published in *Journalism & Mass Communication Quarterly*, *Journal of Media Economics*, *Newspaper Research Journal*, *International Journal of Media Management*, etc. Chyi has worked for several online organizations and has taught theoretical and skills courses such as Economics of New Media, Information Technology and Society, Multimedia Journalism, Directions in News Technology, and Communication Research Methods. She was on the faculty at the University of Arizona (2004–2007) and the Chinese University of Hong Kong (2000–2004). She received her Ph.D. from the University of Texas at Austin, her M.A. from Stanford University, and her B.A. from National Taiwan University.

Mark Deuze has a joint appointment at Indiana University's Department of Telecommunications in Bloomington, the United States, and as Professor of Journalism and New Media at Leiden University, the Netherlands. Recent publications include *Media Work* (Polity Press, 2007), and numerous articles in journals such as *New Media & Society*, *Journalism Studies*, *The Information Society*, and *The International Journal of Cultural Studies*. Weblog: deuze.blogspot.com., e-mail: mdeuze@indiana.edu.

Homero Gil de Zúñiga received a Ph.D. in European Studies at Universidad Europea de Madrid (2006), and a second doctoral degree in Mass Communication at University of Wisconsin–Madison (2008). He currently leads the Center for Journalism and Communication Research at University of Texas–Austin, where he is an assistant professor. Dr. Zuniga's research interest centers on all forms of digital media and their effect on society. In particular, he studies the influence of Internet use in people's daily lives and in the democratic process.

Dan Gillmor is director of the new Knight Center for Digital Media Entrepreneurship and Kauffman Professor of Digital Media Entrepreneurship at Arizona State University's Cronkite School of Journalism and Mass Communication. He is also director of the Center for Citizen Media, an affiliate of the Berkman Center for Internet and Society at Harvard University Law School and Arizona State, and is author of *We the Media: Grassroots Journalism by the People, for the People* (O'Reilly Media, 2004), a book that explains the rise of citizens' media and why it matters.

Wilson Lowrey is an associate professor in the College of Communication and Information Sciences at the University of Alabama (USA). His research focuses on the sociology of news work, with a particular emphasis on the impact of changing social structures and new technologies on decision-making at the organizational and occupational levels. Lowrey's work has been published in a number of journals, including *Journalism & Mass Communication Quarterly*, *Journalism*, *Journal of Media Economics*, and *Mass Communication and Society*.

Donald Matheson is Senior Lecturer in Mass Communication at the University of Canterbury, New Zealand. He is the author of *Media Discourses* (2005), co-author with Stuart Allan of *Digital War Reporting* (forthcoming) and co-editor of the journal *Ethical Space: The International Journal of Communication Ethics*. He writes on journalism practices, with particular emphasis on news language and the communicative ethics of the news, interests which have led him to study weblogs and other digital media. He previously worked at Cardiff and Strathclyde universities in the UK and as a journalist in New Zealand.

Sharon Meraz is an Assistant Professor in the Department of Communication, University of Illinois, Chicago. Her research focuses on the theoretical and practical impact of networked, social media technologies on citizen political engagement, citizen media, digital democracy, and mass media evolution.

Sue Robinson attained her Ph.D. in 2007 from Temple University after a dozen years as a reporter. In January 2007, she began on the tenure track as an assistant professor at the University of Wisconsin-Madison's School of Journalism & Mass Communication where she teaches journalistic skills and press theory and helps direct the School's professional-track MA program. Robinson studies online journalism, narrative writing, and collective memory in the press.

Lou Rutigliano is an Assistant Professor at DePaul University, where he teaches courses in online journalism, alternative and citizen media, and the impact of the Internet on journalism and the news industry. His research is currently interested in the critical and cultural dimensions of networked journalism, and how networked journalism shapes, and is shaped by, newsrooms, journalism schools, and cities.

Ronald A. Yaros is Assistant Professor of Multimedia Journalism in the Philip Merrill College of Journalism at the University of Maryland. He also directs the Lab for Communicating Complexity With Multimedia (http://www. merrill.umd.edu/ronyaros/), which focuses on news about science, health, and technology. Prior to completing a Ph.D. at the University of Wisconsin-Madison, he completed a Master's in education and served as President of a national educational software corporation for nearly ten years. His journalism career began in 1979 as a radio and television anchor and science reporter.

Introduction

Toward a (New) Media Literacy in a Media Saturated World

Dan Gillmor

Summary

In a media-saturated age, amid an evolving ecosystem of journalism and community information, we need to revive and revise media literacy. The need has never been greater, and the benefits more plain. Yet we are missing sufficient participation from the people who should carry this torch: parents, schools, universities and the traditional media themselves.

Media Shift

Media are becoming democratized. This is not so much in the sense of voting—though balloting is one small element in developing technology—but participation. The tools of creating media are growing more powerful, less expensive and easier to use every year. Especially in the developed world, but increasingly in the developing world as well, we own and carry around powerful media-creation tools such as personal computers, digital cameras, smart phones and much more.

The other major democratization is access, but this is less well understood in the context of traditional media. With mass media—newspapers, magazines, radio, television—we created media and then distribute it: We manufactured print products and put them on trucks, delivering them to doorsteps, post offices and news sellers, or we made a TV and broadcast it over the airwaves. We were selling products, in a one-to-many system.

Today, we create media and *make it available, on a many-to-many network of networks*. People who may be interested come and get it. Although there is an element of distribution in this process—namely the marketing so that people know that the content is available—this approach differs from the past methods in fairly radical ways. People can get what they want, from an enormous variety of sources, and they can get it on their own desktop or phone right now, arranged as they choose.

These shifts toward democratized media have also turned the World Wide Web into a read-write medium, where it is nearly as easy to write online (using the broadest form of the word "write" to include all kinds of media) as it is to read. Weblogs, or blogs, were the first major instance of this shift, but the read-write Web is a reality.

These evolutionary changes, as noted, turn mere consumers of media into creators. And, crucially, they encourage some subset of those creators to become collaborators, using the collaborative communications inherent in the Internet. The latter evolution may, in the end, be the most important but, so far, least understood or well developed.

Some of the same tools and technologies that make media creation so easy and ubiquitous have had a dramatic impact on the business of traditional journalism, however. That impact is destructive. While some of the encroachment is journalistic—that is, competition from new entrants who win readers/viewers/listeners away from traditional sources—the key effect is on what we used to call the "business side" of the journalistic house. New competitors for the revenue streams are systematically separating advertising from the journalism ads used to support. Daily newspapers, which once enjoyed monopolies in most American communities and extracted monopoly profits from those places, are finding their business eroding, if not imploding, at an accelerating rate in an era of actual competition for which they are woefully unprepared. Broadcasters are seeing their audiences dwindle quickly, and their own advertising bases are shrinking commensurately.

We are losing something important as we lose our daily newspapers' ability to cover local news and issues. It's too late to imagine their revival, except under radically different management and in radically different form. But we are only the beginning stages of an emerging, more diverse ecosystem of journalism where a host of competitors collectively provides a more nuanced and valuable information flow to the people who need it most—all of us, who function under a system of self-government.

New Creators

When scientists believe they understand something, they test to ensure that they're right. They gather data that either supports or refutes their hypotheses (or, worse than either of those, merely muddles their understanding), and move on from there. Millions of new blogs, online videos, podcasts, social networks, Web 2.0 interactive ventures and much more have become the data set for our emerging media/journalism ecosystem. Let's examine just a few, as anecdotal examples of where we're heading.

- Consider, for instance, the Daily Kos, a website with a leftward political bias that has ardently worked for political change in recent years. It has more readers each day for its political content than most newspapers have readers.
- On Facebook, individuals or groups of people tell each other about their own latest happenings or point each other to wider news. They organize gatherings and games.

- Pambazuka, an African podcasting network, gives us stories we would never have heard in the past. These are stories about the lives of people who, except for the occasional report from major media, have been essentially invisible.
- In the World of Warcraft, a massive multiplayer online game to which millions of people subscribe around the globe, people gather in guilds to accomplish collective tasks.
- Blog Africa and the SFist (the latter is based in San Francisco) have little in common except that they are group blogs covering and aggregating information about geographical places. GigaOm, also based in San Francisco, covers a community of interest—technology—rather than place, deeply and relentlessly.
- People post their homemade videos to YouTube, Blip.TV and many other sites that offer hosting for what we create or remix from other sources. These sites are turning into vast, vital repositories not just for people's randomness, but also for some of the key political and cultural events of our times.
- Wikipedia, the online encyclopedia that (almost) anyone can edit, grows larger and better each day. It is perhaps the singularly most important collaborative experiment on the planet.
- At Flickr, a photo-sharing site, people uploading their pictures "tag" them with keywords describing some element of what they are showing. These tags, created by the millions, are becoming what has been called a bottom-up "folksonomy" as opposed to the top-down taxonomies so laboriously created in the past.
- In Second Life and other "virtual worlds," people assume online identities—often changing gender, as it turns out—to communicate and interact with others in environments that offer physical safety and open-ended imagination.
- Maps with data can tell stories. Everyblock.com is collecting and massaging voluminous data about places, and offering it to people at the micro level: their own street address, for a visual understanding of what is going on around them.
- On Slashdot, an online community for self-described "nerds," users can plumb the moderated comment system—the comments are the content, for the most part—to illuminate issues in considerable depth, though the user ends up doing more work as a result of the free-form nature of the commentary.
- In Brattleboro, Vermont, the iBrattleboro website, created and maintained by volunteers, is often ahead of the local daily newspaper on key stories.

Communities are at the heart of all this activity, whether communities of interest or geography. This is essential for understanding where we are headed. Craigslist, the indispensable classified advertising site, would be nowhere as big were it not for a sense of community about the place and the places it serves. The site's lost-and-found tells you much more about its value than what you can buy and sell.

AND, not OR

One of the eternal questions of our new-media times, as the boundaries of journalism expand, is this: Who is a journalist?

It's the wrong question.

The correct question is: What is journalism? Because in a world where anyone, using widely available tools of media creation, can perform an act of journalism, the key issue is identifying those acts and their results—not trying to decide who is and who is not someone we wish to usher into our traditional priesthood.

Pick up the *New York Times* or visit its website. Even though the newspaper's reports are not always perfectly accurate, and even though the organization sometimes gets things terribly wrong, we can all agree that it performs journalism.

By contrast, the "Blah Blah Say Wat U Want to Say" blog is equally plainly not journalism. This isn't to say that it utterly lacks value; for its (one imagines few) readers it has its own worth. But it isn't journalism and neither is the YouTube video of "Nat and Foxy disco dancing"; a demonstration of enthusiasm but not much else.

But where in the ecosystem do we locate the famous, green-tinged camera-phone photo from the London Underground, showing a man with a cloth over his mouth as he made his way from a smoking train that had just been bombed on July 7, 2005? The picture was taken by a man who himself was escaping from the train. He was not a journalist, but at that moment committed an act of journalism, and his photo made its way around the world in hours because it was authentic—a partial record of a hugely newsworthy event in our planet's history. The same is true of the tourist-captured videos of the late-2004 tsunami that swamped south Asia and killed hundreds of thousands of people; these images are part of the historical record now, deservedly so, and in retrospect were acts of journalism.

An easier case is Talking Points Memo, the online blog collection created and run by Joshua Micah Marshall. The only time this material appears on paper is when someone prints out a page from their Web browser. And much of what Marshall and his team do is to aggregate and point to information from elsewhere on the Web. Yet they (with the help of their audience) are doing some serious reporting as well, and are deservedly winning major journalism awards. Clearly this is journalism.

So is the low-rent online mailing list used by the residents of a small neighborhood in Palo Alto, California, where people regularly report items to each other that are, by any standard we can name, newsworthy. For example, when the tap water turned cloudy in several homes a few years ago, one of the residents called the city to find out what was wrong—some repairs to a water line, it turned out—and then reported back to the neighborhood list the story as explained by the city engineers. If this is not journalism, nothing is.

In Kenya, Ory Okolloh, started a blog to cover the Kenyan Parliament and other governmental issues. She is doing, by various accounts, a better job of telling people what is happening in that legislature than many if not most of the newspapers employing journalists.

The point here is simple: we are not talking about professionals versus everyone else, not talking about one *or* the other. We are moving into a world of one *and* the other—that diversifying ecosystem discussed earlier.

Although a monoculture is easier to understand, diversity is healthier. But it is more confusing, too, where blurred lines are the norm, not the exception.

What are we to make, then, at least in a journalistic sense, of the blog written by Brad DeLong, an economics professor at the University of California, Berkeley? DeLong is a former policy maker in the U.S. Treasury Department, and a renowned expert in economic affairs. His blog is a trove of useful information, told with a distinct political world view, and nearly required reading for those who care about such policy. It is frequently heavily reported, from the author's trove of personal knowledge and research. Is it journalism? By what standard is it not?

Blurrier yet is the line we might draw when looking at the work of advocacy groups such as Human Rights Watch and the American Civil Liberties Union. Like every other organization with a website, they are producing media. They are also doing prodigious amounts of reporting—that is, gathering and sifting information via research and interviews—that is frequently far more detailed than anything coming from traditional media organizations. They are not quite doing journalism, because they are not applying all of the principles of journalism that we'll examine later, but they are very, very close—but they and others are performing a vital information service.

But what of the corporate blog written by Jonathan Schwartz, chief executive of Sun Microsystems, a major technology company? Schwartz discusses his company's and competitors' products, and how he sees his industry developing. Customers and others interested in the topics comment on the blog, directly below his postings. Journalism? No. But it's a far cry from the traditional public relations communications of the past.

All of these examples point to perhaps the most fundamental shift of all in journalism, a change made obvious and necessary by democratizing technology. News is evolving from a lecture into a conversation.

The first rule of a conversation is to listen. Sadly, this is not something most journalists do very well. We pay attention to the sources we interview, and to the people whose press conferences we attend, and to the rich, powerful and/or well-connected people who remain on the trade's semi-official radar. We don't pay much attention, however, to anyone else. We love the readers, plural, but are deeply suspicious of the reader, singular, who can be quirky or even annoying. Yet our readers collectively know more than we do, something true of every beat at every news organization, and listening to them is a crucial part of a smart journalist's job.

More and more news organizations have discovered the value of conversational tools. Journalist blogs are now common. Comment threads, most of which are poorly administered, can be found on many sites under many stories. Podcasts and videos have become a key element of formerly print-only publications, and text is now an element of broadcasters' websites.

Too few media organizations have taken the next steps into audience engagement. And the ones that have are, by the standards of their new-media competition, late to the game. Bloggers take for granted that criticizing someone implies their right to respond, either in the comments below a posting or on their own sites. Contrast this with the traditional letter to the editor in newspapers—the one place where papers are involved in any kind of conversation with their communities. Editors decide whether to run a letter, and feel free to edit it. (That's more than someone writing to or calling a broadcaster is likely to get, however.)

In early December 2008, the *New York Times* website published a long letter signed by U.S. Rep. Charles Rangel, a New York Democrat who had strong objections to an investigative story the paper had recently run about him. Next to the letter was a response from the reporter. The level of detail was impressive, and it demonstrated what all news organizations could do if they cared.

The Times and other organizations have also made strong use of interactive technologies. A notable example is the Washington Post's remarkable "Faces of the Fallen" project: a database of American soldiers killed in Afghanistan and Iraq, which can be sorted by a variety of criteria including age, military branch and home town. Compiled from official releases, news reports and other sources, it's a valuable and important piece of history.

Databases and the Web are made for each other. The ability to display complex, deep information and give users a way to work with it is an opportunity that most organizations have yet to deploy in major ways, but housing-price maps and other such features are showing what's possible with community data. No newspaper or broadcaster is even close, however, to matching what Adrian Holovaty, a former Washington Post staff journalist, and his team at EveryBlock.com are doing to put localized data online.

Another way news organizations could be moving into a participatory journalism world—again, few are doing this—is to recognize a simple reality: they are not oracles. They haven't reported everything, and they don't know everything. They should stop pretending that what they haven't reported isn't important.

The print edition of the *New York Times* carries a slogan that proclaims "All the News that's Fit to Print." It was almost revolutionary, therefore, when the paper's website started linking to articles from blogs and directly competing news organizations, directly under the links to the Times's own journalism and on the home page of the site and the topical home pages. It was an announcement of participation in a wider world, and an extraordinarily important one for the journalism craft.

Links are the fundamental unit of the Web. They are an invitation to see more, to drill deeper, to explore information. *Aftonbladet*, a daily newspaper based in Stockholm, Sweden, is part of a media company that has navigated the online world more adeptly than perhaps any other traditional media operation. The paper recognizes linking's value in many ways, not least its portal to Swedish blogs, where it shows its audience many of the conversations taking place around the nation. Every news organization should recognize that a parallel media universe exists in its own community—and should point to it. This doesn't mean endorsing or vouching for the other material, but simply understanding its existence and relevance.

The world of "mashups"—combinations of data, services and often user input from various parts of the media and the Web—is another arena where traditional organizations have only recently begun to catch up with faster, more nimble startups. Mashups are best understood when looking at things like the Bakersfield Californian newspaper's pothole map, where community residents tell each other where the worst potholes can be found. A community's infrastructure is a newsworthy topic by any measure.

Tunisian political activists have created a more serious mashup: a map of prisons, including some where political dissidents have been held for extended periods under conditions that human-rights groups call cruel. The government of Tunisia thought the locations of some of these prisons were secret; they were not secrets, of course, to the people who'd been imprisoned. The people of Tunisia, if not their rulers, are better off for the availability of this kind of information.

Media organizations long ago learned the value of asking audiences to tell the journalists about newsworthy events—all news operations rely to some degree on tips. That idea has broadened with the wide availability of digital cameras, mobile phones and other network-connected devices. Now it's common to ask audiences for photos and videos of newsworthy events; when a bridge collapsed in Minnesota in 2007, the images and videos captured by non-paid journalists vastly outnumbered the ones by the pros, and some of the former ended up in the pages and broadcasts, not just on Flickr and other photo-sharing sites.

Asking the audience for help can take many forms, some of which can bring high value to the journalism. A Fort Myers, Florida, newspaper asked its readers to help investigate a city-government issue, and the resulting flood of information led to investigative journalism that helped change local policies.

Innovation is Inexpensive

Whether traditional journalists ask for help or not, and whether they recognize the new entrants or not, the trend for a wider and more diverse ecosystem is unstoppable. With democratized media, the major cost in trying something new is talent and time, not money. "(S)omeone with a new idea doesn't have to convince anyone else to let them try it—there are few institutional barriers between thought and action," observes Clay Shirky, author of "Here Comes Everybody: The Power of Organizing Without Organizations" (Penguin, 2008).

So in living rooms and garages and university labs and corporate cubicles around the globe, people are trying. The number of experiments in new media has soared, with uncountable new projects in the works and in the marketplace. Most fail, as is the case with all startups. But because the overall number of people trying is so high, even a tiny percentage of successes means we are seeing a relatively high number of ideas work in sustainable ways.

The successes are visible all around us.

- In Korea, Oh Yeon Ho took a great idea and turned it into OhmyNews.com. More than 40,000 "citizen reporters" from around the nation work with staff editors to produce one of Korea's best-known news reports.
- Om Malik, a journalist in San Francisco, started a blog where he covered technology topics. It has become a mini-empire, growing with the addition of venture capital and talent.
- Lisa Stone and her colleagues at BlogHer.com have created a robust community of female bloggers. With some simple but effective rules, the site has become one of the best examples of the genre.
- Twitter, where people post "micro-blog" content of text messages (140 characters maximum), is finding adherents in the journalism world and everywhere else. Venture capital has flowed in, and few who know the Twitter team doubt that they will find a way to monetize the site.
- Seesmic, a video startup (note: I am an investor), imagines video almost purely as conversation, encouraging people to post their thoughts and then inviting responses.

Not everyone seeks a for-profit business model. Global Voices Online, for which I am an advisor, aggregates blog postings from outside North America. Its purpose is to help us understand the larger world's people and cultures. At a much more local level, Barry Parr covers his small town of Half Moon Bay, California, with his Baysider blog, not because he expects to make money on it but because he cares about his community.

The media-creation process is at heart entrepreneurial. It calls for rapid development amid chaotic conditions, and it recognizes the possibility, if not probability, of failure. But most of all it is about ownership, not necessarily in a corporate sense but equally in the sense of taking responsibility for creating and sustaining something in an iterative method.

How? You start with a good idea. Develop and deploy it quickly; in fact, with consumer Internet products and services it's usually best to put them online *before* you think they're ready. Fix what's broken and improve what's not. Fail fast; don't stick forever with something that is clearly not going to work. Then do it again.

Trust and (New) Media Literacy

The critics of our new world of media often return to a single, crucial issue: How can we know what to trust?

They have a point. The sheer volume of information pouring over us in this media-saturated time defies metaphor, but "drinking from a fire hose" starts to capture the problem. How can we identify the reliable and useful material, separating it from the unreliable and useless.

And what about information that is false? Consider the late-2008 debacle at CNN, when as the *New York Times* reported, Apple's stock price briefly plummeted "after a CNN 'citizen journalist' wrote that an 'insider' reported that Steve Jobs had been rushed to the hospital with chest pains."

The report, posted on the news channel's iReport page where anyone can post videos and other unvetted items, was false. It may have been created by someone whose intention was to briefly torpedo the Apple share price. This was far from the first such occurrence online. False reports have been posted to public-relations wires, including the famous Emulex case many years ago when a fraudster—who was caught and punished—pulled just this kind of stunt.

There were multiple failures in the CNN case, not least of which was the channel's insufficient labeling, since corrected, of the iReport material as unvetted and therefore not necessarily to be trusted. The most critical failure, of course, was the foolish panic that led some Apple shareholders into dumping their stock.

We need to create new tools and updated traditional techniques. It all comes down to some essential principles that, if followed, would lead media consumers to become much more like media activists. The principles include:

- Be skeptical. We need to be skeptical of just about all media. This means not taking for granted the trustworthiness of what we read, see or hear from media of all kinds, whether from traditional news organizations, blogs, online videos or you name it.
- Use judgment; don't be equally skeptical of everything. Imagine a credibility scale ranging from plus 10 to minus 10. I give a *New York Times* or *Wall Street Journal* article an automatic plus 8 or 9; I don't assume perfection but I do trust that, in articles by most reporters for those publications, a strong effort went into getting it right. An anonymous comment on a random blog, by contrast, starts at minus 8 or 9; it would have to go a long way to merely have zero credibility.
- Keep reporting. No one with any common sense buys a car solely based on a TV commercial. We do some homework. It's the kind of research and

follow-up that journalists do. So let's call it reporting. We need to recognize the folly of making any major decision about our lives based on something we read, hear or see—and the need to keep reporting, sometimes in major ways, to ensure that we make good choices.

- Go outside your comfort zone. Look for and read/watch/listen to things that challenge your assumptions, or are from places and cultures you don't know much about. I learn more from people who think I'm wrong than from people who think I'm right.

- Learn media techniques. Younger people are getting pretty good at this already. What I suspect they—and almost everyone else—lack in this regard is understanding how communications are designed to persuade, and how we can be manipulated. We need to teach ourselves, and our children, about how media work in ways that go far beyond knowing how to take a snapshot with a mobile phone or posting something in a blog.

You'll find every one of those principles in the journalist's toolkit. But the media creator who wants to tell other people small or large things about the world in any remotely journalistic way should recognize a few more principles. For journalists, "amateur" or professional, they are:

- Thoroughness. Reporters try to learn as much as they can about a topic. It's better to know much more than you publish than to leave big holes in your story. The best reporters always want to make one more call, check with one more source.

- Accuracy. Accuracy is the starting point for all good journalism. Get your facts right, then check them again. Know where to look to verify claims or to separate fact from fiction.

- Fairness. Whether you are presenting a balanced story or arguing from a point of view, your readers will feel cheated if you slant the facts or present opposing opinions disingenuously.

- Independence. Being independent can mean many things, but independence of thought may be most important. Professional journalists can be relatively independent of conflicts of interest, but sometimes they're so beholden to their sources, and to access to those sources, that they are not independent at all.

- Transparency. Simply, if you have a horse in the race, say so. Reveal—if relevant to what you're talking about—your motives, your background, your financial interests.

Who should be the primary teachers of this new media literacy? We need to look first to parents, then to schools starting in lower grades. If we don't teach our children the kind of critical thinking skills that these principles imply, they will end up hopelessly adrift amid an onslaught of media or so cynical that they will disbelieve trustworthy sources.

Teaching critical thinking, of course, is risky in much of today's America. In many school districts in large swaths of the nation, a teacher who tries this runs the risk of being labeled a dangerous radical.

University journalism educators should make it a priority to impart these principles as well. The mission of journalism schools inevitably is going to broaden—feeding employees into big media companies is plainly a troubled mission—and journalism schools could (and should) lead the effort in universities to help all students understand media literacy.

Traditional media organizations and new journalistic competitors alike should consider media literacy a core mission, too. They stand to gain when their audiences understand what it takes to produce quality reporting, assuming they are doing it, and as time-starved people retreat to quality they will inevitably look to journalists and organizations that produce it.

In the end, media literacy in the 21st century will be all our jobs. We will have to do some work, all of us, to be better consumers and producers. Tactics and techniques will change, but fundamental principles will not. We need to remember them, and put them into practice.

Note

Portions of this work have appeared previously in Dan's blog. Dan's thoughts and insight served as the basis for the keynote, "Media Literacy in a Media-Saturated Age," delivered for the Journalism and Citizenship: New Agendas conference, held at the University of Texas at Austin, July 2007, where contributors to this volume first presented their work include in the following chapters.

Part I

Journalism's Evolution in the Era of the Active Audience

Chapter 1

Journalism, Citizenship, and Digital Culture

Mark Deuze

During the Summer of 2007 temporary or "transient" nightclubs were built in Barcelona and Lisbon (after an earlier 2006 try-out in Berlin) under the brand name *Kubik*. "Designed by Berlin-based urban design agency ModulorBeat and light artist Andreas Barthelmes, Kubik is built from stacked, reused water tanks [. . .] Kubik's 275 illuminated cubes house a bar and lounge from Sunday through Wednesday, and a club from Friday through Saturday."[1] Earlier in 2007, marketing agency Herrmann International Asia together with the Australian arm of Brown-Forman Beverages Worldwide organized the *SoCo Cargo Experiment*, created for the Southern Comfort brand. This equally temporary club concept consisted of 12 metre long shipping containers stacked side by side and on top of each other, with adaptable interiors containing a bar, and stage and lounge areas. The container club premiered on Sydney's Cockatoo Island in October 2006, and then popped up at festivals in Melbourne (February 2007) and Adelaide (March 2007).[2] A similar re-use of shipping containers comes from Singapore-based *Venue VBOX*, offering clients a portable store in a shipping container, which can be set up anywhere temporarily.[3] In May 2007 the Russian vodka brand Stolichnaya launched a *Stoli Hotel* in Los Angeles, working with different agencies such as TTC PR, Legacy Marketing Partners, and Fly Communications.[4] This 10,000 square-foot "pop-up" hotel was designed and built within an empty garage or hall space, and was taken down after a month to be moved to other cities like New York, Chicago, and Miami.[5] Marketing firm Trendwatching explains the growing popularity of "pop-up" retail, hotels, clubs, and other forms of consumerist leisure with the concept of "transumerism": designing and implementing novel and innovative shopping and entertainment opportunities aimed at consumers that are always on the move, "as consumers are slowly but certainly mirroring travel behavior in daily life. After all, in our Experience Economy, the temporary, the transient, is increasingly being valued if not worshipped on a daily basis."[6]

Of course, it would be easy to critique the choice of venues and materials for these marketing efforts. Shipping containers, empty or abandoned urban spaces . . . it all invokes disturbing images of refugees suffocating (as has happened in cargo containers at U.S. and European harbours), of homeless people seeking shelter, of tens of thousands of Hurricane Katrina evacuees forced to temporarily live in the Houston Astrodome. What is a more salient issue here, though, is the shift in focus on living, eating, and socializing towards experiences that are intrinsically temporary, transitory, a moment in time that cannot be relived or revisited. As such, these examples underscore contemporary modern life—a life lived from moment to moment, always in the here and now, in a context of seemingly constant and disruptive change, restlessness, and overall anxious feeling of being part of a "runaway world," as Anthony Giddens (2002) states. In this essay, I would like to couple this crucial observation with a critical debate on the (future) role of professional journalism in developed democratic societies for, as many keen observers of the profession note, it is impossible to conceive of journalism (and the work of journalists) without the larger political and social context within which it operates. Bill Kovach and Tom Rosenstiel (2001, p. 23) similarly argue, that "[w]hether one looks back of three hundred years, and even three thousand, it is impossible to separate news from community, and over time even more specifically from democratic community." The pop-up phenomenon thus is a tool to express my concern with the role of public information and journalism in the experience of community at our particular phase of modernity.

If, as John Hartley (1996) has put it, journalism is the primary sense-making practice of modernity, what kind of modernity does it make? Scholars and practitioners alike often use a normative notion of journalism as providing the social cement of democracies as a point of departure in their work. In journalism, the consensually preferred way of achieving this classical role is through monitoring of bureaucracy, industries, and the state as modernity's key institutions. It is what scholars and newsworkers alike tend to describe as "hard" news—the apex of journalism's informal hierarchy. Presumably, political and economic news forge and reinforce the foundations of social organization. However, contemporary society is anything but solid or socially cohesive. Under conditions of worldwide migration and capital flight, moveable businesses, global conflicts, and widespread environmental apprehension, most people sense a precariousness in everyday life, whether real or perceived. As a response, citizens increasingly retreat into "hyperlocal" enclaves (suburban ghettos or guard-gated communities) and "hyperindividual" personal information spaces (connecting with the world without actually physically engaging with it through online social networks such as *MySpace* and *Second Life*). A fundamental question is whether journalism adds fuel to these flames or effectively patrols the fragile fences of modernity.

As self-proclaimed gatekeepers, journalists have only their occupational ideology and news culture to rely on as a defence against either commercial intrusion or special interests (Deuze, 2005). In doing so, journalism's representation of society tends to stay the same while simultaneously reporting on a rapidly changing world. Considering the tendency among newsworkers to reiterate and reproduce age-old news values, while at the same time surfing on the waves of permanent change amplified by the attitudes and behaviors of the global financial and political elites, journalism makes sense of a modernity that seems unsettling at best, and out of touch with the everyday lives of most of its inhabitants at worst. A key to reorienting journalism studies to the rapidly changing human condition can be found in the works of Polish social theorist Zygmunt Bauman. Bauman's confrontations with modernity led him in his most recent writings to see contemporary society in terms of a "liquid" modernity (2000). Bauman defines a liquid modern society as "a society in which the conditions under which its members act change faster than it takes the ways of acting to consolidate into habits and routines. Liquidity of life and that of society feed and reinvigorate each other. Liquid life, just like liquid modern society, cannot keep its shape or stay on course for long" (2005, p. 1). A liquid modern society is one where uncertainty, flux, change, conflict, and revolution are the permanent conditions of everyday life—indeed, as exemplified by the *SoCo Cargo Experiment* or the *Kubik* nightclubs. Bauman makes a compelling argument how liquid life is neither modern or post-modern, but rather explains how the categories of existence established and enabled by early, first, or solid modernity are disintegrating, overlapping, and remixing. It is not as if we cannot draw meaningful distinctions between global and local anymore. The same goes for other modern categories of everyday life, such as between work and non-work, between public and private, between conservative and progressive, or between mediated and non-mediated experiences. It is just that these and other key organizing characteristics and categories of modern life have lost their (presumed or perceived) intrinsic, commonly held or consensual meaning. As the trendwatchers excitedly proclaim about transumerism: everything (and everyone) is always on the move. Using Bauman's work as an anchoring framework, the challenges to our understanding of the role of journalism are discussed in terms of key political changes articulated with a liquid modern life. The purpose of this approach is to open up new or refreshing ways to ignite the discussion about, for and especially with (young and aspiring) journalists about their role and position in contemporary democratic society.

Politics and Citizenship

The meaning of citizenship has changed in the last few decades. Michael Schudson (1999) argues how most people still tend to be seen by politicians, scholars, and journalists alike as citizens that need to inform themselves widely about all political parties in play, so that they can make an informed decision come election time. However, Schudson also shows how this model of citizenship is a thing of the past—an unrealistic and rather elitist notion of how people should make up their minds, and what political representation means to them. Another reason for the inappropriateness of the "informed" citizen as a benchmark for democratic theory is its reliance on a worldview that is premised on media access in the context of channel scarcity. Whereas the 1950s model of citizenship could be based on a notion of people wishing to inform themselves having access to only a few sources and channels of information, in today's mixed media ecology such an assumption seems rather ridiculous. Media have come to be integrated into every aspect of peoples' daily lives, particularly facilitated by the worldwide proliferation of the Internet and similar services that connect subscribers to a global, always-on, digital information and communication network. The whole of the world and our lived experience in it can indeed be seen as framed by, mitigated through, and made immediate by pervasive and ubiquitous media. This world is what authors such as Marc Schuilenburg and Alex de Jong (2006), and Roger Silverstone (2007) consider as a "mediapolis": a mediated public space where media culture underpins and overarches the experiences of everyday life.

The behavior of the citizen in our contemporary mediapolis is what Schudson calls primarily "monitorial": scanning all kinds of news and information sources—newspapers, magazines, TV shows, blogs, online and offline social networks, and so on—for the topics that matter to her personally. People are not necessarily disengaged from the political process—they just commit their time and energy to it on their own terms. This individualized enactment of citizenship can be linked to the act of the consumer, browsing the stores of the shopping mall for that perfect pair of shoes, comparing prices and sizes with online offerings. Monitoring is indeed the act of the citizen-consumer, participating in society (whether that "society" equals virtual, topical or geographical community, one's role within a democratic nation-state, or within a translocal network) conditionally, unpredictably, and voluntarist.

The way people perceive and enact their role as citizens and consumers increasingly develops in the context of mediated and networked environments, which process loosens—but not destroys—what John Thompson (1996, p. 207) has described as the connection between self-formation and shared locale. Indeed, Barry Wellman (2001) suggests that access to new media like the Internet enhances people's participatory capital, and supplements their social contacts—even though in doing so, we are less likely to feel committed to traditional forms of community. Wellman and his colleagues stress how none of these trends are necessarily new or particular to media:

> Even before the advent of the Internet, there has been a move from all-encompassing, socially-controlling communities to individualized, fragmented personal communities. The security and social control of all-encompassing communities have given way to the opportunity and vulnerability of networked individualism. People now go through the day, week, and month in a variety of narrowly-defined relationships with changing sets of network members. (2001, p. 455)

The worldwide shift towards networked individualized societies has particular consequences for the way people relate to each other. According to Robert Putnam (2004), since the last few decades of the 20th century people around the world have started to withdraw from participating in social institutions such as political parties, religious institutions, as well as from subscription-based news media, large-scale voluntary associations and organized group sports. This does not mean people do not vote, worship, read a newspaper, or engage in league bowling anymore. It does suggest that if we do, we tend to do it whenever we feel like it—rather than because of our membership of a certain collective. This makes our behavior towards such institutions irregular, sporadic, unpredictable, and ultimately dependent on our personal wants and needs.

The Global, the Translocal

The instantaneity in the way people interact and communicate with the world seems to reduce it to their most intimate, direct, and real-time personal environment. Yet the same trend also works the other way around. The world as people experience it not only is getting smaller—it also seems to be getting bigger all the time. The experience of life in the "global village" feels like constantly trying to catch up with Giddens' runaway world, a world constantly on the edge of swerving out of control. In such a world all the traditional institutions that provided the social cement of modern life—most notably the family, the church, the factory or company, mass media, and the state—at times seem nothing but bargaining chips in our individual negotiations with the forces of change that sweep contemporary life. People cannot simply rely on parents, priests, professionals, or presidents for truth anymore—they have to go out and construct their own narrative, to come up with "biographical solutions of systemic contradictions" (Beck, 1992, p. 137). In his more recent work, Ulrich Beck envisions a new type of cosmopolitan democracy, where people as individuals all over the world will have a more or less equal say in world affairs (such as environmental problems, transnational corporate policies, and worldwide migration patterns), as these affect everyone (2006). Several other political and social theorists—such as Daniela Archibugi and David Held (1995)—advocate cosmopolitan solidarity and world citizenship, if only to counter the catastrophic effects of an unbridled globalization in the name of markets and commerce, and to legally and politically acknowledge an "impotence" of national governments (Bauman, 2007a) and the "growing interdependencies of a world society" (Habermas 2001, p. 70). Bauman articulates the cosmopolitan project more critically with individualization and globalization, arguing forcefully that "[t]he new individualism, the fading of human bonds and the wilting of solidarity, are all engraved on one side of a coin whose other side bears the stamp of globalization" (2006, p. 146).

As the contingencies of life, work, and play converge on the shoulders of the individual and traditional social institutions lose their automatic authority, people are at the same time swept up in a world of cosmopolitan politics and a global capitalist economy. As the power of the nation-state to control or protect its individual citizens withers, a new translocal rather than international playground has emerged. Here all kinds of forces and social movements compete for attention, recognition, and cultural acceptance: multinational corporations, cross-border coalitions of social interest groups, globally oriented media, and a growing number of international agencies. These forces increasingly influence interstate decisions and set the agenda of world politics (Archibugi et al., 1998). This does not necessarily mean that people as individuals are completely powerless in the face of global market forces—as the worldwide interconnectedness of markets, industries, economies, and social systems also open up numerous possibilities for the entrepreneurial individual. The point is, however, that the ability, skill, and resources necessary to navigate these global waters are beyond the means and capacities (or even wishes) of many, if not most people. We are supposed to increasingly rely on ourselves—which suggested self-reliance has become an endemic property of late 20th century policymaking, corporate practice, and public discourse, and it seems to warn people to be reluctant to trust the institutions they used to turn to for comfort or protection.

Reporting on studies in 43 countries, Ronald Inglehart (1997) observed a global shift of people in their roles as citizens away from nation-based politics and institutional elites, towards a distinctly skeptical, globally interconnected yet deeply personal type of self-determined civic engagement. Instead of voting at regular intervals in national elections we temporarily join any of the close to 30,000 international non-governmental organizations (INGO) active in the world today. Rather than subscribing to a national newspaper or tuning in to the daily evening newscast we search for news and information online about topics that are only of personal interest to us. We do not form or join unions anymore. We simply move to a different area, city, or country when we become dissatisfied with our working conditions (or when we face permanent unemployment where we live). Although all of these activities may seem beholden to a relatively small group of resourceful financial and cultural entrepreneurs, one cannot forget that blue collar workers now have become a declining minority in most modern countries, whereas a creative class of professionals in knowledge and information industries increasingly dominate the cultural economies of the contemporary information age. As the rift between the individual and the nation-state widens, Pippa Norris (1998) observes the emergence of a new type of deeply critical global citizen, who is excited about the ideals of democracy but is losing confidence in its national practice. "We are undoubtedly living in an anti-hierarchical age," concludes Beck (2000, p. 150).

The distinctly anti-hierarchical character of our time also comes into play in the consumptive world, where advertisers cleverly market to people's desire to be different, to be critical, to be cool. Bauman (2007b) reminds us that under conditions of a consumerist culture people can never really achieve difference, nor should they, for at that moment the act of consuming would stop. On the other hand, once settled in carefully target-marketed brand communities—whether the brand is Shell or Greenpeace, CNN or Indymedia—citizens achieve some kind of collective identity similar to the one achieved by voting (as an act of political allegiance). Mark Poster (2004) stipulates that consumer activity is central to society, as it is the domain where the individual is realized. Considering the act of consumption as productive and creative, Mitzuko Ito (2005) takes this argument even further. In the various ways people engage with each other via the products they consume—whether that product is a political candidate, TV show, or a T-shirt—their consumption becomes a creative and meaningful act. Stated another way, under conditions of liquid life consumer culture and civic engagement seem to be interconnected and co-creative rather than opposing value systems, and as such function to make the daily remix of work, life, and play just a little bit easier.

Roles of Journalism

News has always been a product that commercial companies sold to target audiences as defined by marketing departments (Lampel et al., 2005). As a marketable commodity, it has traditionally competed with the tendency of people to make their own news: pirate radio, alternative media, using the office photocopier as "the people's printing press," activist newsletters pasted on city walls, gossiping in the local pub or market tavern. This was never a real problem for journalists working in the 20th century heyday of mass media where the particulars of audience behaviors remained largely invisible to them—a period Hallin (1992) called the "high modernism" of (American) journalism. It is during this time that journalism, as noted earlier, emerged as the primary sense-making practice of modernity (Hartley, 1996, p. 12). In terms of journalism's "modernist bias of its official self-presentation" (Zelizer, 2004, p. 112), its practitioners came to see their work and their product as the cornerstone of modern society, and more particularly: the nation-state. As Carey (1996) has noted explicitly: "Journalism is another name for democracy or, better, you cannot have journalism without democracy. The practices of journalism are not self-justifying; rather, they are justified in terms of the social consequences they engender, namely the constitution of a democratic social order" (online).

Much has changed since those days. Consider the following conclusion from a series of research projects by the American Pew Research Center for the People and the Press in 2005:

> Sitting down with the news on a set schedule has become a thing of the past for many time-pressured Americans [. . .] More people are turning away from traditional news outlets [. . .] At the same time, public discontent with the news media has increased dramatically. Americans find the mainstream media much less credible than they did in the mid-1980s. They are even more critical of the way the press collects and reports the news.

More ominously, the public also questions the news media's core values and morality.[7]

Reports in most well-established democracies around the world signal similar trends. Corporate journalism has lost its "sense of wholeness and seamlessness" observed by Hallin (1992, p. 14), but not necessarily because of the collapse of political consensus or increasing market forces, as he suggests. I'd like to suggest that journalism—as it is produced within the confines of mainstream news media corporations—has lost touch with Bauman's acute observations of the lived realities of today's citizen-consumers. This is a reality where "liquid modern society and liquid life are locked in a veritable perpetuum mobile" (Bauman, 2005, p. 12). The key to these assumptions about our postmodern condition is the common perception among people of all walks of life that we live in times of fast-paced radical change. In today's global society such a widely shared sense of accelerated change is no longer a break in the otherwise fairly stable routine of everyday existence; instead, it has become the structural condition of contemporary liquid life. It is thus important to note that any consideration of the future of news and political communication has to involve not only an awareness of how the social systems of journalism and politics self-organize to adapt to new circumstances while maintaining their internal power structures, but also how the contemporary condition of liquid modernity and its sense of permanent revolution wreaks havoc on the very foundations of these institutions.

Although people and social systems around the world respond to real or perceived disruptive changes differently, the impact of permanent revolution on society manifests itself most clearly in our increasing uncertainty, anxiety, and disagreement about the exact meaning, role, and function of such well-established features of modern life as the role of the state, the church, the family, and of professional journalism (Bauman, 2000). The added value of a social perspective offers media theory an important marker for understanding this status quo.

Media as social institutions do not escape the sense of accelerated, unsettling change permeating liquid modern life, and it is exactly this notion of volatile, uncertain (global and local) flux that professional journalism fails to come to terms with. If we look at the various ways in which the news industry has tried to integrate or at the very least give some kind of coherent meaning to disruptive technologies like Internet and social trends like individualization or globalization, one can see how journalism still depends on its established mode of production, through which it largely (and unreflexively) reproduces the institutional contours of high (or "solid") modernity. Thus journalism, when it moved online in the late 1990s, has consistently offered shoveled, repurposed, and windowed content for free, cannibalizing on its core product while treating its Web presence as an advertisement for the offline product (Deuze, 2003). In doing so, it remediated not only its product, but also its production process online, including but not limited to its established ways of doing things, its news culture, and its occupational ideology (Deuze, 2005). The primary function of the multitude online thus became the same as people were expected to behave offline, as *publics*: audiences to be sold to advertisers.

In the same vein, journalism has engaged the individualized and networked society in terms of its presupposed "audience fragmentation," which in turn reified professional journalism's position as the primary gatekeeper and information provider in society. Globalization has a particular impact on the making of news, as it forces journalists to translate events occurring all over the world involving all kinds of people to their local constituencies—which communities also increasingly consist of peoples, religions, and cultural practices with roots in different parts of the world. For most of the 20th century the international news media have ignored the complexities when covering the world, and especially after the fall of the Berlin Wall and the end of a convenient Cold War frame primarily reduced it to a vast "global wilderness" (Bauman, 2007b, p. 15). Today, the world enters our homes through news media that tend to combine narrow-minded frameworks like Orientalism (as eminently argued by Edward Said), etnocentrism, and small-town pastoralism (following Herbert Gans), which more adequately represent the homophily of the average corporate newsroom and the make-up of the most affluent cultural groups in society than the kaleidoscopic make-up of citizens in most (Western) multicultural nations.

A New Media Ecology

The 21st century can tentatively be seen as a period when the developed world enters the second "liquid" phase of modernity, where all existing modern social, economical, and political institutions—the church (or mosque, temple), the family, journalism, the nation-state—have become what Beck (1992) has called "zombie" institutions: alive, but dead at the same time. Instead of being able to rely on such institutions for providing some automatic or consensual function in our lives, it is up to each and every one of us to enter into a complex and ongoing negotiation with them, of which the outcome will always be uncertain. This process coincides with the emergence of a post-industrial information culture (Manovich, 2001), shifting the emphasis towards "immaterial" resources like those traded on the international stock exchange and over the World Wide Web, leading scholars to proclaim the establishment of a global network society (Castells, 2000). What is expected of us in such a society is to acquire the skills and resources necessary to navigate complex and interactive social and technological networks. This shifts our core competencies away from so-called "expert" systems to what Levy (1997) sees as a form of collective intelligence particular of cyberculture, where knowledge about any given topic or subject is based on the ongoing exchange of views, opinions, and information between many rather than pulling the wisdom of a few. Hartley (2000) predicts in this context the emergence of a global "redactional" society, where the core competences once exclusively associated with professional journalism are increasingly necessary for every citizen to guarantee survival in a networked information age. Journalism has become not so much the property of what journalists do in order to sell news, but what people all over the world engage in on a daily basis in order to survive, coping with "modernity's extreme dynamism" (Giddens, 1991, p. 16), and the permanent revolution of liquid life (Deuze, 2007).

It is in this context that a new media ecosystem, or new mixed media ecology is taking shape. I have previously drawn distinctions between different and recombinant functions of journalism in such a new media system, where its news professionals will have to find ways to strike a balance between their identities as providers of editorial content but also of public connectivity (as in providing a platform for the discussion the ideal society typically has with itself), as well as between its historical operationally closed working culture strictly relying on "experts" and a more collaborative, responsive and interactive open journalistic culture (Deuze, 2003, p. 219). Of such a complex new media ecology one can see Internet (and all what we do online) as its primary manifestation, where people empowered by increasingly cheaper and easier-to-use technologies participate actively in their own "newsmaking," from responding via e-mail to a breaking news story to collectively producing "citizen journalism" Websites powerful enough to influence presidential elections—as in the case of *Ohmynews* in South Korea.

What is particularly salient about these trends is a further blurring of the carefully cultivated dividing lines between professional and amateurs, between producers and consumers of media. Jenkins (2006) describes this development as the emergence of a "convergence culture," indicating a shift within media companies towards a more inclusive production process fostering a new participatory folk culture by giving average people the tools to archive, annotate, appropriate, and recirculate content. There is no doubt that a future news system will be based—at least in part—on an interactive and connective mode of production where media makers and users will co-exist, collaborate, and thus effectively compete to play a part in the mutual (yet never consensual, as Niklas Luhmann has noted) construction of reality. On a concluding hopeful note, Balnaves, Mayrhofer, and Shoesmith (2004) consider such a shift towards a more engaged, emancipatory, and participatory relationship between media professionals and their publics an example of a "new humanism" in the domains of public relations, journalism, and advertising, constituting "an antidote to narrow corporate-centric ways of representing interests in modern society" (p. 192).

Liquid Journalism

If the old model of journalism was to inform the masses so they could vote intelligently and participate effectively in democracy, the argument as outlined in this essay begs the question how the new media ecology contributes to a new or renewed form of citizenship, and what the role of journalism in such a context would be. Whether one is optimistic or hopeful about the collective intelligence found online, and the networked individualism offline, it seems doubtful that it is possible to call upon citizens to embrace some sense of socially cohesive purpose that is based on their social identity as members of a mass audience: an audience of voters for politics, and audience of consumers for journalism.

Instead of focusing on voter apathy, one could argue that democracy has arrived at its most succesful stage yet: a phase where people trust or believe the political system will function regardless of whether they engage with it or not. If democracy effectively means outsourcing governance to a political elite, it has succeeded. However, this is not exactly what is happening: rather than voter disinterest or civic disengagement, we see another, more anti-hierarchical and deeply individualized type of citizenship emerging. This is the attitude of the citizen-consumer, as Margaret Scammell argues: "The act of consumption is becoming increasingly suffused with citizenship characteristics and considerations. Citizenship is not dead, or dying, but found in new places [. . .] The site of citizens' political involvement is moving from the production side of the economy to the consumption side" (2000, p. 351). Schudson's monitorial citizen is the image of a discerning shopper who has done her research and clipped her coupons before entering the mall. Furthermore, as we have seen, the new media ecology amplifies the act of consumption to a creative level. Consumerism may have all kinds of destructive effects, yet for all its problems it also makes citizens more demanding and critical.

Journalism, until now, has not seemed to be able to find an answer to these developments. It blames the commercial system within which it has always operated. It laments the dominant role of technologies that it has contributed to (desktop editing and publishing software, portable audio/video recording equipment, digitalization). It blames PR spokespeople and spin doctors whose jobs it demands in order to bring the flow of institutional news under control. Despite efforts to "hyperlocalize" or otherwise ground the news in people's everyday lives, as a profession it does not seem to be able to engage the consumer-citizen in a meaningful way.

For journalism, all of this not only means that value attributed to media content will be increasingly determined by the interactions between users and producers rather than the product (news) itself. The real significance of the argument outlined here, is that we have to acknowledge that the key characteristics of current social trends—uncertainty, flux, change, unpredictablilty, or perhaps "kludginess" (paraphrasing Jenkins 2004, p. 34)—are what defines the current and future state of affairs in how people make and use journalism all around the world. In terms of business praxis, this means we see a bewildering variety of top-down, hierarchical, and extremely closed-off types of corporate enclosures of the commons existing next to peer-driven forms of collaborative ownership regarding the manufacture of news. In terms of media production processes, we continue to witness a mix of "one-size-fits-all" content made for largely invisible mass audiences next to (and infused by) rich forms of transmedia storytelling including elements of user control and "prosumer"-type agency. In a way, it will be a mess—which makes the careful and socially realistic study of what people in their shapeshifting identities as consumers as well as producers of (news) media actually do all the more important.

Instead of lamenting or celebrating this process, or trying to find a fixed point somewhere in the future in our failed predictions of where we are going, we should embrace the uncertainty and complexity of the emerging new media ecology, and enjoy it for what it is: an endless resource for the generation of content and experiences by a growing number of people all around the world. Part of what will happen will reproduce existing power relationships and inequalities, for sure. Yet we are also witnessing an unparalleled degree of human agency and user control in our lived experience of mediated reality. A journalism that will successfully embrace and engage this ecology, will have to become fluid itself: a liquid journalism.

Manuscript History

An earlier draft of the material as presented in this contribution was published as: Deuze, M. (2008), The changing context of news work: Liquid journalism for a monitorial citizenry, *International Journal of Communication* 2. URL: http://ijoc.org/ojs/index.php/ijoc/article/view/290.

Notes

1 Source URL: http://www.springwise.com/entertainment/popup_nightclubs_update.
2 Source URL: http://www.springwise.com/food_beverage/popup_nightclubs.
3 Source URL: http://www.venue.com.sg.
4 Press release URL: http://www.prnewswire.com/cgi-bin/stories.pl?ACCT=104& STORY=/www/story/04-27-2007/0004575658&EDATE=.
5 Source URL: http://www.prweek.com/us/news/article/654624/Stoli-Hotel-inspire-buzz-reinforce-brand-message.
6 Source URL: http://www.trendwatching.com/trends/transumers.htm.6.
7 Source URL: http://pewresearch.org/pubs/206/trends-2005.

References

Archibugi, D., & Held, D. (1995). *Cosmopolitan democracy, an agenda for a new world order*. Cambridge: Polity Press.
Archibugi, D., Held, D., & Köhler, M. (Eds.) (1998). *Re-imagining political community: Studies in cosmopolitan democracy*. Palo Alto: Stanford University Press.
Balnaves, M., Mayrhofer, D., & Shoesmith, B. (2004). Media professions and the new humanism. *Continuum: Journal of Media & Cultural Studies, 18*(2), 191–203.
Bauman, Z. (2000) *Liquid modernity*. Cambridge: Polity Press.
Bauman, Z. (2005). *Liquid life*. Cambridge: Polity Press.

Bauman, Z. (2006). *Liquid fear*. Cambridge: Polity Press.

Bauman, Z. (2007a). *Liquid times*. Cambridge: Polity Press.

Bauman, Z. (2007b). *Consuming life*. Cambridge: Polity Press.

Beck, U. (1992). *Risk society: Towards a new modernity*. London: Sage.

Beck, U. (2000). *The brave new world of work*. Cambridge: Polity Press.

Beck, U. (2006). *Cosmopolitan vision*. Cambridge: Polity Press.

Carey, J. (1996). *Where journalism education went wrong* [online]. Presentation at the 1996 Seigenthaler Conference at the Middle Tennessee State University, US. Available: http://www.mtsu.edu/~masscomm/seig96/carey/carey.htm [2002, August 30].

Castells, M. (2000). *The rise of the network society*. 2nd edition. Oxford: Blackwell.

Deuze, M. (2003). The web and its journalisms: Considering the consequences of different types of news media online. *New Media & Society, 5*(2), 203–230.

Deuze, M. (2005) What is journalism? Professional identity and ideology of journalists reconsidered. *Journalism, 6*(4), 443–465.

Deuze, M. (2007) *Media work*. Cambridge: Polity Press.

Giddens, A. (1991). *Modernity and self-identity: Self and society in the late modern age*. Stanford: Stanford University Press.

Giddens, A. (2002). *Runaway world: How globalization is reshaping our lives*. London: Routledge.

Habermas, J. (2001). *The postnational constellation*. Translated by Max Pensky. Boston: MIT Press.

Hallin, D. (1992). The passing of the "high modernism" of American journalism. *Journal of Communication, 42*(3), 14–25.

Hartley, J. (1996). *Popular reality: Journalism, modernity and popular culture*. London: Arnold.

Hartley, J. (2000). Communicational democracy in a redactional society: The future of journalism studies. *Journalism, 1*(1), 39–47.

Inglehart, R. (1997). *Modernization and postmodernization*. Princeton University Press.

Ito, M. (2005). Technologies of the childhood imagination: Yugioh, media mixes, and everyday cultural production. In Joe Karaganis and Natalie Jeremijenko (Eds.), *Structures of participation in digital culture*. Durham, NC: Duke University Press.

Jenkins, H. (2004). The cultural logic of media convergence. *International Journal of Cultural Studies, 7*(1), 33–43.

Jenkins, H. (2006). *Convergence Culture: Where old and new media collide*. New York: New York University Press.

Kovach, B., & Rosenstiel, T. (2001). *The elements of journalism*. New York: Crown Publishers.

Lampel, J., Shamsie, J., & Lant, T. (Eds.) (2005). *The business of culture: Strategic perspectives on entertainment and media*. Mahwah, NJ: Lawrence Erlbaum.

Levy, P. (1997). *Collective intelligence: Mankind's emerging world in cyberspace*. New York: Perseus.

Manovich, L. (2001). *The language of new media*. Cambridge: MIT Press.

Norris, P. (Ed.) (1998). *Critical citizens: Global support for democratic governance*. Oxford: Oxford University Press.

Poster, M. (2004) The information empire. *Comparative Literature Studies, 41*(3), 317–334.

Putnam, R. (Ed.) (2004). *Democracies in flux: The evolution of social capital in contemporary society*. Oxford: Oxford University Press.

Scammell, M. (2000). The Internet and civic engagement: The age of the citizen-consumer. *Political Communication, 17*(4), 351–355.

Schudson, M. (1999). *The good citizen: A history of American civic life*. Cambridge: Harvard University Press.

Schuilenburg, M., & De Jong, A. (2006). *Mediapolis: Popular culture and the city*. Rotterdam: 010 Publishers.

Silverstone, R. (2007). *Media and morality: On the rise of the mediapolis*. Polity Press, Cambridge (UK).

Thompson, J. (1996) *The media and modernity: A social theory of the media*. Palo Alto: Stanford University Press.

Wellman, B., Quan-Haase, A., Witte, J., & Hampton, K. (2001). Does the Internet increase, decrease, or supplement social capital? Social networks, participation, and community commitment. *American Behavioral Scientist, 45*(3), 437–456.

Zelizer, B. (2004) When facts, truth and reality are God-terms: On journalism's uneasy place in cultural studies. *Communication and Critical/Cultural Studies, 1*(1), 100–119.

Chapter 2

The Citizen is the Message

Alternative Modes of Civic Engagement

Zizi Papacharissi

Declining civic participation in conventional forms of political involvements has been interpreted as cynicism (e.g., Cappella & Jamieson, 1996, 1997; Fallows, 1996; Patterson, 1993, 1996), television-induced political apathy (Putnam, 1998, 2001), or a simple reaction to information overload (Schudson, 1998). Simultaneously, increasing civic participation in online political forums, blogs, and online public spaces like YouTube, suggests that alternative forms of political activity are in the making. In contrast to traditional forms of political involvement, such as participation in local community affairs, affiliation with local and national organizations, volunteering, and voting, these newer forms of civic engagement point to an electorate that is seeking more innovative and novel ways for fulfilling civic obligations. Thus, information communication technologies are positioned as vehicles through which civic activity can be reinvented.

Specifically, blogs, vlogs (video blogs), and similar content portals provide ordinary citizens with the opportunity to directly engage the public sphere in a manner previously absent in representative democracies. Growing disinterest in conventional forms of political participation combined with innovative uses of evolving technologies suggest that new models of citizenship or civic engagement could be emerging. These new models inject the representative model of democracy with direct communication opportunities and propose a mutation or deviation from traditional democratic representation. Scholars have used different terms to acknowledge these developments, ranging from Schudson's (1998) monitorial citizen, to Bimber's (1998) accelerated pluralism, or the more recent direct representation model offered by Coleman (2005). The common thread in all lies in enabling the ordinary citizen to potentially become a "gatekeeper" or a "watchdog," appropriating social capital previously colonized by mainstream media. This chapter examines models for civic involvement within a representative democracy and the role online media play in providing opportunities for direct civic interaction. It considers models of journalism and models of civic involvement, and studies how online media allow citizens to combine elements of both so as reinvent themselves as civic monitors.

Modes of Civic Involvement in a Representative Democracy

When examining modes of civic involvement within a democratic infrastructure that is representative, consideration of the following three constants is necessary: (a) limitations to civic involvement imposed by the representative democracy model, (b) decline of the public sphere and how this affects civic engagement, (c) relationship of commercial media to the public sphere. Interaction among these three constants influences interpretations of civic disengagement and contemporary takes on civic involvement that emerge. Overlooking these constants may lead to inflated expectations of public engagement with public affairs. Civic involvement takes shape within a system of democratic representation, devised to manage public affairs in a mass and post-industrial society. Within this system, the public sphere presents the notional locus within which civic deliberation and participation are situated. In mass societies, commercial media present the channels through which this deliberation and participation is broadcast and shared with others. Any discussion of modes of civic involvement, conventional or novel, must be informed by an examination of the aforementioned constants, explicated below.

The Public Sphere in a Representative Democracy

The public sphere is routinely evoked when discussing modes for civic engagement within preceding and contemporary iterations of democracy. As a concept, it sets a standard for civic involvement within representative democracy. Conceptualized by Jürgen Habermas in his seminal work (1962/89), it presents the domain of social life in which public opinion is expressed by means of rational public discourse and debate. The public sphere in a representative democracy is where citizens deliberate and debate on public affairs, with public accord and decision making as implied common goals. In this context, it is defined as "a sphere which mediates between society and state, in which the public organizes itself as the bearer of public opinion, accords with the principle of the public sphere—that principle of public information which once had to be fought for against the arcane politics of monarchies and which since that time has made possible the democratic control of state activities" (Habermas, 1974/2004, p. 351). The value of the public sphere lies in its ability to facilitate uninhibited and diverse discussion of public affairs, thus typifying democratic traditions and enabling citizens to directly interact within a representative political system.

Inclusion in the public sphere is a privilege that citizens of a democracy enjoy; a privilege that in previous incarnations of the public sphere in the Greek and Roman republics was not afforded to those who were not considered citizens. The concept of the public sphere dominates any discussion of civic involvement within a representative democracy, because it suggests a venue through which the public becomes involved in public affairs. Through the public sphere, the public may simultaneously complement and monitor the authority granted to the state and other institutions by the electorate. In previous eras, the public sphere was placed at odds with feudal authorities, and in the modern era, with the state. In the modern era, however, Habermas argues that this ability of the public sphere is compromised by the mass media, which play a critical part in informing and directing public opinion. It is Habermas' argument that the commercialized mass media have turned the public sphere into a space where the rhetoric and objectives of public relations and advertising are prioritized.

This would imply that the mass media direct public opinion in a way that limits civic engagement taking place within the public sphere, a point of view that resonates with other scholars. Carey (1995), for instance, specifically outlined how the commercial influence of a capitalist economy and the private sector crowd out the democratic objectives of a public sphere. Putnam (1996) examined the progression and decline of civic engagement in the US, to conclude that television is responsible for displacing time previously devoted to civic affairs and promoting passive involvement with politics. Similarly, Hart (1994) argued that some media, such as television, "supersaturate viewers with political information," and that as a result, "this tumult creates in viewers a sense of activity rather than genuine civic involvement" (p. 109).

Additional conditions associated with the transition to industrial and post-industrial modern and postmodern society contribute to a deteriorating public sphere and declining interest in politics. For instance, in contemporary representative models of democracy, politicians, opinion leaders, and the media frequently rely on aggregations of public opinion obtained through polls, as opposed to the rational exchange of opinions fostered by the public sphere. Herbst (1993) referred to such aggregations of public opinion as "numbered voices," thus pointing to the substitution of individual and detailed personal opinion on public affairs with a concentration of viewpoints usually expressed in the bipolarity of the yes/no polling response format. Thus, deliberation of public affairs within the public sphere is postponed as citizens are called upon to express agreement or disagreement with prescribed options. Research also indicates that this simplification of complex political issues leads to misinformation and growing civic skepticism. The media frequently employ frames that prioritize politicizing an issue rather than encouraging rational deliberation of it (Fallows, 1996; Patterson, 1993). As the prospect of civic participation is de-emphasized and skepticism is reinforced through negative or cynical coverage in the mass media, growing cynicism spreads in a spiraling manner (Cappella & Jamieson, 1996, 1997) thus further alienating citizens from the prospect of civic activity.

Several disagree with these assessments of civic engagement in contemporary times. For instance, Fraser (1992) characterized the public sphere as an outdated model that excluded marginal and minority opinion. In contrast, she offered the post-industrial model of co-existing public spheres or counterpublics, which form in response to their exclusion from the dominant sphere of debate. These multiple public spheres, though not equally powerful, articulate, or privileged, populate contemporary democracies and broaden the scope of civic deliberation. Focusing on the public sphere could mischaracterize civic engagement, as that would exclude alternative modes of expression that develop in oppositional or analogous directions.

The Lonely Citizen in Post-Industrial Democracy

Arguments that connect civic engagement, the public sphere, and the commercialization of mass media frequently rest on a premise that overestimates and romanticizes political activity in previous eras. To this point, Schudson (1997) argued that public discourse is not the main ingredient, or "the soul of democracy," for it is seldom egalitarian, may be too large and amorphous, is rarely civil, and ultimately offers no magical solution to problems of democracy (Schudson, 1997). In addition, he demonstrated that different models characterized American democracy and periods of political activity, during which the average citizen was much less informed, educated, susceptible to persuasion, and inactive than the contemporary era (Schudson, 1998). Nostalgia for previous eras is sometimes an expression of discomfort or difficulty of acclimation to changing conditions.

Examinations of civic engagement in aggregate seldom incorporate the turn toward individual politics or politics of the self, documented by several scholars (e.g., Lasch, 1979, 1995; Riesman, 1950). They overlook civic engagement that takes place in private, not public spaces, and it is precisely this type of civic engagement that mass and new media enable and that post-industrial lifestyles and work schedules permit. The focus on the public confuses different citizen types and needs. The modern era citizen, for instance, is frequently characterized as passive, cynical, and disconnected, but those trends are not specific to the present era, as several scholars have shown (e.g., Coleman, 2005; Shudson, 1998). Schudson's (1998) historical analysis carefully demonstrates the progression of the American electorate from a period of reliance to the leadership of political elites in the 18th and early 19th centuries, to the dominance of political parties, partisanship, and mob politics in the 19th century, through the emergence of a non-partisan press, civic deliberation, and public opinion polls in the late 19th and 20th centuries, and to the final, contemporary era, characterized by individual and collective rights resolved in the judicial, over the legislative or executive realms. It is this emphasis on individual and collective politics and the reliance on judicial authority for the resolution of public affairs that is neglected when relying on the public sphere, as way of understanding and evaluating civic engagement.

The public sphere model implies that collective issues are resolved via civic deliberation in public space; the present era, however, is dominated by individual and collective issue agendas presented and debated primarily in judicial settings. Riesman (1950) first explicated individual politics in the seminal work, *The Lonely Crowd*, although his primary objective was to map out a process through which political involvement was becoming less inner- more other-directed. In this work, Riesman mapped out the transition from an inner-directed, traditional, pre-industrial society to an industrial, middle-class dominated society defined by other-directed character. He sketched out three types of citizens that dominate the contemporary era: Indifferents, Moralizers, and Inside-Dopesters. These three types are derived from their stance toward tradition and whether they are driven internally, by their own beliefs and values (inner-directed) or externally, by forces and factors external to their control (other-directed). Indifferents are mostly other directed, and view politics from a distance as spectators, and their political attitudes sometimes occasionally fit within the "Don't Know" column. This does not imply ignorance; rather, in Riesman's analysis, it reveals a consumerist approach and lack of ideological allegiance to a political party or emotional involvement with politics that makes Indifferents frequently susceptible to manipulation. Moralizers, on the other hand, are driven by a tendency toward self-improvement and idealism, and approach politics to protect their vested interests, individual and collective. Riesman (1950) distinguishes between Moralizers-in-Power, who pursue the interests of their "class positions, class aspirations or class-antagonisms," and Moralizers-in-Retreat, who experience disillusionment and displacement following lack of success in their political goals (p. 195). Moralizers are inner-directed, and are connected to tradition in varying ways, based on character. The Inside-Dopesters, finally, are those who have given up trying to change political process and find it best to try and understand it instead. They crave to resolve political issues by gaining access to the inside (p. 199). The Inside-Dopester approaches politics with a degree of realism and objectivity that the Moralizer, for instance, does not possess, although that may frequently be accompanied by more of a public relations approach to politics. While several citizens might fit neatly into these categories, most of us exhibit elements of all three behaviors, based on the issue at hand and our vested interest in it. These categories are best understood as behaviors or modes of involvement all citizens in a post-industrial, post-modern democracy engage in, rather than stereotypes.

Even though this brief overview does not do justice to Riesman's more detailed and data-driven characterizations, it helps in discussing civic engagement in more specific terms and avoiding general references to what the public knows or how the public civically engages. Valued as the concept of the public sphere may be, it contains a level of abstraction when it comes down to actual deliberative activities and orientations pursued by citizens. *The Lonely Crowd* describes the ways in which a collection of other-directed individuals compromises leadership, human potential, and autonomy. While this conclusion is conceptually close to Habermas, the distinction between Indifferents, Moralizers, and Inside-dopesters provides a more informed and in-depth way of understanding the connection between the informed citizen, democracy, and civic engagement (or disengagement/apathy). Within these three modes of political involvement, reactions to politics are understood through a more complex set of social and political factors that influence the political behavior of the individual. Riesman's (1950) work is ultimately about the meaning of autonomy in a contemporary era (Gitlin, 2002). Autonomy, over commitment to a public sphere is connected to specific contemporary political behaviors, and could explain how citizens employ both analogue and digital media of representation.

In defense of citizen autonomy, Schudson (1998) presented one citizen model that characterizes most contemporary forms of civic engagement: the monitorial citizen. According to Schudson (1998), monitorial citizens "scan (rather than read) the informational environment . . . so that they may be alerted on a variety of issues . . . and may be mobilized around those issues in a large variety of ways" (p. 310). Monitorial citizens are "defensive," rather than "proactive," surveying the political scene, looking "inactive, but [poised] for action if action is required" (p. 311). Monitorial behavior is motivated by the need to manage information overload delivered by the media and the need to meet minimum civic obligations.

Analogue and Digital Representation

It is through this lens of monitorial activity that the function of mass media and newer media need to be examined, so as to understand how the contemporary citizen re-appropriates media to cast him/herself as a surveyor of civic affairs and occasional civic watchdog, monitoring and occasionally informing the political environment, as necessary. Within a dormant public sphere, colonized by media of commercial focus, the monitorial scope of the citizen is limited. It is within this context that newer information technologies emerge to provide the monitorial citizen with the tools that enable the navigation and management of a complex sphere of information and public affairs. Views on this potential of newer technologies vary, ranging from optimists who perceive them as democratizing forces (e.g., Bell, 1981; Johnson & Kaye, 1998; Kling, 1996; Negroponte, 1998; Rheingold, 1993), to moderates who emphasize the pluralizing effect they have, making democracy more porous (e.g., Bimber, 1998; Blumler & Gurevitch, 2001), to those who question the impact of these technologies on civic deliberation (e.g., Bimber & Davis, 2003; Davis, 1999; Hill & Hughes, 1998; Jankowski & van Selm, 2000; Jones, 1997; Margolis & Resnick, 2000; Scheufele & Nisbet, 2002).

Before examining exactly how newer technologies empower or restrict the monitorial citizen, it is essential to address three aspects of online communication as they directly affect the social and political capital generated by online media: *access* to information, *reciprocity* of communication, and *commercialization* of online space.

Greater *access* to information, enabled by online media, does not guarantee accelerated political activity, increased political interest, or better informed citizens (Bimber, 2001; Kaid, 2002). The advantages of the Internet are avail-able only to the select few who have access to it, thus creating or expanding elite structures (Pavlik, 1994; Sassi, 2005; Williams & Pavlik, 1994; Williams, 1994). Moreover, while digitally enabling citizens (Abramson, Arterton, & Orren, 1988; Grossman, 1995; Jones, 1997; Rash, 1997), online media simultaneously reproduce class, gender, and race inequalities, which define civic involvement and interest (Hargittai, 2008; Hill & Hughes, 1988). Finally, the information access the Internet provides also typically results in entertainment uses of the medium (Althaus & Tewksbury, 2000; Shah, Kwak, & Holbert, 2001), which do not necessarily expand the political horizons of interested citizens.

Several scholars argue that in order for online discussion to be democratizing, it must be characterized by *reciprocity*. Online discussion of public affairs can connect diasporic constituencies but may also reproduce and magnify cultural disparities (e.g., Mitra, 1997a, 1997b; Schmitz, 1997). Scholars routinely point to online political discussions that are amorphous, fragmented, and too specific to bring together a disconnected electorate. Online communication typically takes place among people who already know each other offline (Uslaner, 2004), while online discussions are frequently dominated by elites (Jankowski & van Selm, 2000).

Finally, the *commercialization* of online media concerns scholars, who note its gradual transition from virtual commons to virtual shopping arcade. As a medium constructed within a capitalist context, the Internet is vulnerable to commercial interests (Schiller, 2000, 2006; McChesney, 1995, 2004). Specifically, online media are unable to single-handedly "produce political culture when it does not exist in society at large" (McChesney, 1995, p. 13). Moreover, online content typically overlaps that provided by traditional mass media or fails to attract the masses in the manner traditional media do (Bimber & Davis, 2003; Margolis, Resnick, & Tu, 1997; Scheufele & Nisbet, 2002).

Provided these three conditions are met, then civic interaction fostered by digital technologies could potentially contribute to the social capital generated by previous offline analogue methods of representation and deliberation. A drastic and technologically-induced transformation of political interaction overestimates (and misunderstands) the affordances of online technologies. Concurrently, to dismiss the political potential of online media would overlook some distinct trends developing in response to a representative democracy that frequently isolates its citizens in systems of one-directional communication. Coleman (2005) argues that online technologies combine representative and direct democracy elements to create direct representation capabilities, which offer citizens "the prospect of representative closeness, mutuality, conference, and empathy without expecting them to become full time participating citizens" (p. 211). Direct representation presents the modus operandi for the contemporary *monitorial citizen*, who surveys the political environment may be mobilized when necessary. Whereas analogue media provided limited and structured opportunities for access to information and communication with the political structure, online digital media expand the set of tools monitorial citizens have at their disposal, so that may monitor developments and mobilize if necessary. I illustrate how this dormant political consciousness is supported and activated in two recently formulated modes of civic involvement.

Blogosphere: The Case of the Accidental Journalist

Blogs bear considerable democratizing potential as they provide media consumers with the opportunity to become media producers (Dominick, 1999; Papacharissi, 2007), and are commonly defined as webpages that consist of regular or daily posts, arranged in reverse chronological order and archived (Herring, Kouper, Scheid, & Wright, 2004). Typically, however, most blogs regress to self-confessional posts that resemble diaries, with few exceptions that engage in journalistically informed punditry (Papacharissi, 2007; Scott, 2007; Sundar, Edwards, Hu, & Stavrositu, 2007) of variable impact. Therefore, some find it necessary to distinguish between A-list blogs (popular publicized blogs), blogs that are somewhat interconnected, and the majority of sparsely socially connected and less conversational blogs (Herring et al., 2005).

The blogosphere refers to the collective community of blogs, bearing the assumption that several of these blogs are interconnected and capable of exerting sizable influence on the media. The term implies a word play with the greek root *logos* (meaning word) and employs the term sphere to confer a sense of community and democratic relevance. Because several blog providers track posts and connections between bloggers, but also because blogging thrives on the monitoring of friend and peer posts, the term blogosphere accurately captures the level of interconnectedness among bloggers.

There are several instances in which bloggers direct mainstream media coverage, usually by creating noise over issues or political candidates initially marginalized by mainstream media (Kerbel & Bloom, 2005; Meraz, 2007; Tremayne, 2007). Several major news outlets, including CNN, employ blogs to add a "finger on the pulse of the people" element to their coverage. Most CNN news shows and several major online news web sites (CNN.com, BBC.co.uk) routinely feature stories or content on the mood of the blogosphere on a given issue. Other mainstream outlets, like the *New York Times*, have incorporated blogging into their traditional reporting, and use it to provide in-depth reporting and/or expand on their issue coverage.

Blogs, video blogs (vlogs), and similar expressions may be viewed as an articulation of what Scammell (2000) terms "consumer-style critique," symptomatic of a hedonistic and materialistic culture (p. 354). It should be clarified that most blogs are not news or politically-oriented. Possibly a latter breed of Riesman's (1950) Moralizers, bloggers judge the relevance and importance of political issues subjectively and with the self as the point of reference. Quantitative analyses of blogs find them to be largely self-referential (Papacharissi, 2007) and motivated by personal fulfillment (Kaye, 2007). Even news-oriented, A-list blogs present a blend of public and private factoids and conversation that is subjectively arrived at by standards removed from those of the journalistic profession.

But, it should be noted that blogs do not present or replace journalism, and any such consideration would undermine their potential. The blogger operates as the accidental journalist, engaging in information-gathering that is determined by whim, personal preference, and indulgence in personal interests. Bloggers stumble upon issues in their daily routines that they subjectively decide to feature on their blogs. Professional journalists are guided by commercially viable public interest and restricted by institutional mandates. Bloggers publicize their private agendas of issues they consider important; journalists typically must choose from a public agenda of issues to cover. In fact, the blogosphere's primary contribution lies in challenging what other democratic institutions define as public or private, frequently modifying the established hierarchy of public issues by adding concerns previously considered private. Therefore, blogs exemplify the tendency of online media to "to deinstitutionalize politics, fragment communication, and accelerate the pace of the public agenda and decision making" (Bimber, 2000, p. 333).

Blogs pluralize the public agenda by adopting two modes of media influence: first, by functioning as contemporary opinion-leaders, and second, by monitoring news developments operating as media watchdogs. As opinion leaders, bloggers use their own blogs as public pulpits to express opinions on public affairs (e.g., Scott, 2007; Tremayne, 2007). Through a web of interconnections with other bloggers and with conventional media, they may be able, on occasion, to create sufficient noise that allows a direct impact on the media, public, and policy agendas. As watchdogs, they employ their blogs and the blogosphere to draw attention to issues marginalized or ignored by mainstream media (e.g., Meraz, 2007; Sundar et al., 2007) Therefore, blogs are meaningful in their ability to dilute the agenda setting influence of traditional news sources, and to present novel, more personal private standards for what should be considered news.

For monitorial citizens, blogs present the space where what is defined as private and what is defined as public can be challenged, and where hierarchies of issues determined by power elites can be revised, and agendas re-aligned. Within a traditional representative democracy, the monitorial citizen surveys information but has limited avenues of becoming involved, should it become necessary to do so. However, within the more porous political environment blogs enable, monitorial citizens are afforded (a) a wider scope of issue and coverage to monitor, (b) guidance on issues based on standards that resemble their own, and (c) direct route of mobilization and exerting influence.

YouTube: Reconstruction and Satire

Much like blogging, YouTube presents another illustration of citizen journalism. Similar to the blogosphere, YouTube contributes to political conversation by expanding the agenda of issues covered and providing individuals with a forum through which they can articulate their opinions. YouTube, like the blogosphere, is based on amorphously organized and anarchically determined presentation of user generated content, except, for YouTube most of the content is audio/visual, and carries little, if any, written commentary.

YouTube premiered in February 2005, and unlike competing video providers, took advantage of an open and convenient architecture to attract user contributions. The appeal of YouTube has been described as "Easy to use and does not tell you what to do" (Boutin, 2006), while others highlight the diversity of content featured, making mention of the "Many Tribes of YouTube" (Hefferman, 2007), or the authenticity of communication featured (Story, 2007; Young, 2007). YouTube contains vast amounts of audiovisual content, presented in an unstructured format that makes the site virtually impossible to monitor or regulate. Some of this content violates copyright, in that it manifestly reproduces content already copyrighted by other entities, and had been the subject of prior lawsuits against YouTube and its parent company, Google (e.g., Broache & Sandoval, 2007). Other types of content present creative re-workings of media content in ways that endorse the audience member as media producer, and promote political satire and dialogue. The main draw is that YouTube user generated content serves a variety or purposes, ranging from catching a politician in a lie to impromptu karaoke, with no restrictions.

The broad appeal of YouTube has been generating economic and political interest. CNN partnered with YouTube to run the much advertised YouTube debates during the 2008 Presidential primaries. Barack Obama's campaign had used the portal to post video content and take questions from voters, and as president-elect, he employed the medium to broadcast frequent addresses to the public. These more traditionally-oriented uses of YouTube do not capture the unique appeal of the portal, however, best known for its satirical reconstruction of the Apple "1984" ad (in support of Obama and in critique of Hillary Clinton) or for posting content catching Senator George Allen, a Republican from Virginia using inappropriate language.

Where blogging provides the pulpit, YouTube provides the irreverence, humor, and unpredictability necessary for rejuvenating political conversation trapped in conventional formulas. As participatory citizen journalism, YouTube illustrates a contemporary take on the editorial cartoon and satire, elements of reporting that are popular and typically generate more emotional reactions, yet not central to news portals at present. It is no accident that YouTube generated early attention by routinely featuring satirical quips by *The Daily Show with Jon Stewart*. The prominence of satirical content reveals a playful mood that results in a creative and no-sense pastiche of content that is befitting of post-modern political tastes and orientations. YouTube content completes the media and news sphere that the monitorial citizen scans while surveying the political environment, by adding various and diverse takes on political reality. YouTube also provides an opportunity for expression different from conventional mobilization, opinion expression, or protest. Not all issues on the monitorial citizen radar warrant these types of reaction; several simply evoke sarcasm, humor, or satire, which are equally important forms of political thought and expression.

The Private and the Public

The present review of civic engagement, as it persists with representative democracy and the public sphere and is enabled by online digital channels, traces the progression of a citizen who has retreated from public sphere of inter-action to a private space of thought, expression, and reaction. Some have argued that the trend Riesman had begun to describe in *The Lonely Crowd* should be reversed, marking a turn from the other-directed condition back to the inner-directed condition (Sennett, 1978). In the context of self-absorption and evolving narcissism (Lasch, 1979), determining what is inside is prone to "confusion [that] has arose between public and intimate life; people are working out in terms of personal feelings public matters which properly can be dealt with only through codes of impersonal meaning" (Sennett, 1978). The contempo-rary citizen functions civically in a cultural environment which is founded upon the tension between that which is considered public and that which is consid-ered private. Civic apathy also expresses a dissatisfaction with how the state or media institutions have prioritized public and private issues, including certain private concerns in the public affairs agenda while excluding others. Subsequently, any online digital media are employed by individuals to rectify perceived inconsistencies between what citizens deem as public, but other civic institutions have excluded from their agenda as private. This view acknowl-edges the limited opportunities for direct communication and reaction within a representative democracy. It also incorporates the inadequacy of commercial media in forwarding an agenda that is consistent with the public's understand-ing of what merits public coverage. Finally, it is aligned with a contemporary understanding of the citizen who evaluates public affairs with the self as the point of reference, and with the tools afforded him/her in post-industrial repre-sentative democracies at hand. A post on a blog, a video log in YouTube, even the practice of following a blog represent public expressions of private dissent, albeit mild, with a mainstream media agenda determined by elite power con-stellations.

The citizen in a representative democracy, previously enabled within the public sphere and through civic deliberation, is now enabled via a private sphere and through the use of private media environments. This private citizen is not politically disinterested; on the contrary, this citizen is politically inter-ested in modes that are not easily captured via aggregate measures, such as polls, and has a political appetite that is not satiated by mass produced content. Therefore, the personalized content provided by online media fits well within this citizen's private sphere of contemplation, evaluation, and action, in which the self remains the point of reference. This citizen is alone, but not lonely or isolated.

Online media take the overlap and tension between the private and the public under consideration and contain the architecture to support and articulate it. Contemporary media and political institutions, on the other hand, are successful in their attempts to engage the public in so far as they acknowledge the tension between the private and the public, and ineffective when this tension is ignored. Future models of journalism should directly engage the tension between the meaning of private and public information, as they redefine journalistic roles and modes of communication.

References

Abramson, J. B., Arterton, F. C., & Orren, G. R. (1988). *The electronic commonwealth: The impact of new media technologies on democratic politics*. New York: Basic Books.

Althaus, S. L., & Tewksbury, D. (2000). Patterns of Internet and traditional media use in a networked community. *Political Communication, 17*, 21–45.

Bell, D. (1981). The social framework of the information society. In T. Forester (Ed.), *The microelectronics revolution* (pp. 500–549). Cambridge, MA: MIT Press.

Bimber, B. (1998). The Internet and political transformation: Populism, community, and accelerated pluralism. *Polity, 3*, 133–160.

Bimber, B. (2000). The study of information technology and civic engagement. *Political Communication, 17*(4), 329–333.

Bimber, B. (2001). Information and political engagement in America: The search for effects of information technology at the individual level. *Political Research Quarterly, 54*, 53–67.

Bimber, B., & Davis, R. (2003). *Campaigning online: The Internet in U.S. elections*. Oxford: Oxford University Press.

Blumler, J. G., & Gurevitch, M. (2001). The new media and our political communication discontents: Democratizing cyberspace. *Information, Communication & Society, 4*, 1–14.

Boutin, P. (2006). A grand unified theory of YouTube and MySpace. *Slate*, posted April 28, 2006, http://www.slate.com/id/2140635/.

Broache, A., & Sandoval, G. (2007, March 13). Viacom sues Google over YouTube clips. CNET News, http://news.cnet.com/Viacom-sues-Google-over-YouTube-clips/2100-1030_3-6166668.html, url accessed 2008/11/25.

Cappella, J., & Jamieson, K. H. (1996). News frames, political cynicism, and media cynicism. *Annals of the American Academy of Political and Social Science, 546*, 71–85.

Cappella, J., & Jamieson, K. H. (1997). *Spiral of cynicism: The press and the public good*. New York: Oxford University Press.

Carey, J. (1995). The press, public opinion, and public discourse. In T. Glasser & C. Salmon (Eds.), *Public opinion and the communication of consent* (pp. 373–402). New York: Guilford.

Coleman, S. (2005). The lonely citizen: Indirect representation in an age of networks. *Political Communication, 22*(2), 197–214.

Davis, R. (1999). *The web of politics: The Internet's impact on the American political system*. New York: Oxford.

Delli Carpini, M. X. (1999). In search of the informed citizen: What Americans know about politics and why it matters. Paper presented at the conference on The Transformation of Civic Life, Middle State Tennessee State University, Murfreesboro and Nashville, Tennessee, November 12–13, 1999.

Dominick, J. (1999). Who do you think you are? Personal home pages and self-presentation on the world wide web. *Journalism and Mass Communication Quarterly, 76,* 4, 646–658.

Fallows, J. (1996, February). Why Americans hate the media. *The Atlantic Monthly, 277,* 2, 45–64.

Fraser, N. (1992). Rethinking the public sphere: A contribution to the critique of actually existing democracy. In C. Calhoun (Ed.), *Habermas and the public sphere* (pp. 109–142). Cambridge, MA: MIT Press.

Gitlin, Todd (May 24, 2002). David Riesman, Thoughtful Pragmatist. *The Chronicle of Higher Education* (http://chronicle.com/free/v48/i37/37b00501.htm, retrieved on 2008–11–25).

Grossman, L. K. (1995). *The electronic republic.* New York: Viking.

Habermas, J. (1962/1989). *The structural transformation of the public sphere: An inquiry into a category of a bourgeois society* (T. Burger & F. Lawrence, trans.). Cambridge, MA: MIT Press. (Original work published 1962.)

Habermas, J. (1974/2004). The public sphere. In F. Webster (Ed.), *The Information society reader* (pp. 350–356). London: Routledge.

Hargittai, E. (2008). The digital reproduction of inequality. In D. Grusky, (Ed.), *Social Stratification,* Edited (pp. 936–944). Boulder, CO: Westview Press.

Hart, R. P. (1994). Easy citizenship: Television's curious legacy. *Annals of the American Academy of Political and Social Science, 546,* 109–120.

Hefferman, V. (May 27, 2007). The many tribes of YouTube. *New York Times,* p. 1, 23, Section 2.

Herbst, S. (1993). *Numbered voices: How opinion polling has shaped American politics.* Chicago: University of Chicago Press.

Herring, S. C., Scheidt, L. A., Kouper, I., & Wright, E. (2007). Longitudinal content analysis of blogs 2003–2004. In M. Tremayne (Ed.), *Blogging, citizenship, and the future of media* (pp. 3–20). New York: Routledge.

Hill, K. A., & Hughes, J. E. (1998). *Cyberpolitics: Citizen activism in the age of the Internet.* New York: Rowman and Littlefield Publishers, Inc.

Jankowski, N. W., & van Selm, M. (2000). The promise and practice of public debate in cyberspace. In K. Hacker, & J. van Dijk (Eds.), *Digital democracy: Issues of theory and practice.* London: Sage.

Johnson, T. J., & Kaye, B. K. (1998). A vehicle for engagement or a haven for the disaffected? Internet use, political alienation, and voter participation. In T. J. Johnson, C. E. Hays, & S. P. Hays (Eds.), *Engaging the public: How the government and media can reinvigorate democracy* (pp. 123–135). Lanham, MD: Roman and Littlefield.

Jones, S. G. (1997). The Internet and its social landscape. In S. G. Jones (Ed.), *Virtual culture: Identity and communication in cybersociety* (pp. 7–35). Thousand Oaks, CA: Sage.

Kaid, L. L. (2002). Political advertising and information seeking: Comparing exposure via traditional and Internet channels. *Journal of Advertising, 31,* 27–35.

Kaye, B. K. (2007). Blog use motivations. In M. Tremayne (Ed.), *Blogging, citizenship, and the future of media* (pp. 127–148). New York: Routledge.

Kerbel, M. R., & Bloom, J. D. (2005). Blog for America and civic involvement. *Harvard International Journal of Press Politics*, 10 (4), 3–27.

Kling, R. (1996). Hopes and horrors: Technological utopianism and anti-utopianism in narratives of computerization. In R. Kling (Ed.), *Computerization and controversy* (pp. 40–58). Boston: Academic Press.

Lasch, C. (1979). *The culture of narcissism.* New York: Norton & Co.

Lasch, C. (1995). *The revolt of the elites and the betrayal of democracy.* New York: Norton & Co.

Margolis, M., & Resnick, D. (2000). *Politics as usual: The cyberspace Revolution.* Thousand Oaks: Sage.

Margolis, M., Resnick, D., & Tu, C. (1997). Campaigning on the Internet: Parties and candidates on the World Wide Web in the 1996 primary season. *Harvard International Journal of Press/Politics*, 2, 59–78.

McChesney, R. (1995). The Internet and U.S. communication policy-making in historical and critical perspective. *Journal of Computer-Mediated Communication* 1(4), URL (consulted Jan. 2001): http://www.usc.edu/dept/annenberg/vol1/issue4/mcchesney.html#Democracy.

McChesney, R. (2004). Media policy goes to main street: The uprising of 2003. *Communication Review*, 7(3), 223–258.

Meraz, S. (2007). Analyzing political conversation on the Howard Dean candidate blog. In M. Tremayne (Ed.), *Blogging, citizenship, and the future of media* (pp. 59–82). New York: Routledge.

Mitra, A. (1997a). Virtual community: Looking for India on the Internet. In S. G. Jones (Ed.), *Virtual culture: Identity and communication in cybersociety* (pp. 55–79). Thousand Oaks, CA: Sage.

Mitra, A. (1997b). Diasporic web sites: Ingroup and outgroup discourse. *Critical Studies in Mass Communication*, 14,158–181.

Negroponte, N. (1998). Beyond digital. *Wired*, 6(12), 288.

Papacharissi, Z. (2007). The blogger revolution? Audiences as media producers. In M. Tremayne (Ed.), *Blogging, citizenship, and the future of media* (pp. 21–38). New York: Routledge.

Patterson, T. (1993). *Out of order.* New York: Knopf.

Patterson, T. (1996). Bad news, bad governance. *Annals of the American Academy of Political and Social Science*, 546, 97–108.

Pavlik, J. V. (1994). Citizen access, involvement, and freedom of expression in an electronic environment. In F. Williams, & J. V. Pavlik (Eds.), *The people's right to know: Media, democracy, and the information highway* (pp. 139–162). Hillsdale, NJ: Lawrence Erlbaum.

Putnam, R. D. (1996). The strange disappearance of civic America. *The American Prospect*, 24, 1, 34–48.

Rash, W. (1997). *Politics on the nets: wiring the political process.* New York: W. H. Freeman & Co.

Rheingold, H. (1993). *The virtual community: Finding connection in a computerized world.* Boston, MA: Addison-Wesley Longman Publishing.

Riesman, D. (1950). *The lonely crowd.* New Haven Yale University Press.

Sassi, S. (2005). Cultural differentiation or social segregation? Four approaches to the digital divide. *New Media Society*, 7(5), 684–700.

Scammell, M. (2000). The Internet and civic engagement: The age of the citizen-consumer. *Political Communication*, http://www.informaworld.com/smpp/title~content=t713774515~db=all~tab=issueslist~branches=17 – v17 *17*(4), 351–355.

Scheufele, D. A., & Nisbet, M. (2002). Being a citizen online: New opportunities and dead ends. *Harvard International Journal of Press/Politics*, 7, 55–75.

Schiller, D. (1999). *Digital capitalism: Networking the global marketing system*. Cambridge, MA: MIT Press.

Schiller, D. (2006). *How to think about information*. Urbana: University of Illinois Press.

Schmitz, J. (1997). Structural relations, electronic media, and social change: The public electronic network and the homeless. In S.G. Jones (Ed.), *Virtual culture: Identity and communication in cybersociety* (pp. 80–101). Thousand Oaks, CA: Sage.

Schudson, M. (1997) Why conversation is not the soul of democracy. *Critical Studies in Mass Communication*, *14*, 1–13.

Schudson, M. (1998). *The good citizen: A history of American civic life*. New York: Free Press.

Scott, D. T. (2007) Pundits in Muckrakers' clothing: Political blogs and the 2004 US presidential election. In M. Tremayne (Ed.), *Blogging, citizenship and the future of media* (pp. 39–58). New York: Routledge.

Sennett, R. (1978). *The fall of public man*. New York: Alfred A. Knopf.

Shah, D. V., Kwak, N., & Holbert, R. L. (2001). Connecting and disconnecting with civic life: Patterns of Internet use and the production of social capital. *Political Communication*, *18*, 141–162.

Story, L. (May 26, 2007). Putting amateurs in charge. *New York Times*, pp. B1, B9.

Sundar, S. S., Edwards, H. H., Hu, Y., & Stavrositu. C. (2007). Blogging for better health: Putting the "public" back in public health. In M. Tremayne (Ed.), *Blogging, citizenship, and the future of media* (pp. 83–102). New York: Routledge.

Tremayne, M. (2007). *Blogging, citizenship and the future of media*. New York: Routledge.

Uslaner, E. M. (2004). Trust, civic engagement, and the Internet. *Political Communication*, *21*(2), 223–242.

Williams, F. (1994). On prospects for citizens' information services. In F. Williams & J. V. Pavlik (Eds.), *The people's right to know: Media, democracy, and the information highway* (pp. 3–24). Hillsdale, NJ: Erlbaum.

Williams, F., & Pavlik, J. V. (1994). Epilogue. In F. Williams & J. V. Pavlik (Eds.), *The people's right to know: Media, democracy, and the information highway* (pp. 211–224). Hillsdale, NJ: Erlbaum.

Young, J. R. (May 11, 2007). An anthropologist explores the culture of video blogging. *Chronicle of Higher Education*, 53 (36), accessed http://chronicle.com/, July 2007.

Chapter 3

Institutional Roadblocks

Assessing Journalism's Response to Changing Audiences

Wilson Lowrey

In a mid-sized daily newspaper in the American South, administrators have mounted a giant board covered with rows of newspaper front pages from previous weeks. Each page accompanies a chart with circulation and penetration figures for that day. The board's purpose is clear—it's an oracle, offering cryptic truths about the hidden connection between news content and audience behavior. And the truths remain cryptic. As one editor puts it, "If anyone in this building tells you they know how to interpret this, they're full of it."

The divide between news media and audience is not new. Historically, journalists have ignored, rationalized away, or redefined audiences to suit their own needs or to conform to constraints (e.g., Ettema & Whitney, 1994; McQuail, 1997, 2005; Ryan & Peterson, 1982; Sumpter, 2000). The newsroom's wall of uncertainty and the editor's reaction to it suggest the disconnect continues, and that journalists are still able to shrug it off.

How much longer will this be the case in our age of connectedness, where distance is passé and anyone can commit acts of journalism? Shouldn't journalists now be compelled to answer the gate-knocking from the audience—or from those "formerly known as the audience" (Rosen, 2006)? To what degree is technological change spurring journalists to bridge the journalist-audience divide? This essay examines these questions and assesses the most likely responses by news organizations to today's increasingly uncertain audience dynamics.

There are signs that those within news organizations have become more familiar with those outside it. Words like "interactivity" and "participatory" are now common in the journalist's vocabulary. The number of news-oriented blogs and traditional news sites hosting blogs has increased dramatically over the last two years (Lenhart & Fox, 2006; Lowrey & Mackay, 2008; Pew Research Center, 2008). Journalists report receiving more feedback from audiences via e-mail and discussion forums (Hendrickson, 2006; Rosenberry, 2005), as well as through site-use data (Domingo, 2008a; MacGregor, 2007; McKenzie, et al., 2008), and there is some evidence that awareness of local blogs leads journalists to adopt blogs as sources (Dylko & Kosicki, 2006; Lowrey & Mackay, 2008). Rising online traffic and ad sales, coupled with stagnant audience and sales figures for traditional news forms (Newspaper Association of America,

2008; The Project for Excellence in Journalism, 2007), and increasing profit pressures from public ownership of news companies suggests these trends may continue.

Scholars and news professionals have focused much attention on these changes in technologies and news practices and structures. Yet, equally as interesting is the stability. Much has not changed, and many change efforts by news organizations have been skin-deep and fleeting. Formal efforts to reach online audiences—blogging, citizen journalism projects, convergence partnerships—have been criticized as superficial (Gade, 2004; Lowrey, 2005; Singer, 2004, 2005), and there is evidence the traditional work routines of journalism practice still dominate decision-making (Cassidy, 2006; Domingo, 2008a; Singer, 2004, 2005). The reluctance of news organizations to accept new practices is well-documented, reaching back to the introduction of half-tone and wirephoto technologies (Zelizer, 1995). What accounts for this intractability? It is unclear whether intimacy with, and challenges from, audiences will lead to greater openness, or whether journalists will seek to maintain distance, legitimacy, and authority—or some combination of these.

To shed light on these questions, this essay adopts the framework of "new institutionalism" from the sociology of organizations.[1] New institutionalists hold that all organizations seek public legitimacy through conformity with wider cultural "accounts" of how an organization or field is supposed to behave and in accord with the needs of other social, political, and economic institutions. Pursuit of legitimacy may supersede interest in the organization's efficiency and optimization, and adoption of organizational forms and practices may become independent of their functionality. In fact, change for the sake of short-term efficiency can present problems for institutional organizations so that managers may ignore new trends or merely adopt them superficially. Organizations may buffer themselves from the demands of external realities, ducking concrete feedback and ignoring evaluation—examples of what institutionalists call "loose coupling"—in order to maintain accordance with wider institutions, and thus their sanctioned appearance. New institutional theory has been most frequently applied to government institutions and non-profits, for which it is difficult to measure success, but more recently researchers have applied the theory to commercial firms (Budros, 2004; Fligstein, 1991) including news organizations (Cook, 1998, 2006; Kaplan, 2006; Lowrey, 2005; Ryfe, 2006) and public relations organizations (Wehmeier, 2006).

It is argued here that traditionally, journalists have acted institutionally—at least in part—in their behavior toward audiences, and that they are loosely coupled from audience response. Unlike other professionals such as doctors and accountants, journalists do not meet one-on-one with their clients,[2] and direct impact of audiences on professional and organizational practice is relatively weak (Pritchard & Berkowitz, 1991; Weaver, et al., 2007). Distance from their clientele has prompted journalists to substitute conventional stand-ins for the relatively unknown audience, including professional colleagues, friends and family (McQuail, 1997, 2005; Sumpter, 2000). Journalists redefine the nature of audiences in order to win political battles within and outside their organizations (Gans, 1979; Webster & Phalen, 1994), and they often eschew audience research data, preferring "gut instinct" over aggregated opinions they consider ill-informed and low brow—or a threat to their autonomy (Gans, 1979; McQuail, 2005).

For a news organization to allow its content producers to ignore or reshape client responses flies in the face of business sense. It is irrational from the framework of the traditional "rational choice" model of economics, which assumes managers and their firms seek efficiency and optimization by responding rationally to information about their environment (DiMaggio & Powell, 1991). But it makes sense from an institutional perspective. Hard, visible evidence of performance quality, or lack of quality, may confound efforts to conform to the accepted accounts of other social institutions and the wider culture. Thus, New Institutional theory offers explanation for the persistence and widespread homogeneity of routines such as audience typification, and for the industry's sluggish adaptation to new technologies and changing audience dynamics.

It should be noted that news organizations are by no means entirely institutional—managers certainly do make optimized choices in response to market pressures, and these pressures are increasing in intensity. But this essay focuses on the institutional orientation, which has been less thoroughly examined in relation to recent uncertainties in the news organization's environment.

Before examining how organizations are likely to respond to increased activity by online audiences, two areas of literature need to be fleshed out. One is the literature on institutionalism, particularly as it relates to journalism and the news industry. In this framework, wider institutions and cultures are the antecedent, and organizational and professional behavior related to audiences is the outcome. Another is the literature on "audiencemaking" (Ettema and Whitney's term [1994]), which examines journalists' conceptions and constructions of audiences, and possible reasons for these. Literature on audiencemaking is explored first.

Mass Communicators' Conceptions of Audiences

Scholars have suggested that journalists cannot truly grasp the diverse, complex nature of those who experience the products of their work. So journalists, like other mass communicators, rely on constructed audiences. Early research on journalists' perceptions of audiences suggested communicators need some conception of the message receiver in their heads—an "imaginary interlocutor" or "reference group"—in order to communicate (Ball-Rokeach & Cantor, 1986; McQuail, 1997, 2005). The reference group perspective is found in research on various types of symbol producers, such as TV and print journalists (Burns, 1977; Gans, 1979; Sumpter, 2000), children's TV production (Wartella, 1994), and fine art production (DiMaggio & Hirsch, 1976).

Journalists and news managers may define audience response as response from professional colleagues. Gans (1979) found that news managers valued feedback from their own cultural milieu—e.g., fellow professionals, friends and family members—partly because these substitute audiences were likely to reinforce managers' own views. Other studies acknowledge the importance of occupational reference groups as well, in newspapers (Tuchman, 1978; Tunstall, 1971), TV production (Burns, 1969; Wartella, 1994; Pekurny, 1982), movie production (Gans, 1957), the production of news blogs (Lowrey & Latta, 2008), and in the production of fine art (Becker, 1982).

Mass communicators may hold audiences in contempt, perceiving them to be less intelligent and unappreciative (Burns, 1977; Schlesinger, 1978), uncritical and culturally low brow (Gans, 1979). Similar characterizations have been applied to online audiences, which journalists have perceived as uncivil, even dangerous—a "jerk swarm," according to one trade publication (Palser, 2006, p. 70). This animosity may spring from a concern that direct audience demands constrain media professionals' autonomy (McQuail, 2005).

Perhaps for a similar reason, media professionals historically have held audience research in contempt, eschewing findings from surveys and focus groups and doubting the validity and helpfulness of ratings (McQuail, 1997, 2005; Schlesinger, 1978) and online metrics such as page views (Quinn & Trench, 2002). News managers for national print and TV sometimes ignore or reject the intangible mass audience of marketing research (Gans, 1979). Wartella (1994) found that producers of children's television rely on "guts and instinct" to estimate audience preferences. As one producer said, "If you have to go to research to find out what children like, then there is something wrong with you" (p. 49).

Ettema and Whitney (1994) question whether audience substitutes in the heads of media professionals have much impact on decision-making, suggesting such "fantasies" may be "harmless ghosts in the production machine" (p. 8). Rather, they say audience constructions may be produced in strategies and interactions at the organizational level. Audiences are "reconstituted" as having social meaning or financial value for groups within and outside organizations. For example, both groups within media organizations and external entities that regularly interact with media organizations (such as news sources), create and adopt different accounts of the audience to gain strategic advantage (Cantor, 1971; Gans, 1957). Through a "contest of wills, cabals and behind-the-scene alliances, contestants rationalize their self-interests in terms of what the audience will like" (Ryan & Peterson, 1982, p. 24). Within newsrooms, visual journalists push portrayals of audiences as impatient, busy and distracted, and print reporters are more likely to view audiences as taking time to read in-depth (Lowrey, 2002). Similarly, online journalists pushing for more use of multimedia are likely to portray audiences as technically savvy (Boczkowski, 2004). Audience constructions are used to reinforce arguments about the need for regulation, with TV companies portraying audiences as astute consumers, and regulators and external pressure groups portraying them as helpless victims

(Webster & Phalen, 1994). Even audience metrics can be strategic constructions. They are used to show advertisers "a heretofore unmeasured audience, to correct a damaging impression of an audience, or to highlight flattering new details about an audience" (Miller, 1994, p. 60).

In planning meetings, claims are made about the nature of audiences that correlate with characteristics of media products that have proven successful in the past (Ryan & Peterson, 1982). Thus, uncertainty is reduced by mimicking products with proven track records (McQuail, 1997, 2005; Ryan & Peterson, 1982), and the validity of these decisions is increased by invoking the audience. Mimicry is particularly likely for Internet media, as successful product forms are conveniently available for monitoring (Boczkowski & de Santos, 2007).

These strategic perceptions of audiences become taken-for-granted typifications within media organizations and media professions, and they constrain decision-making invisibly. Typifications correlate with the needs of other institutions on which journalism depends: advertisers rely on audience data for their decision-making, and they value quantified measures; regulatory bodies find useful the typification of audiences as victims; media chains and syndicates benefit from the static typification of audience in the product-image framework, thus easing coordination and decision-making. The notion that journalists typify audiences and that news organizations buffer internal decision-making from the impact of daily audience feedback fits well with the institutional approach. These typifications and loose coupling allow conformity with wider institutional needs.

New Institutional Theory

The new institutional approach, with roots in political science, economics, and sociology, is a reaction to social science frameworks that have viewed human agents as purely calculating, goal-oriented, and acontextual. New institutionalists have focused instead on the power of habits, norms, and unquestioned typifications in shaping decision-making, the fruitfulness of loose coupling, and the crucial context of organizations' environments.

As early as 1898, the economist Thorstein Veblen emphasized the role of environmental influences and taken-for-granted conventions in shaping behavior. However, it is Max Weber's notion of legitimacy that most obviously informs today's institutionalism. While Weber recognized the pull of materialism and the power of economic constraints, he also emphasized the influence of widely-held beliefs, norms, and traditions (DiMaggio & Powell, 1991; Scott, 1995). Weber offered the example of soldiers, who may easily overthrow their officers at any time through sheer numbers, but who instead obey orders, because they expect others to obey them and because they unquestioningly accept the legitimacy of military authority and rules (Collins & Makowsky, 1998). Subsequent institutional scholarship has focused on the gap between formal and informal organizational behavior, on the development of organizational routines, on the mimicry of convenient models, and on decision makers' adherence to familiar, previously taken paths (DiMaggio & Powell, 1991).

The "new institutionalism" was initiated in the 1970s with an influential piece by Stanford sociologists John Meyer and Brian Rowan (1977), and the framework has been elaborated in subsequent research (e.g., DiMaggio & Powell, 1983; Scott & Meyer, 1991; Scott, 1995; Tolbert & Zucker, 2001). These scholars distinguished institutional settings from "relational" or "technical" settings, in which organizations are highly responsive. Competitive marketplace conditions are an example of a relational setting. Divisions within relational organizations are tightly coordinated, and internal rules and policies ostensibly lead to efficiency and optimized practices (Meyer & Rowan, 1977; Scott & Meyer, 1991). In contrast, institutional settings are based on typifications and on interpretations that are taken for granted and sanctioned by society. Conformity with institutionalized rules and expectations leads the organization to Weberian legitimacy, which elicits resources from other organizations: "Organizations compete not just for resources and customers, but for political power and institutional legitimacy, for social as well as economic fitness" (Aldrich, 1979, p. 265). Institutionalized policies and practices acquire myth-like status, and organizations follow them ceremonially, regardless of the effectiveness of these policies and practices. Meyer and Rowan (1977) offer the example of the powerful social status of modern medicine, which is based on institutionalized rules for managing illness. Doctors adopt a social role and behaviors that conform with these rules, and spotty success rates with client-customers do little to dampen their authority (Abbott, 1988; Freidson, 1994).

The intrusion of a relational environment can cause trouble for institutional organizations. When output can be easily monitored and evaluated, "consumers gain considerable rights of inspection and control" (Meyer & Rowan, p. 354), and organizations must then respond directly. As a strategic defense against relational pressures, institutionalized organizations adopt "loose coupling," or a slackening of the bonds among divisions within organizations, between goals and ends, between administration and performance, and between provider and client. In contrast, relational organization may be said to be "tightly coupled," as goals are coordinated and attached to ends, output quality and efficiency are monitored and evaluated, and evaluation shapes subsequent product changes. Meyer and Rowan offer examples of loose coupling:

> Hospitals treat, not cure, patients. Schools produce students, not learning. In fact, data on technical performance are eliminated or rendered invisible. Hospitals try to ignore information on cure rates, public services avoid data about effectiveness, and schools deemphasize measures of achievement.
>
> (p. 357)

Research by Meyer, Scott and Deal (1983) on schools provides examples of loose coupling. They found that school administrations did not control classroom instruction in a direct, rigorous way; administrators conducted relatively little evaluation of the impact of instruction on students, and any evaluation tended to be invisible from stakeholders; administration did little to coordinate agendas of different subunits, allowing inconsistent programs and practices; and novel practices were not coordinated and enforced in a systematic way, resulting in an ongoing parade of inconsequential, trendy innovations. These methods of loose coupling allowed these schools to continue to conform to a public typification of "modern schooling" regardless of actual results, thereby maintaining legitimacy (Meyer, Scott & Deal, 1983).

How can this level of stability and success coincide with such seemingly irrational, inefficient practices? The most plausible explanation, say Meyer and Rowan (1978) is that "schools produce education for society, not for individuals or families" (p. 82). Schools serve largely as a stratifying mechanism for wider society, providing individuals with credentials and status, enabling the personnel needs of other social institutions, and helping to legitimate these institutions. Changing in response to individual students or families could make it difficult to conform to the legitimated perception society has about schools and their practices.

Institutionalism and Journalism

Just as educational instruction tends to occur in the isolation of the classroom, relatively removed from organizational coordination and control, the practice of journalism occurs on one side of "the wall" between editorial and the organization's revenue engines, though this buffer has eroded considerably in recent years (see, e.g., Gade, 2008; Sylvie & Witherspoon, 2002). Journalists' neutrality and autonomy are also forms of decoupling, serving "as a way to preclude attempts by individual news people to be more interactive and supportive of community engagement in their work" (Deuze, 2005). As will be discussed later, it is not uncommon for online news operations to be loosely coupled from main news operations, a structure that buffers the core product from the online product and the uncertainty it entails. And in their study of schools in the 1980s, Meyer, Scott and Deal found that 20 percent of teachers reported frequent teachers' evaluations. In comparison, Weaver and Wilhoit found in their 1983 survey of U.S. journalists that 35 percent reported "regularly receiving comments about their work" from supervisors (Weaver et al., 2007). These findings reinforce previous findings that many news organizations have not regularly, systematically, and formally monitored performance of newsroom professionals (Beaupre, 1991), and that feedback is often latent and indirect (Breed, 1955; Sigelman, 1973; Weaver et al., 2007).

Barriers between editorial and revenue production, loose evaluation by newsroom administrators, ideologies of neutrality and autonomy, and a distance from audiences are all forms of loose coupling that make it easier for news operations to cushion themselves from the uncomfortable fact that a substantial amount of news content does not address popular consumer preferences. That the Senate plans to bring up a foreign spending bill, or that the Democratic candidate has taken a six-point lead in the polls, or that the city council votes funds for downtown development is not information most find crucial for functioning successfully in their daily lives (though certainly some do). And judging by declining news consumption, fewer and fewer are entertained by such information. If, as Meyer and Rowan say, "Hospitals treat, not cure, patients" and "schools produce students, not learning," it may also be that journalists produce "news" rather than an informed, engaged public. Yet, regardless of whether or not journalism has been effective on an individual or social level, audiences have been buying news they don't necessarily need for generations, and they continue to do so, though news consumption rates have diminished. Historically, journalism seems to have survived—even thrived—by maintaining public legitimacy as an institution rather than by successfully analyzing and meeting the wishes and needs of customers or citizens. From where has journalism drawn this crucial public legitimacy? What wider institutional and cultural purposes does journalism serve?

Environmental Approaches in News Sociology

A number of scholarly approaches in news sociology are similar to new institutionalism in that they assume news media draw clout, credibility, and legitimacy from their environment.

Scholars of media and culture distinguish instrumental, technical processes and functions from wider cultural and social purposes—i.e., the media do the work of presenting and maintaining the dominant culture or cultures. James Carey observed that producing and reading news is like "attending a mass, a situation in which nothing new is learned but in which a particular view of the world is portrayed and confirmed" (Carey, 1985, p. 20). Kevin Barnhurst and John Nerone (2001) note that the daily output of journalism's "profane commercial operation" is decoupled from its "sacred political work," and that although news content is commonly disparaged, "the form of the newspaper is almost sanctified" (p. 1). Similarly, Altheide and Snow's (1978) media logic thesis suggests the form and grammar of the media become culturally sanctioned and concordant with the processes and structures of other social institutions. Likely, the lack of a strong legitimating media logic for Internet news slowed its initial acceptance by audiences and journalists (see e.g., Singer & Gonzalez-Velez, 2003), though that is changing (Deuze, 2004; Lowrey, 2004).

Other scholars suggest American journalism's most relevant cultural environment derives from the Progressive Era (Kaplan, 2006). The era coincided with the end of the party press, and it swept in a technocratic culture, where social problems are naturally addressed through facts, and solutions are technical. They say journalism derived its present legitimacy from the culture's belief in attainable solutions, applicability of detached, expert knowledge, and in the notion of an engaged public. The public has needed to know that an institution exists to provide public information, and check the powerful, and to report on pressing problems. It is less important that this institution perform effectively or even that the public pay much attention to it. Michael Schudson (2002) says journalists work to maintain an aura of sacredness and legitimacy, regardless of effectiveness or efficacy. Citing Manoff, he says, "Reporters deploy experts in stories not so much to provide viewers with information but to certify the journalist's effort, access, and superior knowledge [Manoff 1989, p. 69]."

Journalism's legitimacy also derives from fundamental association with powerful governmental, political, and corporate institutions. According to the power structure framework of Tichenor, Olien, and Donohue (1980), news media reflect the degree to which powerful institutions are concentrated in communities, and community powers monitor and send messages to, or about, one another through the news media. Similarly, media system dependency theory posits that news organizations strive to maintain ties to other social systems because they depend on their resources: "especially crucial . . . are strong connections with the political system that controls regulatory, trade and legitimacy resources and the economic system that controls profit-related resources" (Ball-Rokeach et al., 1999). Ryfe (2006) and Cook (1998) describe the national news media as a creature of dominant political institutions. Powerful politicians use the media to build coalitions and to send strategic messages, and "newsmaking and policymaking are . . . intertwined to the point of being indistinguishable (Cook, 2006, p. 167).

Responses to the Online Audience

Because the institution of news exists, publics can believe in at least the possibility of a mechanism for obtaining "right answers," and in the public's involvement in this mechanism. As Kaplan (2006) says, the press is "part and parcel of the democratic public sphere. Its authority derives from its service to the public's deliberations" (p. 177). Powerful sources depend on news media to serve as vessels for their messages, and these vessels must be credible and legitimate for the messages to be credible and legitimate (Hallin, 1997). Thus, New Institutionalism suggests journalism seeks to maintain its role as expert, objective carrier of public discussion about social problems, and thereby maintain its legitimacy with powerful political institutions. Evidence of news media inefficiency and inefficacy would undermine efforts to maintain this ceremonious role, and thus news organizations buffer themselves and journalists from the uncertain consequences of their daily work—including economic uncertainty and challenges from audiences.

What impact then, is increased audience interactivity through the Internet likely to have? Will journalists choose stasis and simply reconstruct the audience in order to deal with the audience's new proximity and immediacy? Or, will journalists be forced to make fundamental changes in the ways they practice their work? Deuze (2005) has noted that journalists negotiate their values in the face of external change, sustaining "operational closure, keeping outside forces at bay." However, news organizations and their environment may be becoming less institutional and more relational, as TV news did in the 1970s. Jay Rosen characterizes this challenge to the mainstream news media: "The people formerly known as the audience are simply the public made realer, less fictional, more able, less predictable. You should welcome that, media people. But whether you do or not, we want you to know we're here" (Rosen, 2006).

Institutional theory predicts a number of possible responses by journalists, journalism, and news organizations, ranging from institutional to relational responses. Anecdotal accounts in industry and academic literature offer some insight into the most likely responses. One possible response is what Scott (1995) calls "avoidance," and there are several ways an institution may avoid the relational environment, thereby avoiding fundamental change.

Define the Audience as Unknowable

Journalists traditionally have considered audiences unknowable, and audiences have been constructed in more familiar forms—colleagues and bosses, family members and friends (McQuail, 1997, 2005; Sumpter, 2000). There is some evidence journalists perceive the online audience as unfathomably numerous, complex, and unruly. The online audience has been called a "jerk swarm" (Palser, 2006, p. 20) and a "motley lot of bloggers [and] partisans" (Smolkin, 2006, p. 18). Audience response has been called mere complaint, with audiences depicted as incapable of resolution and sense-making (Brown, 2004; MacGregor, 2007). Frustration over time spent with online audiences is also evident (Hendrickson, 2006; Quinn & Trench, 2002).

Evidence from research over the last five years has suggested that news managers—even online news managers—have seemed more interested in business as usual than in online feedback. Cassidy (2006) found that decision-making about online news was driven by the same routines driving print news decisions. Weaver et al. (2007) found in their 2002 survey of American journalists that 39 percent thought "letting people express views" was extremely important, ranking seventh in a list on which "investigating government claims" ranked first (71 percent), and "getting information to the public quickly" ranked second (59 percent). A December 2005 study of online news managers found that 34.7 percent perceived "managing user-generated content" as a job requirement, and 29.5 percent saw "cultivating online communities" as a requirement (Magee, 2006). And in a 2006 survey of U.S. daily newspaper managers, fewer than 20 percent said they regularly discussed blog postings about their newspaper's content in news meetings or regularly used blogs as news sources (Lowrey & Mackay, 2008).

Journalists have also expressed doubt about the helpfulness of readership data. Thirty percent in the study by Weaver et al. (2007) reported that audience ratings influenced the concept of newsworthiness, compared to 77 percent who cited journalistic training, 58 percent who cited supervisors, and 43 percent who cited peers. Some journalists see online metric data as inadequate and even irrelevant. A 2002 analysis of 24 European online news operations found "markedly weak interest in tracking usage of their sites as a basis for redesigning those sites" (Quinn & Trench, 2002). In a recent national survey of U.S. editors, 38 percent said site-use data "often" had an impact on news coverage decisions (McKenzie et al., 2008). A comment from one online journalist in MacGregor's 2007 study of British online news reveals an institutional attitude: "If I just wanted to chase what people on the Internet wanted to click on, I would do stories about porn and football and nothing else. We are a news site, so we have to be treated as news, and we have to cover stories which do not always have mass appeal."

Adopt Half-Measures

A second strategy of avoidance is to embrace outward forms that acknowledge changes in the nature of the audiences—for example, offering special pages with citizen content, community blogs, or links to "talk back" forums at the ends of stories—without fundamentally altering core structures and practices. This is a form of loose coupling that institutional scholars call "disimplementation," which buffers core activities from innovation, and which may lead only to skin-deep changes (Scott, 1995). Managers keep up with changing fashions, and the superficial acquisition of newly correct technical procedures and structures take on a ritual aspect (DiMaggio & Powell, 1983). Whether or not these innovations are effective, or even assessed, these institutionalized practices "establish an organization as appropriate, rational, and modern. Their use displays responsibility and avoids claims of negligence" (Meyer & Rowan, 1977). Schools routinely adopt innovation as cosmetic rather than structural change, serving to show external and internal groups they are up with the latest practices (Cuban, 1992).

News organizations appear to do the same: periodically instituting popular new newsroom structures, such as topic teams, that ultimately change core routines little (Gade, 2004); claiming involvement in "convergence" efforts that amount to TV stations and newspapers swapping company logos on their Web sites (Lowrey, 2005); adopting the rhetoric of civic and citizen journalism, but rarely moving beyond the occasional community project (Heider, McCombs, & Poindexter, 2005; Nichols Friedland, Rojas, Cho, & Shah, 2006); and offering the form of blogging, shorn of a feisty spirit and short on links to alternative voices (Lowrey, 2006; Singer, 2005). In each case, the fundamental practices and routines continue, while change efforts receive minimal, perhaps fleeting resources.

Disimplementation may also be seen in the segregation of online production from core news production. In the past, online news staffs have sometimes reported to advertising or marketing managers, they have not regularly voiced opinions in news planning meetings, and typically they have not been seen as opinion leaders (Singer, Tharp, & Haruta, 1999; Singer, 2004). More recently, Bressers (2006) found the newsrooms of large dailies to be increasingly integrated, but still only 58 percent reported housing the online staff within the newsroom and only 22 percent of print journalists reported frequently or always generating copy for the online operation.

Mainstream journalists, and to some degree audiences, have adopted a "wait-and-see" attitude toward online news production, partly because it has not been solidly grounded in journalism's traditional institutional environment. The fact that some online journalists report to marketing directors and have technical or graphics backgrounds rather than journalism backgrounds, reinforces this reluctance to fully accept online journalism. In many cases, newsrooms have offered interactive features for audiences without backing them with staffing resources or promoting them (Cawley, 2008; Domingo, 2008b; Singer & Gonzalez-Velez, 2003).

During times of uncertainty, organizations often mimic other organizations that are perceived to be similar, legitimate, and successful (DiMaggio & Powell, 1983). Mimicry is further evidence that changes are often skin deep. Lowrey (2005) found evidence that newspapers and TV stations mimicked practices of nearby large news organizations in determining the nature of TV-newspaper partnerships. The online environment is particularly conducive to imitation. Boczkowski and de Santos (2007) has shown that monitoring of the online environment correlates with increased homogeneity among newspapers.

"Civilize" the Audience

A third avoidance strategy is to tame the swarm. Journalists can attempt to maintain traditional institutional connections, procedures, and structures by redefining online journalism and blogging as "tools" for journalists, thereby safely incorporating them into the routine procedures of legitimated, institutional forms of journalism. This form of loose coupling involves reconstructing the audience as civil or not civil—i.e., as those who are sufficiently socialized to legitimated practices of journalism, and those who are not. Industry online news authorities such as Steve Outing (2005) encourage news organizations to "take advantage [of the] alternative press" by "managing the army of temporary journalists" (p. 80), incorporating citizen reporting into the main news product, requiring citizen contributions to meet news organizations' published standards, and by socializing them to the field. Such efforts have "no staff or operational cost . . . citizen bloggers are volunteers" (Smith, 2005). The name "citizen journalism" fits well with the institutional fields from which journalism has traditionally drawn its legitimacy.

Occupational sociologists have noted a similar phenomenon in professional competition, in which one occupation will co-opt the practices of another occupation in order to stave off a jurisdictional threat (Abbott, 1988). Lowrey and Mackay (2008) found that news managers' awareness of local blogging activity correlated with the adoption of the blogging form on news Web sites, as well as adoption of blogs as "reporting tools."

Efforts at "transparency" in news practices serve the function of socializing audiences to the field, giving them "explanation of news decisions, coverage priorities and newsroom values." Such efforts may be seen as subtle forms of control, or at least of persuasion. Attempts at "intimacy at a distance" and "pseudo-participation" is nothing new in journalism, stretching back to the 1800s (Griffen-Foley, 2004). Examples include calls for readers' stories (Griffen-Foley, 2004), telephone call-ins, homey, familiar forms of address, and even canned laughter for sitcoms (McQuail, 1997).

Statements from the news industry suggest that attempts at transparency represent both public relations and efforts at control. New York Times Editor Bill Keller says transparency efforts can repair the image of news organizations as being aloof: "It's a healthy thing to let readers know how much work we put into things to get them right and to get them fair." American Journalism Review's Rachel Smolkin (2006) asks whether or not "readers [are] swayed by the answers news organizations provide" (p. 20). Barb Palser, a director with Internet Broadcasting Systems says that when mainstream media do open themselves to audience participation, audiences must exercise civility: "Professional news sites have a reputation for being comfortable, civil places to be, and—inconceivable though it may be for some bloggers—many people visit them for that reason" (Palser, 2006, p. 70).

Become More Relational: Let the Market Dictate

The first three responses represent avoidance by loose coupling, and therefore suggest stasis, with perhaps some minimal change. A fourth possible response suggests more substantial change: Journalists and news organizations may become more tightly coupled with audiences, moving away from an institutionalist orientation and toward a relational orientation in which direct assessment of audience responses dictates managers' decisions about content. As is true of many organizations, news organizations are partly relational and partly institutional, and response to both public and market have always played a role in managers' decisions, despite journalists' proclivity to construct audiences or ignore marketing. TV news has been particularly sensitive to audience ratings, starting in the late 1960s when consultants advocated moving away from traditional notions of public affairs news to news that audiences "could use" in their daily lives, such as consumer and weather news. As one consultant put it, "we decided we were not beholden to politicians [and would] not cover government for the sake of covering government" (Allen, 2005, p. 376). Sumpter's (2000) case study research of audience construction at newspapers revealed that editors were beginning to grudgingly select stories in order to court the unknown, but contested market, rather than only for a "near audience" of other reporters and editors (p. 344).

As discussed, research within the last year indicates news managers are increasingly monitoring and responding to site-use feedback from online audiences (Lowrey & Mackay, 2008; MacGregor, 2007; McKenzie et al., 2008). Partly this is because metrics such as page views offer instant quantitative measurement of audience behavior. MacGregor (2007) found that journalists were increasingly checking "their hunches against the statistical data," obsessively consulting the data and instantly adapting content: "In doing so, editorial priorities are re-weighted and in consequence a basic practice of news judgment is being affected in the online newsroom" (p. 290). As a Philadelphia Inquirer online journalist puts it, "Web journalism is a shot of adrenaline . . . The feedback is immediate. I know almost instantly what's working. It's like I'm back in my father's hardware store, deciding what to put in the front window to bring in customers" (p. 290). This is a change from Quinn and Trench's 2002 finding of "remarkably weak interest" in use of online metric data.

Public investment in parent companies has encouraged a relational orientation in some ways, but discouraged it in others. The drive for profit encourages the view that readers are consumers rather than members of a public, as well as an emphasis on determining and meeting consumer demands. Hirsch and Thompson (1994) say increasing public ownership has moved newspapers toward a relational approach: "The journalistic ideal of serving democracy by reporting what the community needs to know is seen as less legitimate than using survey research to offer what the market wants to see" (p. 154). Yet, public investment has led to diminished newsroom resources and staff cuts, and depleted newsrooms are more likely to follow routine practices—many of which conform to the institutionalized account of news.

The fragmentation of audiences online is another source of journalists' increased responsiveness. Research shows that online news sites are becoming more specialized—a cause and consequence of audience fragmentation—thereby making it easier for content producers and advertisers to track and effectively respond to audience feedback. And theoretically, the ability to monitor audience patterns makes it more likely content will be tailored to meet specialized needs (Dimmick, 2003; Tewksbury, 2005).

Yet MacGregor (2007) also notes that managers have some skepticism about the completeness of online data, echoing journalists' traditional skepticism about audience research (Gans, 1979; McQuail, 2005): "Slavery to audience whim is sharply defined as perilous, from exactly the same principles outlined in pre-Internet studies." The need to conform to institutional accounts of what constitutes news is a major obstacle to full adoption of online metrics as a determinant of content. Hard audience data makes it more difficult to justify reporting on political and public affairs, thus undermining journalists' professional orientation, the communication needs of the powerful, and public faith in the institution that ostensibly watchdogs the powerful and facilitates the public search for solutions.

Follow a New Logic

Finally, journalists and news organizations may change by embracing participatory news forms, open sourcing, and audience interactivity in a substantial, meaningful way. But to do so, journalists and news organizations would need to draw legitimacy from some alternative cultural logic in the industry's environment. This is not impossible, as the cultural and social logics of institutions can be multiple, contradictory, and impermanent: "Some of the most important struggles between groups, organizations and classes are over the appropriate relationships between institutions, and by which institutional logic different activities should be regulated" (Friedland & Alford, 1991). Actual organizational change can derive from fundamental institutional conflict (Friedland & Alford, 1991).

There are indications of a new logic. Other traditional social and political institutions are showing signs of decentering, and some authority is devolving into the hands of the populace. Membership in political parties and labor unions are at a record low; professional control in medicine has been challenged by online knowledge, alternative health approaches, and a consumerist culture; institutional education is being increasingly undermined by the home schooling movement; and the social institution of marriage is being destabilized by an increasing preference for fleeting, temporary relationships. Such changes may reflect a larger cultural shift, one that could destabilize the existing institutional order and bring about new social, political, and economic arrangements.

A number of scholars suggest journalists are beginning to adapt to a new multicultural, post-modern, post-structural environment, in which openness, flux, and discourse among many voices are increasingly valued, and top-down media and the logic of detachment and neutrality is less valued (Deuze, 2005; Moore, 1999). In such a cultural environment, substantive dialogue is esteemed over official pronouncement (Ettema & Peer, 1997), and news embraces no particular view of the world, for "there is no reality, only redescribings of events by many different people" (Ettema & Glasser, 1994). There is some evidence of news organizations opening up to multiple, diverse voices in their communities, through hosted blogs and forums, and citizen journalism sites. More evidence may surface yet.

But it appears that at least at present, most organizational change is not fundamental change. This is not surprising, given that existing political and social institutions are still dominant, even if threatened, and that these institutions depend on consistency, credibility, and legitimacy in the mainstream media. Powerful source institutions and advertisers are still likely to direct most of their finite communication resources to mainstream news media. The credibility of the news media is grounded in a publicly accepted account, or typification, of news media, and fundamental deviation from this accepted account seriously undermines legitimacy in the eyes of external traditional institutions. Superficial deviation probably does not. This is not to suggest that fundamental change in journalism and news organizations is not possible—only to show that fundamental change is bound to the slow changes of the wider culture and society.

Conclusion

Pursuit of institutional legitimacy is likely to remain important for news organizations, but relational pressures should not be underestimated. They are mounting on all sides. Audiences are fragmented and purposive. Public ownership of news companies is growing more common, and pursuit of profit is growing in importance. As the anecdote introducing this essay demonstrates, there is a growing expectation that the news side will observe fluctuation in market appeal and shape content accordingly. Editors are becoming more accommodating to the business side, and though data on audience consumption is not paramount, it is becoming more relevant to news decisions (Gade, 2004, 2008; Weaver et al., 2007). Under growing relational pressure, journalists and news organizations are likely to overtly embrace audience participation in the production of news information—not to spark engagement in public issues or to encourage meaningful, diverse storytelling—but to increase the number of eyes on the product. A relational approach could widen the door for new ideas and social change through media, but only to the extent that audience participation does not clash with pursuit of profit.

Still, journalists and news organizations are unlikely to make imminent *fundamental* changes in practices related to audiences because the wider institutional realm in which journalism takes place is not likely to make imminent, fundamental changes. Powerful institutional forces stemming from government, politics, and large corporations have an important stake in the current public account of traditional journalism and its practices, processes, and forms. Such practices and forms have been roundly and justifiably criticized, but no other existing communication institution possesses the level of cultural legitimacy of traditional journalism, even if this legitimacy is tarnished. Thus, news organizations are likely to continue to take half measures, bowing to increasing pressure from relational market forces by adopting new forms and trends, but buffering many core practices from these changes.

So, as with all organizations, there are both relational and institutional pressures on news operations. This duality has been observed in different ways by previous scholars: Beam (2003) proposed that news organizations have orientations toward both audience marketing and public service; McQuail's (2005) "field of social forces" model depicts separate economic and social/political pressures in the media environment; and Benson (2006) suggests news production lies along a continuum between poles of market and civic power. Research is needed to reveal where news organizations sit along such continuums, why they sit where they do, and what impact the position on a continuum is likely to have for news content, for society, and for active audiences.

The relational-institutional continuum need not be exclusively adopted for examining change and stasis in existing news organizations. Individual-level production such as citizen journalism sites and blogs may be eventually subject to these same forces. While current scholarship characterizes the rhetorical nature of blogging as deeply personal, in contrast to the institutional rhetoric of traditional news content, the nature of this content may change if individual production moves toward organizational production, and as these sites gain public and institutional legitimacy. There is evidence that as bloggers' audience numbers grow, blog content becomes less personal and more conservative and careful (Lowrey & Latta, 2008). Bloggers are also pursuing advertising and corporate money gifts for mentions in postings, and some bloggers have accepted paying positions with news organizations (Lasica, 2005). It stands to reason that dense connectivity, predicted for early entrants into networks (Barabasi & Albert, 1999), would increase work load, which could in turn lead to task differentiation and the beginnings of organizational forms. Original reporting also increases work load, and there is some evidence that reporting is a determinant of blog popularity on the Internet (Singer, 2005; Tremayne, Zheng, Lee & Jeong, 2006). Of course, existing news organizations do not stand to gain from the transformation of personal Web sites to organizational forms, suggesting one reason for present efforts to control or co-opt the budding participatory journalism/blogging phenomenon.

Might the wider cultural and institutional logic change so that the decentered, egalitarian network becomes the dominant system by which information is generated and distributed? This possibility is noted in response number five, above, and modest transformations to flatter teams structures in news organizations, as well as experimentation with participatory news forms suggest some movement in this direction. But it does not seem a strong possibility for the foreseeable future. The rule-bound, bureaucratic, institutional form continues to reduce uncertainty in daily and necessary social, political, and economic exchanges; it manages the growing complexity of internal differentiation and external relationships; and the legitimacy that organizations acquire over time is crucial to other institutions that depend on them. It seems more likely that change could come through relational pressures, though again, this may not be core change. As mentioned above, relational needs may lead to listening to audiences and incorporating more audience content. But, as the purpose is the pursuit of profit, they may also lead to typifying audience as marketing data, and to cutting staff.

Finally, this essay's emphasis on structure and stasis is not meant to suggest the absence of human agency or the impossibility of change. Weber makes clear that culture and social structure derive from the activity of real, individual people, and that organizations are a mix of the ideal types of bureaucratic and personal control, with political struggles within organizations often generating change (Collins & Makowsky, 1998). Changes in news organizations and practices do come through internal agitation, such as the realization that news about women need not be sequestered in "society pages" (Barnhurst & Nerone, 2001) or that photographs may be considered news and not just illustration (Zelizer, 1995). To be sure, such changes derive from normative acceptance in the wider culture—they must first be "thinkable." But they cannot come to be without human action, from both management and the rank and file, and increasingly, from voices beyond the organization. Thus, while this essay has emphasized the organizational and institutional reasons for staying put vs. pursuing superficial or fundamental innovation, it is human change agents, socialized to norms in the broader culture, who perform the acts that stabilize or catalyze.

Nevertheless, both news scholars and industry analysts have a tendency to magnify signs of change and ignore the stubborn stasis of routines and typifications. So as both scholars and professionals justifiably strive and hope for change, it is important to also take a sober look at the forces holding journalism in place, as well as the lengths to which journalists and their news organizations will go to leave core principles, routines, and practices untouched. It is hoped that a greater understanding of stasis will lead to an enhanced ability to predict or bring about change.

Notes

1 For reasons not very applicable to this essay, this framework is called "new institutionalism" to distinguish it in from traditional "institutionalism," a framework adopted by social scientists in the first half of the 20th century. The essential difference has to do with an emphasis on cognitive typfication in new institutionalism as opposed to normative socialization in traditional institutionalism. As institutionalists and new institutionalists frequently argue whether or not this subtle distinction even matters, it is ignored here.

2 Whether or not journalism "qualifies" as a professional is not of interest here. Most sociologists of work and the professions have long since turned away from assessing areas of work by lists of professional criteria and focus instead on the way areas of work seek control. As Andrew Abbott (1988) put it, "whether journalism's inability to monopolize makes it 'not a profession' is not particularly interesting"—of greater importance is the external competition that "shaped it decisively" (p. 225).

References

Abbott, A. (1988). *The system of professions: An essay on the division of expert labor.* Chicago: University of Chicago Press.

Aldrich, H. E. (1979). *Organizations and environments.* Englewood Cliffs, NJ: Prentice-Hall.

Allen, C. (2005). Discovering "Joe Six Pack" content in television news: The hidden history of audience research, news consultants and the Warner Class model. *Journal of Broadcasting and Electronic Media, 49,* 363–382.

Altheide, D. L., & Snow, R. P. (1979). *Media Logic.* Beverly Hills, CA: Sage.

Ball-Rokeach, S. J., & Cantor, M. (1986). *Media, audience, and social structure.* Thousand Oaks, CA: Sage.

Ball-Rokeach, S. J., Hale, M., Schaffer, A., Porras, L., Harris, P., & Drayton, M. (1999). Changing the media production process: From aggressive to injury-sensitive traffic crash stories. In D. Demers & K. Viswanath (Eds.), *Mass media, social control and social change* (pp. 229–262). Ames, Iowa: Iowa State University Press.

Barabasi, A. L., & Albert, R. (1999). Emergence of scaling in random networks. *Science, 286,* 509–512.

Barnhurst, K. G., & Nerone, J. (2001). *The form of news.* New York: The Guilford Press.

Beam, R. A. (2003). Content differences between daily newspapers with weak market orientations. *Journalism & Mass Communication Quarterly, 80,* 368–390.

Beaupre, L. K.(1991). Rating the performance of newsroom professionals. *Newspaper Research Journal, 12,* 22–27.

Becker, H. (1982). *Art worlds.* University of California Press.

Benson, R. (2006). News media as a "journalistic field": What Bourdieu adds to new institutionalism, and vice versa. *Political Communication, 23,* 187–202.

Boczkowski, P. (2004). *Digitizing the new: Innovation in online newspapers.* Cambridge, MA: The MIT Press.

Boczkowski, P., & de Santos, M. (2007). When more media equals less news: Patterns of content homogenization in Argentina's leading print and online newspapers. *Political Communication, 24,* 167–190.

Breed, W. (1955). Social control in the newsroom: A functional analysis. *Social Forces, 33,* 326–355.

Bressers, B. (2006). Promise and reality: The integration of print and online versions of major metropolitan newspapers. *The International Journal of Media Management, 8,* 134–145.

Brown, F. (2004, Sept.). Questions about "accessibility" draw complaints, not solutions. *Quill, 92,* 31.

Budros, A. (2004). Causes of early and later organizational adoption: The case of corporate downsizing. *Sociological Inquiry, 74,* 355–380.

Burns, T. (1969). Public service and private world. In P. Halmos (Ed.), *The sociology of mass media communicators* (pp. 53–73). Keele: University of Keele.

Burns, T. (1977). *The BBC: Public institution and private world.* London: Macmillan.

Cantor, M. (1971). *The Hollywood TV producer: His work and his audience.* New York: Basic Books.

Carey, J. (1985). *Communication as culture: Essays on media and society.* Boston: Unwin Hyman.

Cassidy, William P. (2006). Gatekeeping similar for online, print journalists. *Newspaper Research Journal, 27,* 6–23.

Cawley, A. (2008). News production in an Irish online newsroom: Practice, process and culture. In C. Paterson & D. Domingo (Eds.), *Making online news* (pp. 45–60). New York: Peter Lang.

Collins, R., & Makowsky, M. (1998). *The discovery of society.* Boston: McGraw-Hill.

Cook, T. E. (1998). *Governing with the news: The news media as a political institution.* Chicago: University of Chicago Press.

Cook, T. E. (2006). The news media as a political institution: Looking backward and looking forward. *Political Communication, 23,* 159–171.

Cuban, L. (1992). Curriculus stability and change. In P. Jackson (Ed.), *Handbook of research on curriculum* (pp. 216–247). New York: Macmillan.

Deuze, M. (2004). What is multimedia journalism? *Journalism Studies, 5,* 139–152.

Deuze, M. (2005). What is journalism? *Journalism, 6,* 442–464.

DiMaggio, P. J., & Hirsch, P. M. (1976). Production organization in the arts. *American Behavioral Scientist, 19,* 735–752.

DiMaggio, P., & Powell, W. (1983). The iron cage revisited: Institutional isomorphism and collective rationality in organizational fields. *American Sociological Review, 48,* 147–160.

DiMaggio, P. J., & Powell, W. W. (1991). Introduction. In P. J. DiMaggio & W. W. Powell, *The new institutionalism in organizational analysis* (pp. 1–40). Chicago: The University of Chicago Press.

Dimmick, J. (2003). *Media competition and coexistence: The theory of the niche.* Mahwah, NJ: Lawrence Erlbaum.

Domingo, D. (2008a). Interactivity in the daily routines of online newsrooms: Dealing with an uncomfortable myth. *Journal of Computer-Mediated Communication, 13,* 680–704.

Domingo, D. (2008b). When immediacy rules: Online journalism models in four Catalan online newsrooms. In C. Paterson & D. Domingo (Eds.), *Making online news* (pp. 113–126). New York: Peter Lang.

Dylko, I. B., & Kosicki, G. (2006). Sociology of news and new media. Paper presented to the Association for Education in Journalism and Mass Communication, San Francisco, California.

Ettema, J., & Glasser, T. L. (1994). The irony in—and of—journalism: A case study in the moral language of liberal democracy. *Journal of Communication, 44,* 5–28.

Ettema, J., and Peer, L. (1997). Good news from a bad neighborhood. Toward an alternative to the discourse of urban pathology. *Journalism and Mass Communication Quarterly, 73,* 835–856.

Ettema, J. S., & Whitney, D.C. (1994). The money arrow: An introdution to audiencemaking. In J. S. Ettema & D. C. Whitney (Eds.), *Audiencemaking: How the media create the audience* (pp. 1–18). Thousand Oaks, CA: Sage.

Fligstein, N. (1991). The structural transformation of American industry: An institutional account of the causes of diversification in the largest firms, 1919–1979. In P. J. DiMaggio & W. W. Powell (Eds.), *The new institutionalism in organizational analysis* (pp. 311–336). Chicago: The University of Chicago Press.

Freidson, E. (1994) *Professionalism reborn: Theory, prophecy, and policy.* Chicago: University of Chicago Press.

Friedland, R., & Alford, R. R. (1991). Bringing society back in: Symbols, practices and institutional contradictions. In P .J. DiMaggio & W. W. Powell (Eds.), *The New Institutionalism in Organizational Analysis* (pp. 108–142). Chicago: University of Chicago Press.

Gade, P. (2004). Newspapers and organizational development: Management and journalist perceptions of newsroom cultural change. *Journalism & Communication Monographs, 6,* 3–55.

Gade, P. (2008). Journalism guardians in a time of great change: Newspaper editors' perceived influence in integrated news organizations. *Journalism and Mass Communication Quarterly, 85,* 371–392.

Gans, H. (1957). The creator-audience relationship in the mass media: An analysis of movie making. In B. Rosenberg & D. White (Eds.) *Mass culture: The popular arts in America* (pp. 315–324). New York: Free Press.

Gans, H. J. (1979). *Deciding what's news: A study of CBS Evening News, NBC Nightly News, Newsweek, and Time.* New York: Pantheon.

Griffen-Foley, B. (2004). From Tit-Bits to Big Brother: A century of audience participation in the media. *Media, Culture & Society, 26,* 533–548.

Hallin, D. C. (1997). Commercialism and professionalism in the American news media. In J. Curran & M. Gurevitch (Eds.), *Mass media and society* (pp. 243–262). New York: St. Martin's Press.

Heider, D., McCombs, M., & Poindexter, P. M. (2005) What the public expects of local news: Views on public and traditional journalism. *Journalism and Mass Communication Quarterly, 82,* 952–967.

Hendrickson, R. D. (2006). Publishing e-mail addresses ties readers to writers. *Newspaper Research Journal, 27,* 52–68.

Hirsch, P. M., & Thompson, T. A. (1994). The stock market as audience: The impact of public ownership on newspapers. In J. S. Ettema & D. C. Whitney (Eds.), *Audiencemaking: How the media create the audience* (pp. 142–158). Thousand Oaks, CA: Sage.

Kaplan, R. L. (2006). The news about new institutionalism: Journalism's ethic of objectivity and its political origins. *Political Communication, 23,* 173–185.

Lasica, J. D. (2005, Feb. 17) The cost of ethics: Influence peddling in the blogosphere. *Online Journalism Review.* Retrieved November 26, 2008 from http://www.ojr.org/ojr/stories/050217lasica/

Lenhart, A., & Fox, S. (2006, July 19). Bloggers: A portrait of the Internet's new storytellers. *Pew Internet & American Life Project.* Retrieved November 26 from http://www.pewinternet.org/PPF/r/186/report_display.asp

Lowrey, W. (2002). Word people vs. picture people: Normative differences and strategies for control over work among newsroom subgroups. *Mass communicatin and society, 5,* 411–432.

Lowrey, W. (2004). More control, but not clarity, in non-linear Web stories. *Newspaper Research Journal, 25,* 83–97.

Lowrey, W. (2005). Commitment to newspaper-TV partnering: A test of the impact of institutional isomorphism. *Journalism and Mass Communication Quarterly, 82,* 495–514.

Lowrey, W. (2006). Mapping the journalism-blogging relationship. *Journalism, 7(4),* 477–500.

Lowrey, W., & Latta, J. (2008). The routines of blogging. In C. Paterson & D. Domingo (Eds.), *Making online news.* Cresskill, NJ: Hampton Press.

Lowrey, W., & Mackay, J. (2008). Journalism and blogging: A test of a model of occupational competition. *Journalism Practice, 2,* 64–81.

MacGregor, P. (2007). Tracking the online audience: Metric data start a subtle revolution. *Journalism Studies, 8,* 280–298.

Magee, C. M. (2006, November 1). The roles of journalists in online newsrooms. *Online News Association.* Retrieved November 30, 2008 from http://journalist.org/news/archives/MedillOnlineJobSurvey-final.pdf.

Manoff, R. K. (1989). Modes of war and modes of social address: The text of SDI. *Journal of Communication, 39,* 59–84.

McKenzie, C., Hays, H., Woo, C. W., Chung, J. Y., & Lowrey, W. (2008). The influence of community structure and economic factors on the evaluation of reader feedback. Paper presented at the annual convention of the Association for Education in Journalism and Mass Communication, Chicago, IL.

McQuail, D. (1997). *Audience analysis.* Thousand Oaks, CA: Sage.

McQuail, D. (2005). *Mass communication theory: An introduction.* London: Sage Publications.

Meyer, J. W., Scott, W. R., & Deal, T. E. (1983). Institutional and technical sources of organizational structure: Explaining the structure of educational organizations. In J. W. Meyer, & W. Scott (Eds.), *Organizational environments: Ritual and rationality* (pp. 45–70). Sage, New York.

Meyer, J., & Rowan, B. (1977). Institutionalized organizations: Formal structure as myth and ceremony. *American Journal of Sociology, 83(2),* 340–363.

Meyer, J. W., & Rowan, B. (1983). The structure of educational organizations. In J. W. Meyer & W. R. Scott. *Organizational environments: Ritual and rationality* (pp. 71–98). Beverly Hills, CA: Sage.

Miller, P. V. (1994). Made-to-order and standardized audiences: Forms of reality in audience measurement. In J. S. Ettema & D. C. Whitney (Eds.), *Audiencemaking: How the media create the audience* (pp. 57–74). Thousand Oaks, CA: Sage.

Moore, R. C. (1999). Where epistemology meets ecology: Can environmental news reporting survive postmodernism? *Mass Communication and Society, 2,* 3–25.

Newspaper Association of America (23 October 2008). Newspaper Web site audience increases sixteen percent in third quarter to 68.3 million visitors. Retrieved November 26, 2008, from http://www.naa.org/presscenter.aspx.

Nichols, S. L., Friedland, L. A., Rojas, H., Cho, J., & Shah, D. V. (2006). Examining the effects of public journalism on civil society from 1994 to 2002: Organizational factors, story frames and citizen engagement. *Journalism and Mass Communication Quarterly, 83,* 77–100.

Outing, S. (2005, spring). Managing the army of temporary journalists. *Nieman Reports,* 79–80.

Palser, B. (2006 April/May). Coping with jerk swarms. *American Journalism Review, 28,* 70–70.

Pekurny, R. (1982). Coping with television production. In J. S. Ettema & D. C. Whitney (Eds.), *Creativity and constraint: Individuals in mass media organizations* (pp. 131–143). Beverly Hills, CA: Sage.

The Pew Research Center (2008 July 21). The changing newsroom. *Journalism.org.* Retrieved Nov. 26, 2008 from http://journalism.org/node/11961.

Pritchard, D., & Berkowitz, D. (1991). How readers' letters may influence editors and news emphasis: A content analysis of 10 newspapers, 1948–1978. *Journalism Quarterly, 68,* 388–395.

The Project for Excellence in Journalism (2007). State of the News Media 2007. *Project for excellence in journalism.* Retrieved November 26, 2008 from http://www.stateofthenewsmedia.org/2007/.

Quinn, G., & Trench, B. (2002). Online news media and their audiences. Heerlen, Netherlands: European Centre for Digital Communication. Retrieved November 26, 2008 from http://mudia.ecdc.info/abstracts.html

Rosen, J. (2006 June 27). The people formerly known as the audience. *PressThink.*

Retrieved November 26, 2008, from http://journalism.nyu.edu/pubzone/weblogs/pressthink/2006/06/27/ppl_frmr.html

Rosenberg, B., & White, D. (Eds.), *The popular arts in America* (pp. 315–334). New York: Free Press.

Rosenberry, J. (2005). Few papers use online techniques to improve public communication. *Newspaper Research Journal*, *26(4)*, 61–73.

Ryan, J., & Peterson, R. A. (1982). The product image: the fate of creativity in country music songwriting. In J. S. Ettema & D. C. Whitney (Eds.), *Individuals in mass media organizations: Creativity and Constraint* (pp. 11–32). Beverly Hills, CA: Sage Publications.

Ryfe, D. (2006). Guest editor's introduction: New institutionalism and the news. *Political Communication*, *23*,135–144.

Schlesinger, P. (1978). *Putting "reality" together: BBC news*. London: Constable.

Schudson, M. (2002). The news media as political institutions. *Annual Review of Political Science*, *5*, 249–269.

Scott, W. R. (1995). *Institutions and organizations*. Thousand Oaks, CA: Sage.

Scott, W. R., & Meyer, J. W. (1991). The organization of societal sectors: Propositions and early evidence. In P.J. DiMaggio & W. W. Powell (Eds.), *The new institutionalism in organizational analysis* (pp. 108–142). Chicago: The University of Chicago Press.

Sigelman, L. (1973). Reporting the news: An organizational analysis. *American Journal of Sociology*, *79*, 132–151.

Singer, J. (2004). Strange bedfellows? The diffusion of convergence in four news organizations. *Journalism Studies*, *5*, 3–18.

Singer, J. (2005) The political j-blogger: "Normalizing" a new media form to fit old norms and practices. *Journalism 6*, 173–198.

Singer, J. M, & Gonzalez-Velez, M. (2003). Envisioning the caucus community: Online newspaper editors conceptualize their political roles. *Political Communication*, *20*, 433–452.

Singer, J., Tharp, M.P., & Haruta, A. (1999). Online staffers: Superstars or second-class citizens? *Newspaper Research Journal*, *20(3)*, 29–47.

Smith, S. (2005, October 18). Managing the transparent newsroom. *redOrbit*. Retrieved November 26, 2008 from http://www.redorbit.com/news/technology/274863/managing_the_transparent_newsroom/.

Smolkin, R. (2006, April/May). Too transparent? *American Journalism Review*, *28(2)*, 17–23.

Sumpter, R. (2000). Daily newspaper editors' audience construction routines: A case study. *Critical Studies in Mass Communication*, *17*, 334–336.

Sylvie, G., & Witherspoon, P. D. (2002). *Time, change, and the American newspaper*. Mahwah, NJ: Lawrence Erlbaum Associates, Inc.

Tewksbury, D. (2005). The seeds of audience fragmentation: Specialization in the use of online news sites. *Journal of Broadcasting and Electronic Media*, *49*, 332–348.

Tichenor, P. J., Donohue, G. A. & Olien, C. N. (1980). *Community conflict and the press*. Beverly Hills, CA: Sage.

Tolbert, P. S., & Zucker, L.G. (2001). The institutionalization of institutional theory. In S. Clegg, C. Hardy, & W. R. Nord (Eds.), *Handbook of organization studies* (pp. 175–190). London: Sage.

Tremayne, M., Zheng, N., Lee, J. K., & Jeong, J. (2006). Issue publics on the web:

Applying network theory to the war blogosphere. *Journal of Computer-Mediated Communication, 12,* Retrieved November 26 from http://jcmc.indiana.edu/vol12/issue1/tremayne.html.

Tuchman, G. (1978). *Making the news: A study in the construction of reality.* New York: The Free Press.

Tunstall, J. (1971). *Journalists at work.* London: Constable.

Wartella, E.A. (1994). Producing children's television programs. In J. S. Ettema & D. C. Whitney (Eds.), *Audiencemaking: How the media create the audience* (pp. 38–56). Thousand Oaks, CA: Sage.

Weaver, D. H. Beam, R. A., Brownlee, B. J., Voakes, P. S., & Wilhoit, G. C. (2007). *The American journalist in the 21ˢᵗ century.* Mahwah, NJ: Lawrence Erlbaum.

Webster, J. G., & Phalen, P. F. (1994). Victim, consumer of commodity? Audience models in communication policy. In J. S. Ettema & D. C. Whitney, *Audiencemaking: How the media create the audience* (pp. 19–37). Thousand Oaks, CA: Sage.

Wehmeier, S. (2006). Dancers in the dark: The myth of rationality in public relations. *Public Relations Review, 32,* 213.

Zelizer, B. (1995). Journalism's "last" Stand: Wirephoto and the discourse of resistance. *Journal of Communication, 45,* 78–92.

Part II

The Public's Relationship with Digital Content

Producing Citizen Journalism or Producing Journalism for Citizens

A New Multimedia Model to Enhance Understanding of Complex News

Ronald A. Yaros

What is already an overwhelming amount of complexity in news appears to be growing exponentially. Add to the list of complex stories—such as the global economic crisis—other long-term issues such as science and health literacy. For years, the National Institute of Health has noted the need to increase scientific literacy ("Healthy People 2010," 2000) in a citizen population that possesses only a limited understanding of science, health and technology (Dunwoody, 1992; Lewenstein, 1992, 1994; Miller, 1987a, 1987b, 2000, 2001, 2004). Although the proportion of U.S. citizens qualifying as scientifically literate has doubled between 1980 and 2000, the current level remains problematic for a democratic society that values citizen understanding of major policies and participation to resolve policy disputes (Miller, 2004). At the same time, younger citizens claim the Internet as their primary news source and no other medium compares in terms of available information (Magid Associates, 2004).

Although more user-generated content can blur the line between professional and citizen journalism, there is evidence to suggest that when a low knowledge public is forming opinions about controversial scientific issues, citizens continue to trust and rely heavily on the scientific community (Brossard & Nisbet, 2007).

Clearly, the Web medium satisfies citizens who want shorter, fact-driven accounts as well as those seeking specific context, interpretation, and opinion (Tremayne, 2004). Others maintain that news about science, health and technology is produced primarily for the "science attentive public" (Miller, 1986). The challenge, therefore, is determining when and how more citizens will engage with and understand news about complex issues in a complex Web medium.

Such a discussion cannot ignore the ongoing debate about the similarities of the brain's nonlinear structure to the Web, what some label "structural isomorphism" (Bieber et al., 1997; Eveland & Dunwoody, 2001; Shirk, 1992). Or is it a myth that enhanced learning can occur from the Internet's ability to manipulate information (Dillon, 1996)?

> To date, the claims have far exceeded the evidence and few hypertext systems have been shown to lead to either greater comprehension or

significantly better performance levels. Clearly, mere exposure to information is not enough for learning to occur, which we really always knew. (Dillon, 1996, pp. 31–32)

Studies of learning across media have claimed either significant differences in learning (Chen & Rada, 1996) or little difference (Dillon & Gabbard, 1998), which leads one to conclude that it's not the medium but the ways messages are structured and users' patterns (Eveland & Dunwoody, 2001).

The questions are why and how should citizens with limited expertise engage in complex news issues on a medium that offers so many other choices. The new cognitive model proposed here attempts to answer with the hypothesis that more citizens might better understand complex news if the content was presented with more personalization, involvement and coherent multimedia structures. The model proposed does not stop there, however. This chapter synthesizes traditional research with newer concepts for a more integrated model to facilitate more effective production of news by both citizens and professionals to enhance understanding.

Conceptualizing "understanding" is key because merely informing a citizen about a complex issues such as the global financial crisis or climate change does not mean citizens are always provided with sufficient details to discuss the issues and influence policy.

Not surprisingly, several factors affect an individual's ability to comprehend information. As one example, non-experts who read science and health news text online benefited significantly from more explanation in linear "structure building" writing. This linear structure is often absent in traditional "inverted pyramid" news stories (Yaros, 2006). The research also found significant differences in how the organization of facts within a complex news story affected readers' deep comprehension of the content (Yaros, 2005b). Interestingly, these effects changed significantly when hypertext links were added to the same stories (Yaros, 2005a).

These data lend support to those who believe that the so-called "digital natives" who were born with the Internet probably process information differently than those from an older generation. John Palfrey, Director of the Berkman Center for Internet and Society at Harvard's Law School, observes that "grazing digital natives" hear, read or view a story's headline, bare facts, or at most a paragraph with little or no context. Only those who take a deep dive into the content make sense of the news by putting it into a frame or offering an analysis of it (Palfrey, 2006).

If these assertions are true, one goal for the cognitive model proposed here is to address behaviors that might be indigenous to users of a nonlinear medium with endless choices. A second goal is to identify more effective methods for communicators to engage citizens in issues that are important and complex yet competing with so much other information online. This suggests a need to go

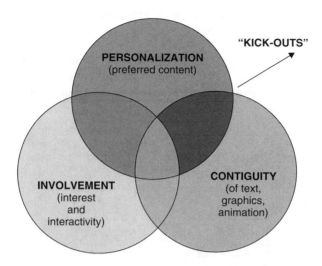

Figure 4.1 The "PICK" model for multimedia news (Yaros 2008, 2009).

well beyond current formats to address amounts of information never before seen by consumers of information.

The proposed "PICK" model for complex news (Figure 4.1) synthesizes a collection of concepts and research from the fields of educational psychology and communication. The four concepts in PICK include (1) personalization; (2) involvement; (3) contiguity; and (4) cognitive "kick-outs." The Venn diagram differs from more linear "cause and effect" models in that the processing of multiple elements on a Web page occurs simultaneously and nonlinearly before user engagement and subsequent understanding occur. Although two or more processes in the model could occur at any one time, it is the *combination* of all four PICK concepts that represent the new theory to maximize interest in and understanding of complex news by non-expert citizens.

Arguably, these processes could apply to more than just news information. The premise of this discussion, however, is to review the ample evidence for why the combination of these four processes may be especially important if more citizens are to produce effective journalism and/or understand complex issues.

Situational Understanding

The concept of understanding is defined in the seminal work by Kintsch (1988) in the field of cognitive psychology. "Situational" understanding represents robust comprehension because it depends on both the explicitly stated information within a message plus inferences and elaborations generated by a citizen's world knowledge. A citizen's well-established situation model provides many of the semantic and contextual features necessary for reactivation of relevant information presented in news (O'Brien & Myers, 1999). The fact that high-knowledge readers are significantly better at making bridging inferences from a message than low-knowledge readers (Britton & Gulgoz, 1991; McNamara, 2001) suggests that a citizen who does not possess the appropriate knowledge with which to make gap-filling inferences from a text requires more coherent and explicit text to understand it (McNamara et al., 1996).

In short, if a citizen is unable to make inferences from a complex news story (such as a financial crisis) and integrate that information with his or her prior knowledge, the potential for situational understanding is reduced (Kintsch, 1988).

Conversely, the more commonly measured "text-based" understanding is a more shallow form of comprehension. Text-based understanding is typically measured by simple recall or recognition of information (as in multiple choice tests) to which one is previously exposed. Therefore, one's text base understanding may explain why a citizen can recall a particular phrase from a news story but fails to elaborate on its meaning or context.

It is important to note that since text-based understanding can also contribute to a citizen's situational understanding of an issue, the distinction between the two types of understanding can be a matter of degree rather than absolute.

The PICK model assumes that the audience's familiarity with news about complex issues differs significantly from the audience's familiarity with more commonly reported news such as accidents, fires, and entertainment. The obvious difference between these stories is that news about complex issues often contains terminology that requires more analytical understanding (Lemke, 1990).

The Four "PICK" Components

Who and what determine the structures of various media? Historically, scholars with expert knowledge have driven the publishing of textbooks. Educational psychologists, who conducted empirical research of the teaching and learning processes, developed methods for classroom instruction. On the Web, it is less clear who (or what) is driving the evolution of designs for assembling and presenting content. Obviously, programmers who code content management technologies—including RSS feeds, podcasts, blogs, flash, etc.—play an integral role. Other than usability studies or research of the number of page views or click streams, there is limited research of how traditional methods of learning might or might not apply to learning from news on the Web.

Browse the major news sites. The dominant strategy continues to be the presentation of a large amount of information with the producers apparently hoping that the user will find, select and engage with *something* of interest. This is not to say that the graphic principles of dominance, hierarchy, balance, space, color, and unity aren't important to make content visually appealing. In addition to those concepts, however, the theory discussed in this chapter posits that assembling information in nonlinear media is an "orchestration" of factors and methods that work in synchrony if citizens are to process an endless stream of text, graphics and multimedia free-choice environment. In short, we haven't yet figured out the best way to effectively communicate in an environment with an overwhelming amount of choices and information. This conclusion supports the first concept in the PICK model, personalization of the information.

The Concept of Personalization

Personalization is conceptualized as the degree to which content is tailored for an individual for consumption. Web servers can instantly implement pre-set user preferences to collect, combine and deliver personalized content to the user on demand (Brusilovsky & Maybury 2002; Mostafa 2002). Citizens embrace personalized Web sites in a medium associated with an overwhelming amount of information (Eppler & Mengis, 2004) and those who personalize their choices become their own "gatekeepers" of information (Shoemaker 1991). The challenge for future producers of content, therefore, is not whether citizens should be provided with personalized content of interest but to what extent that content should be personalized.

It has already been shown that Web portals that provide personalized content of interest generate more positive user attitudes (Kalyanaraman & Sundar, 2006). According to the researchers, the positive attitude is the outcome of: (1) a user's ability to customize; (2) the user's perceived relevance of the content; and (3) the novelty of the content. However, Sundar and Marathe (2006) found that user attitudes for differing levels of personalization are mediated by a user's expertise with the medium. Specifically, the more experienced the user, the more customization is desired.

Interestingly, Sundar and Nass (2001) also found that users who could choose their own news stories rated the content lower in quality, newsworthiness and likeability than those who read the same stories without choice. While this suggests that some users prefer professionals or computers to filter stories, another subsequent study concluded that "affectively true self-as-source will foster positive attitudes toward content by invoking a greater sense of "me-ness." Citizens "may see their content gate-keeping decisions as reflecting their identity" (Sundar & Marathe, 2006, p. 5). At the same time, Sundar (2007) noted that merely manipulating the level of choice (i.e., user vs. professional journalist) may not always enhance positive attitudes if the content is judged to be "mediocre." Users, therefore, seem to be saying don't just give me a choice for content; give me content that is good. In summary, citizen involvement with a complex news story can be motivated by personalizing the delivery of that content to the user, but personalization is not the only factor that stimulates involvement.

The Concept of Involvement

The PICK model explicates the concept of involvement along the two dimensions of interest in and interactivity with the content. Since these terms have been used in an ill-defined sense, specific conceptualizations of interest and interactivity follow.

Interest

Interest in specific content can influence one's selective exposure to the content (Ettema et al., 1983; Genova & Greenberg, 1979; Kwak, 1999; Viswanath et al., 1993). On the Web, that process can occur instantaneously. Results from three studies that measured how individuals judge the visual appeal of a Web page, for example, suggest most users take approximately 50 milliseconds to form an opinion about the page (Lindgaard et al., 2006).

For the PICK model proposed here, conceptualizing a broad concept such as interest draws from the literature on the role of interest in learning (Renninger et al., 1992). In this application, interest is differentiated as either "individual" or "situational."

Individual interest is one's attention to and learning from a content domain that develops slowly over time. Individual interest tends to have long-lasting effects on a person's knowledge and values (Hidi, 1990; Hidi & Baird, 1986, 1988; Hidi & McLaren, 1990; Krapp, 1988; Miller, 1986). This definition suggests that individual interest should be detectable prior to exposure to content because individual interest is established a priori. Presumably, the content interest is already familiar to the individual. To illustrate, a communication scholar can self-report individual interest in a Web site about communication research prior to exposure to a specific communication study.

On the other hand, situational interest is the extent to which specific but less familiar stimuli influence cognitive engagement across individuals. On the Web, situational interest could be influenced by characteristics on a specific page structured with text or graphics that capture attention, regardless of the user's expertise and prior knowledge (Hidi & Baird, 1986; Hidi & McLaren, 1990). A reader with little or no interest in nanotechnology prior to exposure to a news story about nanotechnology might exhibit situational interest in the specific nanotechnology story because it is structured in a way that attracts identification and interest. If so, the situational interest generated was evoked suddenly by the content, which might have only a short-term effect and marginally influencing the knowledge and values of a user who had little or no familiarity with the content's domain prior to exposure. Pertinent to complex news, situational interest could be elicited if someone with little or no individual interest in a story's topic reads the first words or graphics of the unfamiliar news story and continues his or her engagement with the story (Krapp, 1988).

Obviously, individual interest in a domain does not guarantee that an individual with expertise for the domain will attend to every news story about that domain. In this case, the expert could exhibit high individual interest on a pretest of interest but low situational interest in a particular story. Conversely, a citizen with little interest in a complex news story who chooses to ignore the complex news story exhibits both minimal individual and minimal situational interest. For researchers, it may be most helpful to measure individual interest prior to exposure to content so that it can be later teased from situational interest.

As detailed later in this chapter, the PICK model predicts that an effective strategy for content producers is to combine content that satisfies a citizen's long-term individual interest (i.e., well written and easy to understand text) with content that also generates short-term situational interest (an explanatory graphic or animation). In support of this strategy, a 2007 pilot study of text and graphics conducted by Yaros and Cook tested participants who claimed little or no individual interest in health news. Participants were exposed to four different story structures (two different text structures with or without an explanatory graphic). Following exposure, participants rated the stories on how interesting participants perceived the stories to be. Participants also answered a battery of questions to measure deeper situational understanding of the complexity. Despite a small pilot sample ($N = 17$), results confirmed a statistically significant positive correlation between interest and situational understanding ($r = .26$).

It has also been shown that one's motivation for seeking information can play a role in one attending to content. However, in the context of the earlier differentiation between individual interest and situational interest, more research is needed to explore how one's long-term individual interest in content is linked to the motivation to seek that content. Surprisingly, Eveland and Dunwoody (2001b) found that readers who self-reported a motivation to learn from news actually learned *less* than readers who did not claim such motivation. It may be impossible to know exactly why motivation and learning did not correlate in that study, but there is ample empirical evidence to support a significant correlation between interactivity and learning.

Interactivity and Involvement

The PICK theoretical model assumes that once a Web user becomes situationally interested in complex news, continued interest benefits learning. Sundar and Shyam (2007) noted "greater interactivity breeds more involvement, focusing more user attention on content" (p. 96). This suggests that strategies to involve citizens by retaining the citizens' interest should be employed as quickly as possible for all the message elements, including text. For example, instead of vague headlines, users' involvement can be enhanced with explanatory headlines, which offer more meaningful information. Explanatory headlines that, in effect, become lead sentences, help to increase the chances that users will continue engagement because less time is needed to "figure out" what the story is about.

This process is represented in the PICK Venn diagram where personalization and interactivity overlap. Related research from the fields of advertising and marketing has also shown that interactivity also increases users' positive perceptions of brands (Cho & Leckenby, 1999; Macias, 2003; Sundar & Kim, 2004), political participation (Stromer-Galley, 2000), and telepresence (Coyle & Thorson, 2001; Nelson et al., 2006; Stuer, 1992). Applied to news, interactivity could also enhance a citizen's attitude for a news Web site (Kalyanaraman & Sundar, 2006).

Unfortunately, and similar to interest, there is currently no universally adopted conceptualization of interactivity. One reason is that interactivity with new media has varied from links on a Web page to the more sophisticated Web 2.0 tools that offer user-generated input and networking (Rafaeli & Ariel, 2007). The researchers write, "a conceptual definition should be considered more broadly than just a single situation, determined by a specific environment and tools" (p. 73). Others conceptualized interactivity by multi-level features of modality such as audio, video, animation, source (or the extent to which citizens serve as sources) and traits of the hypertext such as external links or buttons to click.

The PICK theoretical model defines interactivity as the degree to which content assists citizens to input choices, responses or content. This means that a news organization that transfers or "shuffles" content from a printed newspaper product or an evening newscast to the Web provides minimal opportunity for user interactivity. Merely clicking a "play" button does not accurately define the PICK's term of interactivity. Conversely, any ability for citizen journalists to serve as the source of content—through blogs, forums, uploaded video, etc.—represents more meaningful interactivity because the model focuses on the user. The association of interactivity and direct user involvement is supported by the agency model of customization (Sundar, 2006), which states that online experiences that facilitate feelings of "self-as-source" or agency produce different cognitive and attitudinal outcomes by focusing the user's attention on content.

One might also argue that the validity of this conceptualization is enhanced when the user also demonstrates situational understanding of the content presented. This may appear to be rather obvious at first, but it becomes less obvious when one acknowledges that complex news is often prepared for consumption by a "general" audience and with producers often imputing audience knowledge for the content. Although it has been shown that interactivity can facilitate learning (Young, 1996), too much user involvement can inhibit comprehension when the interactivity overwhelms a user's cognition (Darken & Sibert, 1996; McDonald & Stevenson, 1996). The challenge for substantiating the value of citizen involvement, therefore, is recognizing when too much interactivity distracts from learning and citizen involvement.

One possible answer is to consider how interactivity has been operational-ized. Several studies used features such as online polls or a number of clickable links and images to quantify interactivity (Coyle & Thorson, 2001; Massey & Levy, 1999; McMillan & Hwang, 2002). Other studies solicited users' per-ceived interactivity (Cho & Leckenby, 1999; Wu, 1999). A few researchers tracked "click streams" of how users navigated through websites to determine interactivity (Coyle & Gould, 2002). Regardless of the method used, the PICK model argues that the notion of interactivity is an increasingly important factor in an increasingly complex world. This complexity stems from the increasing number of technological tools for interactive production, including sophisti-cated Flash animation and social networking tools such as "Twitter." Interactively feeding one or two lines of text live during a presidential debate is obviously easier to read than watching a debate on line with the live text and real-time "ratings" being generated by an audience with real-time reaction devices. Between the two, there is a threshold when interactivity overwhelms the audience reducing the effectiveness of the communication.

Again, an important point to keep in mind as this discussion of the PICK's Venn diagram is that interactivity alone cannot guarantee a citizen's interest in and understanding of complex issues. As detailed in the next section, there is substantial evidence for the importance of how the collection of the elements presented thus far are combined in a single structure to communicate one coherent message. This is no different from structuring a well-written news text. That single structure, however, is more difficult and more complex when mul-tiple elements, such as including links, video, slideshows, blogs and animation, are presented as part of the message. The extent to which layout structures have varied in the past is significant. Traditionally, most newspapers featured one main lead story and photo to focus citizens on what is perceived to be the "lead-ing" story of the day. Despite the Web's environment of free choice, many sites continue this single lead story structure online. Limiting the number of such choices for citizens also limits exposure and interactivity for citizens who not only seek a variety of information but increasingly demand it.

On the opposite end of the choice scale, newer content management systems instantly assemble and place multiple media into predetermined templates. Regardless of the content within the individual elements, such pages are often robotically structured based on the organization of topics or the aesthetic appeal of the design, not how coherent the stories are. Coherence in multimedia is referred to as contiguity.

The Concept of Contiguity

Linear news text printed in newspapers or books is considered to be well written when it is organized and coherent. Virtual content online, however, include hypertext as just one in a collection of digital elements that are electronically linked (Bolter, 1991) and then combined with other media. In that sense, the

Web is considered to be interconnected nodes of hypertext with nonlinear processing of content as users move from one informational node to another. Some scholars believe that once citizens arrive at a Web site they revert to the traditional linear processing of text (Alexander & Jetton, 1996; Goldman & Rakestraw, 2000). Others disagree. Bolter (1998) stated, "Literacy in electronic environments may have more to do with the production and consumption of images than the reading and writing of either hypertextual or linear prose" (p. 7). So what exactly is contiguity in multimedia?

First, a multimedia environment occurs when content is presented in more than one form, such as when news is presented visually *and* textually (Mayer, 1997; Moore, Burton, & Myers 1996). Several studies have shown that text is remembered better when it is illustrated by images compared to text without images (Levie, 1982; Levin, 1987; Mayer, 1989a; Mayer, & Gallini, 1990). At the same time, some have claimed that multimedia is often developed on the basis of its technological capacity instead of research-based principles (Kozma, 1991; Moore, Burton, & Myers, 1996). Others add that multimedia designs are often the products of intuitive beliefs from designers rather than on empirical evidence from research (Park, 1994). To effectively utilize advances in technology, developers need to better understand the ways in which people learn from words and pictures (Mandl, 1989; Willows, 1987). Mayer and Anderson (1991) remind us that potentially powerful animations, for example, are meaningless if the comprehender "cannot determine to what the elements and actions in the animations refer" (p. 490).

All of this informs the third component of the PICK model labeled contiguity. Contiguity in multimedia news is the extent to which the combinations of hypertext, photos, animation, slides, links, blogs, video and audio relate to each other to maximize coherence of the single message while preventing cognitive overload. Contiguity, and the benefits of the so-called contiguity principle are already well-researched within the field of educational psychology.

The contiguity principle states that the effectiveness of multimedia learning increases when words and pictures are presented contiguously in time or space (Moreno & Mayer, 1999). Through replication, Mayer and his colleagues demonstrated that individuals who learn from multimedia outperformed others when the design: (1) combined words with pictures rather than words alone; (2) placed words close to corresponding pictures; (3) used narration with corresponding animation and; (4) avoided extraneous words, pictures, and sound effects. According to Mayer, the results should be interpreted in light of individual differences, particularly with low-experience, high-imagery learners.

Contiguity does not imply that every news story should have a related photo or graphic. A more important process to consider for citizen and professional journalists is the extent to which all of the elements on a page or within a single story relate to each other to form one coherent message. To illustrate, when describing steps in a complex process, news text accompanied by an animated timeline of events and graphics that collectively relate to the story should be structured and presented with contiguity—not redundancy or independence—to communicate one message. This is different from writing an entire news story and then having another person—such as an artist—design what is perceived to be a separate but related graphic to be inserted by a content management. The PICK theoretical model posits that contiguity in multiple media will become increasingly important when communicating complexity to technologically savvy citizens and may eventually help citizens to differentiate well-produced storytelling from someone merely uploading random video for viewing.

More specifically, spatial contiguity describes the importance of text being physically close to related pictures or graphics. Studies show that participants generated a median of nearly 50 percent more creative solutions to problems when different forms of explanations were integrated together (Chandler & Sweller, 1991; Paas, 1994). Others found that individuals who read explanations placed near text in captioned illustrations generated significantly more solutions to problem-solving questions than those who read the same text and illustrations presented on separate pages (Mayer, 1989a; Mayer, Steinhoff, Bower, & Mars, 1995).

More recent research suggests that contiguity between the structures of text and hypertext links can significantly influence both user interest and learning (Yaros, 2005a). To test competing comprehension theories with linear versus nonlinear content, two complex news stories were modified into two text and hypertext structures. Participants ($N = 301$) with little or no expert knowledge for the content were tested for situational interest in and understanding. In support of traditional linear reading (such as the Construction-Integration Model), significant enhancement to situational interest and understanding occurred, but only when linear text was combined with linear link structures. Conversely, in support of a nonlinear model (such as cognitive flexibility theory) enhanced interest and understanding were measured for nonlinear text but only when combined with nonlinear link structures. These results suggest that contiguity within the *structures* of text and hypertext is important. The reasons for this remain unclear but it may relate to one's level of cognitive load.

Instructional designers have known for some time that multimedia instruction is sensitive to cognitive load (Clark, 1999; Sweller, 1999; van Merrienboer, 1997). The PICK model brings this issue to the forefront for professional and citizen journalism because users familiar with new media now respond to information that is designed to be both efficient and effective. A 2007 experimental study by Yaros and Cook tested participants' cognitive load and situational understanding of four health news stories by correlating eye-tracking data with post exposure questionnaires. The goal was to explore the relationship of how non-expert citizens process complex stories presented in one of two text structures (nonlinear vs. linear) with or without explanatory graphics. Timed eye measurements, including fixation durations on the text, graphics, and both, were recorded for 17 participants plus their pupil diameter to measure cognitive load. After viewing four counterbalanced stories, participants' situational understanding was measured along with participants' self-reported perceptions of story complexity and interestingness.

Again, the results showed the importance of contiguity between the text and graphics. Longer reading times—associated with more complexity and cognitive load for the content—produced a significant main effect of the text structure condition. Participants spent significantly more time viewing text in the nonlinear condition than they did for the more linear explanatory text. There was also a significant main effect of graphic presence on pupil diameter (i.e., more cognitive load), with larger pupil diameters measured when the graphic was present than when it was absent.

These data substantiate the need for news producers to keep graphics as simple as possible. The results also support previous research that suggested when individuals view news text and pictures about less familiar complex issues, individuals take more time to actively search and select particular information and then build a knowledge structure that accommodates present or anticipated demands (Gernsbacher, 1990a; Gernsbacher, Varner, & Faust, 1990b; Kintsch, & van Dijk, 1978; Schuell, 1988).

Comprehension was also affected. When correlating the eye-tracking data with post exposure measures of situational understanding, each of the four linear news stories with explanatory graphics enhanced understanding than the traditional linear texts with graphics. Interestingly, three of the four stories were rated higher in participants' perceived complexity when the stories were read in the traditional news structure. These results were interpreted as the importance of explanatory graphics and their contiguity with text to user comprehension (Mayer & Gallini, 1990).

Why hasn't contiguity been a concern for producers of multimedia news? This skill is not yet discussed in journalism schools. The focus to data continues to be on learning the new tools than it is on how to assemble content produced by the tools. Whatever the reason, the logical but important design principle of contiguity will eventually help to engage more citizens with complex news. In the interim, less contiguious texts, graphics, video, slides or animation may reduce engagement of citizens with complex content. This reduction of engagement describes the fourth concept of the PICK model. The reduction is produced by a cognitive "kick out."

The Concept of "Kick Outs"

The first three concepts of the PICK model presented in this chapter focused on the production elements that could enhance user engagement with multimedia journalism. The fourth and final component of the model—called the "kick out"—addresses those elements that threaten engagement.

Obviously, if a citizen becomes uninterested in a news story for any reason, he or she is likely to instantly terminate engagement with the content (Eveland & Dunwoody, 2001). The PICK model defines anything that terminates interest as a cognitive "kick out." In some ways, a kick out is a potential force as one interacts with the content and the available choices that constantly compete for one's attention. This persistent force eventually contributes to a user's decision to terminate engagement and choosing other content. The PICK model considers a kick out to be equal in importance to anything that generates interest and engagement in content.

Based on the previously discussed information, if news is not personalized enough for the user's experience, prior knowledge or interest, or is not interactive enough for citizen involvement or is not contiguous enough to quickly form a coherent message, the content itself will likely "kick out" citizen engagement.

Although some kick-outs are obvious (i.e., a broken link or long download time), it can be challenging to empirically detect kick-outs and their effects. Yes, the terminating moments of engagement with content might be easily found by tracking users' click streams of navigation, but identifying the specific element or elements of a page that produced the "kick out" can be difficult. Experimentation using eye-tracking hardware to reliably tabulate micro-level eye movements that lead to kick-out sequences may hold some promise in identifying elements in news that either reduce or increase engagement.

Recall from an earlier section that at least one study found motivated Web users failed to learn more from news than users who did not claim such motivation (Eveland & Dunwoody, 2001). This raises the possibility that "kick outs" could have played a role in this failure to learn despite the users' motivation to learn. Logically, motivated learners must also possess the appropriate knowledge with which to generate inferences for understanding the content. Second, a motivated citizen may not be exposed to a contiguous message structure that facilitates understanding. A partial list of other potential "kick outs" includes:

- technical difficulties
- information perceived to be outdated
- ads that are annoying
- unacceptably slow download times
- confusing information
- content perceived to have little or no perceived relevance by the user
- too much time required to comprehend the content
- unavailable products or information (i.e., broken links)
- an overwhelming amount of information
- too many or too few graphics
- too much or not enough text
- irritating or offending comments from others
- web sites or page content with ideologies inconsistent with those of the user

Ideally, the structure of complex news would minimize kick-outs while maximizing the other concepts in the PICK model. To illustrate, suppose an animation accompanies a complex news story and users terminate interest in the animation because they find it, too, increases in complexity too quickly. In that case, adding user-controlled buttons or offering the user self-paced controls to select events in the animation could simultaneously minimize or eliminate kick-outs while increasing personalization, involvement and contiguity.

Conclusion

It is not that the news of the future produced by citizens and professionals will need to include one or more of the PICK concepts. That already exists. It's that the most effective multimedia news will embrace the four concepts combined if the content is to engage a future audience that is dominated by "digital natives" who grew up with interactive, nonlinear technology. Of course, the concepts in the PICK model do not guarantee that a more informed citizenry will result. It is without question, however, that technology used by multitasking users will need to supply content that effectively captures audience interest. The combination of the PICK concepts addresses this anticipated demand for future journalists who will have to compete for the largest possible audience in an increasingly fragmented media environment.

The trends in Web production and the research to date suggest that the traditional ways to structure news text (inverted pyramid) and layouts (i.e., dominance, hierarchy, balance, space, color, and unity) are now only a subset of all the important variables to be considered when producing multimedia news. Based on the literature summarized in this chapter, *simultaneously* personalizing the content to the citizen, involving the citizen through interactivity, presenting hypertext, graphics and animation with contiguity and minimizing "kick outs" that instantly terminate user interest in the content are steps future journalists will need to consider in a world of overwhelming content.

Future research is needed to test how the "repackaging" of news influences the younger audience. How will news alerts compete with services such as "Twitter"? To what extent will personalization by services such as Google and The DailyMe gain popularity with the general audience? Research questions of the future will extend beyond the appeal of layouts or usability of general Web sites and explore different ways to instantly share information preferred by various fragments of the audience. Equally important, the PICK model predicts that the four concepts need to be applied not only at the macro (Web site) level, but also at the micro (story) level. In other words, once an audience member engages in the first words of a complex news story, the model predicts that ongoing personalization, involvement and contiguity with minimal kick-outs continue to be paramount if the audience member is to be retained.

Obviously, it is always more challenging to engage a citizen with complex issues than it is with more familiar and presumably easier to understand information. The PICK model anticipates and addresses the antecedents needed for engagement and learning from multimedia. The model is the first to synthesize the multiple concepts, supported by the previous research presented here.

Miller (2004) wrote, "The tools for communication and learning are unparalleled in both quality and access and will undoubtedly have a substantial impact on adults' information seeking and acquisition, but the nature and direction of this impact are not clear" (p. 291). The goal of this chapter was to explain why the PICK concepts will need to be addressed by citizen and professional journalists alike if they are to produce engaging content for the technologically savvy audience of the future. There are, of course, already plenty of examples online of ineffective Web sites, page formats and generic graphics. These exemplify the accurate conclusion that almost anyone can produce and post almost anything on the Web. However, much like the evolution of radio and television newscasts during the past decades, the bar for producing the most effective multimedia will continue to rise. The conclusion is that based on the current research and observation of the next generation of media users, concepts in the PICK model will be the determining factors that separate mediocre content with content that will be truly worth the time and effort for the audience to engage.

References

Alexander, P. A., & Jetton, T. L. (1996). The role of importance and interest in the processing of text. *Educational Psychology Review*, 8(1), 89–122.

Bieber, M., Vitali, F., Ashman, H., Balasubramanian, V., & Oinaas-Kullonen, H. (1997). Fourth generation hypermedia: Some missing links for the World Wide Web. *International Journal of Human-Computer Studies*, 47, 31–65.

Bolter, J. D. (1991). *Writing space: The computer, hypertext, and the history of writing.* Hillsdale, NJ: Lawrence Erlbaum Associates.

Britton, B. K., & Gulgoz, S. (1991). Using Kintsch's computational model to improve instructional text: Effects of repairing inference calls on recall and cognitive structures. *Journal of Educational Psychology*, 83, 329–404.

Brossard, D., & Nisbet, M. C. (2007). Deference to scientific authority among a low information public: Understanding U.S. opinion on agricultural biotechnology. *International Journal of Public Opinion Research*, 19(1), 24–52.

Brusilovsky, P., & Maybury, M. T. (2002). From adaptive hypermedia to the adaptive web. *Communications of the ACM*, 45, 5, 30–33.

Chandler, P., & Sweller, J. (1991). Cognitive load theory and the format of instruction. *Cognition and Instruction*, 8, 293–332.

Chen, C., & Rada, R. (1996). Interacting with hypertext: A meta-analysis of experimental studies. *Human-Computer Interaction*, 11, 125–156.

Cho, C.-H., & Leckenby, J. D. (1999). Interactivity as a measure of advertising effectiveness. In M. S. Roberts (Ed.), *Proceedings of the American Academy of Advertising* (pp. 162–179). Gainesville, FL: University of Florida.

Clark, R. C. (1999). *Developing technical training* (2nd ed.). Washington, DC: International Society for Performance Improvement.

Coyle, J. R., & Gould, S. J. (2002). How consumers generate clickstreams through web sites: An empirical investigation of hypertext, schema and mapping theoretical explanations. *Journal of Interactive Advertising, 2*(2), 55–73.

Coyle, J. R., & Thorson, E. (2001). The effects of progressive levels of interactivity and vividness in Web marketing sites. *Journal of Advertising, 30*(3), 65–79.

Darken, R. P., & Sibert, J. L. (1996). Navigating large virtual spaces. *International Journal of Human-Computer Interaction, 8,* 49–71.

Dillon, A. (1996). Myths, misconceptions, and an alternative perspective on information usage and the electronic medium. In J. J. Levonen, J. F. Rouet, A. Dillon, & R. J. Spiro (Ed.), *Hypertext and Cognition* (pp. 25–42). Mahwah, NJ: Erlbaum.

Dillon, A., & Gabbard, R. (1998). Hypermedia as an education technology: A review of the quantitative research literature on learner comprehension, control, style. *Review of Educational Research, 68,* 322–349.

Dunwoody, S. (1992). Comparative strategies for making the complex clear. In B. V. Lewenstein (Ed.), *When science meets the public* (pp. 101–102). Washington: American Association for the Advancement of Science.

Eppler, M. J., & Mengis, J. (2004). The concept of information overload: A recent review of literature from organization, science, accounting, marketing. MIS and related disciplines. *The Information Society, 20,* 325–344.

Ettema, J. S., Brown, J. W., & Luepker, R. V. (1983). Knowledge gap effects in a health information campaign. *Public Opinion Quarterly, 47,* 516–527.

Eveland, W. P., & Dunwoody, S. (2001). User control and structural isomorphism or disorientation and cognitive load? Learning from Web versus print. *Communication Research, 28,* 48–78.

Genova, B. K. L., & Greenberg, B. S. (1979). Interests in news and the knowledge gap. *Public Opinion Quarterly, 43,* 79–91.

Gernsbacher, M. A. (1990). *Language comprehension as structure building.* Hillsdale, NJ: L. Erlbaum.

Gernsbacher, M. A., Varner, K. R., & Faust, M. (1990). Investigating differences in general comprehension skill. *Journal of Experimental Psychology: Learning, Memory, and Cognition, 16,* 430–445.

Goldman, S. R., & Rakestraw, J. A., Jr. (2000). Structural aspects of construction meaning from text. In M. L. Kamil, P. B. Mosenthal, P. D. Pearson, & R. Barr (Eds.), *Handbook of reading research: Volume III* (pp. 311–335). Mahwah, NJ: Lawrence Erlbaum Associates.

Healthy People 2010. (2000). 2006, from http://www.healthypeople.gov/document/

Hidi, S. (1990). Interest and its contribution as a mental resource for learning. *Review of Educational Research, 60*(4), 549–571.

Hidi, S., & Baird, W. (1986). Interestingness: A neglected variable in discourse processing. *Cognitive Science, 10,* 179–194.

Hidi, S., & Baird, W. (1988). Strategies for increasing text-based interest and students' recall of expository texts. *Reading Research Quarterly, 23,* 465–483.

Hidi, S., & McLaren, J. (1990). The effect of topic and theme interestingness on the production of school expositions. In H. Mandl, E. De Corte, N. Bennett, & H. F. Friedrich (Eds.), *Learning and instruction: European research in an international context* (Vol. 2.2, pp. 295–308). Oxford: Pergamon.

Kalyanaraman, S., & Sundar, S. S. (2006). The psychological apeal of personalized online content in web portals: Does customization affect attitudes and behaviors? *Journal of Communication, 56,* 110–132.

Kintsch, W. (1988). The role of knowledge in discourse comprehension: A construction-integration model. *Psychological Review, 95,* 163–182.

Kintsch, W., & van Dijk, T. A. (1978). Toward a model of text comprehension. *Psychological Review, 85,* 363–394.

Kozma, R. B. (1991). Learning with media. *Review of Educational Research, 61,* 179–211.

Krapp, A. (1988, September). Interest, learning and academic achievement. Paper presented at the Third European Conference of Learning and Instruction (EARLI). In P. Nenniger (chair), Madrid.

Kwak, N. (1999). Revisiting the knowledge gap hypothesis: Education, motivation, and media use. *Communication Research, 26,* 385–413.

Lemke, J. L. (1990). *Talking science: Language, learning, and values.* Norwood: Ablex.

Levie, H. W., & Lentz, R. (1982). Effects of text illustrations: A review of research. *Educational Communication and Techology Journal, 30,* 195–232.

Levin, J. R., Anglin, G. J., & Carney, R. N. (1987). On empirically validating functions of pictures in prose. In D. M. Willows & H. A. Houghton (Eds.), *The psychology of illustration* (Vol. 1, pp. 51–86). New York: Springer.

Lewenstein, B. V. (1992). *When science meets the public.* Washington, DC: American Association for the Advancement of Science.

Lewenstein, B. V. (1994). A survey of activities in public communication of science and technology in the United States. In B. Schiele (Ed.), *When science becomes culture: World survey of scientific culture (Proceedings I)* (pp. 119–178). Boucherville: University of Ottawa Press.

Lindgaard, G., Fernandes, G., Dudek, C., & Brown, J. (2006). Attention web designers: You have 50 milliseconds to make a good first impression! *Behaviour & Information Technology, 25*(2), 115–126.

Macias, W. (2003). A preliminary structural equation model of comprehension and persuasion of interactive advertising brand web sites. *Journal of Interactive Advertising.* Retrieved June 5, 2007, from http://www.jiad.org/vol3/no2/macias/index.htm.

Magid Associates, F. (2004). Generational media study. Retrieved April 25, 2005, from www.online-publishers.org/pdf/opa_generational_study_sep04.pdf.

Mandl, H., & Levin, J. R. (1989). *Knowledge acquisition from text and pictures.* Amsterdam: North-Holland.

Massey, B. L., & Levy, M. R. (1999). Interactivity, online journalism and English-language web newspapers in Asia. *Journalism & Mass Communication Quarterly, 76*(1), 138–151.

Mayer, R. E. (1989). Systematic thinking fostered by illustrations in scientific text. *Journal of Educational Psychology, 81,* 240–246.

Mayer, R. E. (1997). Multimedia learning: Are we asking the right questions? *Educational Psychologist, 32*(1), 1–19.

Mayer, R. E., & Anderson, R. B. (1991). Animations need narrations: An experimental test of a dual-coding hypothesis. *Journal of Educational Psychology, 83,* 4, 484–490.

Mayer, R. E., & Gallini, J. K. (1990). When is an illustration worth ten thousand words? *Journal of Educational Psychology, 82*(4), 715–726.

Mayer, R. E., Steinhoff, K., Bower, G., & Mars, R. (1995). A generative theory of textbook design: Using annotated illustrations to foster meaningul learning of science text. *Educational Technology Research and Development, 43,* 31–43.

McDonald, S., & Stevenson, R. J. (1996). Disorientation in hypertext: The effects of three text structures on navigation performance. *Applied Ergonomics, 27*, 61–68.

McMillan, S. J., & Hwang, J. S. (2002). Measures of perceived interactivity: an exploration of the role of direction of communication, user control and time in shaping perceptions of interactivity. *Journal of Advertising, 31*(3), 14–29.

McNamara, D. S. (2001). Reading both high-coherence and low-coherence texts: Effects of text sequence and prior knowledge. *Canadian Journal of Experimental Psychology, 55*(1), 51–62.

McNamara, D. S., Kintsch, E., Songer, N. B., & Kitsch, W. (1996). Are good texts always better? Interactions of text coherence, background knowledge, and levels of understanding in learning from text. *Cognition and Instruction, 14*(1), 1–43.

Miller, J. D. (1986). Reaching the attentive and interested publics for science. In S. Friedman, S. Dunwoody, & C. Rogers (Eds.), *Scientists and Journalists: Reporting Science as News* (pp. 55–69). New York: Free Press.

Miller, J. D. (1987a). Scientific literacy in the United States. In D. Evered & M. O'Connor (Eds.), *Communicating Science to the Public* (Vol. 19–40). London: Wiley.

Miller, J. D. (1987b). The scientifically illiterate. *American Demographics, 9*(6), 26–31.

Miller, J. D. (2000). The development of civic scientific literacy in the United States. In D.D. Kumar & D. Chubin (Eds.), *Science, technology, and society: A sourcebook on research and practice* (pp. 21–47). New York: Plenum Press.

Miller, J. D. (2001). Who is using the Web for science and health information? *Science Communication, 22*(3), 256–273.

Miller, J. D. (2004). Public understanding of, and attitudes toward, scientific research: What we know and what we need to know. *Public Understanding of Science, 13*, 273–294.

Moore, D. M., Burton, J. K., & Myers, R. J. (1996). Multiple-channel communication: The theoretical and research foundations of multimedia. In D. H. Jonassen (Ed.), *Handbook of research for educational communication and technology* (pp. 851–875). New York: Macmillan.

Moreno, R., & Mayer, R. E. (1999). Cognitive principles of multimedia learning: The role of modality and contiguity. *Journal of Educational Psychology, 91*(2), 358–368.

Mostafa, J. (2002). Information customization. *Intelligent Systems, IEEE, 17*, 6, 8–11.

Nelson, M. R., Yaros, R. A., & Keum, H. (2006). Examining the influence of telepresence on spectator and player processing of real and ficticious brands in a computer game. *Journal of Advertising, 35*(4), 87–99.

O'Brien, E., & Myers, J. L. (1999). Text comprehension: A view from the bottom-up. In S. R. Goldstein, Grasser, A.C., & van den Broek, P. (Eds.), *Narrative comprehension, causality, and coherence: Essays in honor of Tom Trabasso* (pp. 35–54). Hillsdale: Erlbaum.

Paas, F. G. W. C., & Van Merrienboer, J. J. G. (1994). Variability of worked examples and transfer of geometrical problems solving skills: A cognitive load approach. *Journal of Educational Psychology, 86*, 122–133.

Palfrey, J. (2006). How digital natives experience news. Retrieved November 21, 2006, from   http://blogs.law.harvard.edu/palfrey/2006/05/20/how-digital-natives-experience-news/

Park, O., & Hannafin, M. (1994). Empirically-based guidelines for the design of interactive multimedia. *Educational Technology Research and Development, 41*, 63–85.

Rafaeli, S., & Ariel, Y. (2007). Assessing interactivity in computer-mediated research. In A. Joinson, K. McKenna, T. Postmes, & U. Reips (Eds.), *The Oxford handbook of internet psychology* (pp. 71–88). Oxford, UK: Oxford University Press.

Renninger, K. A., Hidi, S., & Krapp, A. (1992). *The role of interest in learning and development.* Hillsdale: Erlbaum.

Rieber, L. P. (1990). Animation in computer-based instruction. *Educational Technology Research and Development, 38,* 77–86.

Schuell, T. J. (1988). The role of the student in the learning from instruction. *Contemporay Educational Psychology, 13,* 276–295.

Shirk, H. N. (1992). Cognitive architecture in hypermedia instruction. In E. Barrett (Ed.), *Sociomedia: Multimedia, hypermedia, and the social construction of knowledge* (pp. 79–93). Cambridge: MIT Press.

Shoemaker, P. J. (1991). *Communication concepts 3: Gatekeeping.* Newbury Park, CA: Sage Publications.

Stromer-Galley, J. (2000). Online interaction and why candidates avoid it. *Journal of Communication, 50*(4), 73–93.

Stuer, J. (1992). Defining virtual reality: Dimensions determining telepresence. *Journal of Communication, 42*(4), 73–93.

Sundar, S. S. (2007). Social psychology of interactivity in human website interaction. In A. Joinson, K. McKenna, T. Postmes and U. Reips (Eds.), *The Oxford handbook of Internet psychology.* Oxford, UK: Oxford University Press.

Sundar, S. S., & Kim, J. (2004). Interactivity and persuasion: influencing attitudes with information and involvement. Paper presented at the annual convention of the International Communication Association, Communication and Technology division, New Orleans, LA.

Sundar, S. S., & Marathe, S. S. (2006). Is it tailoring or is it agency? Unpacking the pyschological appeal of customized news. In *Association for education and journalism & mass communication.* San Francisco, CA.

Sundar, S. S., & Ness (2001). Conceptualizing sources in online news. *Journal of Communication, 51,* 1, 52–72.

Sweller, J., & Chandler, P. (1999). *Instructional design in technical areas.* Camberwell, Australia: ACER Press.

Tremayne, M. (2004). The Web of context: Applying network theory to the use of hyperlinks in journalism on the Web. *Journalism & Mass Communication Quarterly, 81*(2), 237–253.

van Merrienboer, J. J. G. (1997). *Training complex cognitive skills.* Englewood Cliffs, NJ: Educational Technology Press.

Viswanath, K., Kahn, E., Finnegan, J. R., Hertog, J., & Potter, J. (1993). Motivation and the "knowledge gap": Effects of a campaign to reduce diet-related cancer risk. *Communication Research, 20,* 546–563.

Willows, D. M., & Houghton, H. A. (1987). *The psychology of illustration: Volume 1. Instructional issues.* New York: Springer-Verlag.

Wu, G. (1999). Perceived interactivity and attitude toward websites. Paper presented at the American Academy of Advertising.

Yaros, R. A. (2005a, August). Building a coherent web: Using structure building text and hypertext to facilitate engagement and understanding of news about complex issues. Paper presented at the Association for Education in Journalism & Mass Communication, San Antonio, TX.

Yaros, R. A. (2005b, August). Communicating complex news: Structuring stories to enhance public engagement and understanding of science. Paper presented at the Association for Education in Journalism & Mass Communication, San Antonio, TX.

Yaros, R. A. (2006). Is it the medium or the message? Structuring complex news to enhance engagement and situational understanding by non-experts. *Communication Research, 33*(4), 285–309.

Yaros, R.A. (2008). *Communicating complex news online. How users process information about science, health and technology.* VDM Publishing: Saarbrucken, Germany.

Yaros, R.A. (2009). Digital natives: Following their lead on a path to a new journalism. In *Nieman Reports.* Winter 2009 Edition: Nieman Foundation for Journalism at Harvard University.

Young, J. D. (1996). The effect of self-regulated learning strategies on performance in learner controlled computer-based instruction. *Educational Technology Research & Development, 44,* 17–27.

Chapter 5

Information Surplus in the Digital Age

Impact and Implications

Hsiang Iris Chyi

It was not until recently that journalism practitioners and scholars came to realize the real power of the technological changes brought about by the Internet, a technology they have been watching for more than a decade. Discussions on the future of journalism surround old and new issues such as interactivity, convergence, multi-platform storytelling, citizen journalism, blogsphere, and, perhaps most practically, the decline in newspaper circulation. These discussions share a sense of crisis.

This study attempts to identify one key factor—information surplus—which explains why audiences worldwide are changing their information-seeking behavior and why traditional news media are losing control during the process (Farhi, 2008; Gillmor, 2004; Stepp, 2008). Without fully understanding the nature of the changes due to information surplus, discussions surrounding the newspaper crisis might be missing the point.

Equally important implications exist for media scholars. As traditional news media's roles, i.e., gatekeepers or agenda setters, are being redefined by the abundance of information made available to the public by new media technologies, how should theorists redefine theories to make sure they stay relevant in the digital age?

This article examines the impact of "information surplus" from a media economics perspective and analyzes its implications for journalism and communication research. Specifically, my analysis addresses the following questions:

- How does the proliferation of online content, both media-generated and user-generated, change the public's demand for news?
- If the amount of information available exceeds what users can consume even at the price of zero, what are the implications for news production and presentation?
- How can media scholars effectively study media use, content, and effects in a digital era characterized by information surplus without being confined by existing, possibly outdated, theoretical frameworks?

Decline in News Consumption

Newspaper circulation has been on the decline since 1987 (weekday) and 1993 (Sunday) despite a growing U.S. population (Newspaper Association of America, 2007). The State of the News Media, the annual report of American journalism, documented that the losses have accelerated since 2004 (The State of the News Media, 2006). During the past three years, newspaper daily circulation dropped 6.3 percent and Sunday circulation 8 percent (The State of the News Media, 2007).

Readership decline is most obvious among young readers. In 1972, among the youngest age group (18–22), 46 percent read a newspaper every day (Peiser, 2000). By 2002, only 21 percent of the same age group did so (Mindich, 2005, p. 28). In 2007, 66 percent of Americans over 65 read a newspaper in an average week, while only 33 percent of 18-to-24-year-olds and 34 percent of 25-to-34-year-olds did so ("The State of the News Media," 2008). Such "cohort replacement" (p. 11)—more younger people who read less frequently and fewer older people who read more frequently—predicts further declines in the future (Peiser, 2000).

Faced with the unprecedented readership crisis, the newspaper industry has been asking (and has been asked) questions like: "What should newspapers do to retain readership, especially among young people?", "What is the essential content value of newspapers?", "Will there still be a place for newspapers in the future?" (Avriel, 2007; Wilkinson, 2003).

Other traditional news media—such as network TV news, local TV news, and radio news—are all losing audiences, too. The percentage of Americans who watched network TV news regularly dropped from 60 percent in 1993 to 28 percent in 2006 (Pew Research Center for the People & the Press, 2006). The median age of the network evening news audience is 60 (The State of the News Media, 2007).

Some newspaper practitioners believe that young people are turning to the Internet for their news. But according to David Mindich (2005), author of *Tuned out: Why Americans under 40 don't follow the news*, most young people go online "for anything but news" (2005, p. 4). The Pew study shows that even the Internet news audience is aging—while 47 percent of the 30–34 year-olds get news online regularly, only 30 percent of those 18–24 do so—which is about the same as the group ages 50–64 (Pew Research Center for the People & the Press, 2006).

Even among the general public, the picture is not encouraging. Two-thirds of U.S. adults have not turned to online news and appear unlikely to do so (Ahlers, 2006). And only 31 percent of Americans access online news regularly (Pew Research Center for the People & the Press, 2006).

So, what is happening?

Information Surplus

One key factor that is very often underestimated, if not neglected, during the discussion about the decline in news consumption is "information surplus"— the oversupply of information, which in large part is caused by the Internet's capacity of distributing content at minimal cost, particularly in the web 2.0 era, when the amount of user-generated content is growing exponentially.

Two related concepts are "information explosion" and "information overload." Information explosion refers to "an extreme increase in the supply of information" (Rudd & Rudd, 1986, p. 304). For example, "the Sunday *New York Times* contains more factual information in one edition than in all the written material available to a reader in the fifteenth century" (Davenport & Beck, 2001, p. 4). Information overload focuses on the psychological effect of information explosion on users. The effect represents "a state of affairs where an individual's efficiency in using information in their work is hampered by the amount of relevant, and potentially useful, information available to them" (Bawden, Holtham, & Courtney, 1999, p. 249). None of these concepts is novel.

What's novel is the speed at which digital information is being created and distributed. The proliferation of online content is on an unprecedented scale and is challenging the orthodox assumption of scarcity in economics (Ghosh, 1998). It is estimated that the world produced about five exabytes of new information in 2002, that's the equivalent of the amount of information stored in 37,000 new libraries the size of the Library of Congress (Varian & Lyman, 2003). Of this vast body of information, 92 percent was stored on magnetic media (mostly hard disks) in digital format. Overall, the amount of new information doubled between 2000 and 2003; the amount of information on the Web tripled between 2000 and 2003 (Varian & Lyman, 2003). And this was before Web 2.0 took off.

As of March 2007, Technorati, the popular search engine for the blogsphere, was tracking some 70 million weblogs and reported about 120,000 new blogs and 1.4 million posts being created worldwide each day, and the blogsphere would double its size in about 320 days (Sifry, 2007). YouTube, launched in December 2005, was serving more than 100 million videos per day by mid 2006 (BBC News, 2006). The number of YouTube video clips grew 20 percent to 6.1 million in August 2006 (Gomes, 2006). The overabundance of information and the speed at which more information is created carry important implications.

To explain the information surplus phenomenon in economic terms, Figure 5.1 illustrates a simple demand and supply analysis of the information market in general. D is the demand curve. S_1 is the supply curve. As factors such as technological innovations, an increasing number of suppliers, and the decreasing price of input are present, the supply curve would shift to the right (Boyes & Melvin, 1996)—from S_1 to S_2, for example. As a result, price drops from P_1 to P_2

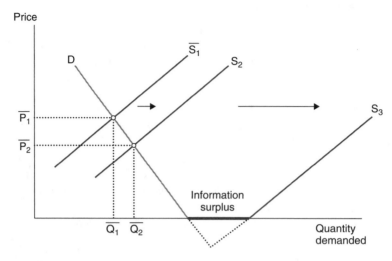

Figure 5.1 Information surplus.

and the quantity demanded increases from Q_1 to Q_2. In other words, in the new equilibrium, more information is consumed at a lower price. This used to be how we conceptualized the effect of an increase in supply.

However, if one considers the volume of information that is now available to users and the speed at which new information is being created and distributed in the Web 2.0 era, we may need to go beyond S_2, as the actual supply curve might have been approaching S_3, resulting in a huge gap between content supplied and content consumed even at the price of zero. The demand for information, on the other hand, remains stable, as users have only limited capacities to process information given time and attention constraints. Attention, or the "human bandwidth," is a scarce resource in the attention economy (Davenport & Beck, 2001, p. 2).

In other words, what is happening is beyond information explosion; it is information surplus, meaning the amount of information available far exceeds what users can consume even if they want to and even at the price of zero. An information market characterized by information surplus has profound implications for the traditional media industry.

First, the decline in news consumption should not surprise anyone. Today, with all kinds of information readily accessible online or offline, users get to pick what to consume. News is becoming just one of the many, if not unlimited, choices. One can visit news sites, watch videos on YouTube, listen to music from Pandora.com, blog, check email, chat with friends, pay bills, do shopping, to name just a few.

Users pick whatever information they want—news or non-news. In economic terms, news and non-news information in general are substitute goods, given limited time and attention. In media history, the growth of media choices is the norm, and so is the fact that media have always competed for audience's time and attention (Fidler, 1997). The decline in news consumption started in the 1960s as the first TV generation grew up (Mindich, 2005). Today, however, the volume and diversity of information available has transformed the information landscape from "information explosion" to "information surplus," from "information abundance" to "information overabundance," from "there ain't no such thing as a free lunch" to "information *has* to be free."

Moreover, today's information environment suggests that the information surplus phenomenon is an on-going process. There is little reason to believe that the supply curve would stop shifting to the right after reaching S_3, suggesting future decline in news consumption. It is therefore important to examine news consumption in the context of information surplus.

Product Differentiation Strategies in the Attention Economy

News Consumption in the Attention Economy

From now on, information is probably never going to be in short supply—attention is. The authors of the book *Attention Economy* argue that "attention is the real currency of businesses and individuals" and that attention management is the most important determinant of business success (Davenport & Beck, 2001, p. 3). As the amount of information keeps growing, holding people's attention is difficult, but you can purchase attention or pay for someone to receive your information (Davenport & Beck, 2001), which is not surprising if there is too much information floating around at the price of zero.

Given that attention has become the most valuable resource in the information society, it is no wonder the online news industry has found it difficult, if not impossible, to charge for access to online content. Effective September 19, 2007, the New York Times on the Web dropped its fee-based program TimesSelect. In an open letter to readers, Vivian Schiller (2007), senior vice president and general manager of NYTimes.com, wrote:

> Since we launched TimesSelect in 2005, the online landscape has altered significantly. Readers increasingly find news through search, as well as through social networks, blogs and other online sources. In light of this shift, we believe offering unfettered access to New York Times reporting and analysis best serves the interest of our readers, our brand and the long-term vitality of our journalism.

In response to NYTimes.com's move away from the subscription model, Jeff Jarvis (2007), a media professor and blogger, in a post titled "Times deselected," declared that "TimesSelect is dead . . . With it goes any hope of charging for content online. Content is now and forever free."

So online news has to be free. But offering free news online does not necessarily boost readership. Research showed that the majority of online newspaper readers in the local market tend to be readers of the print edition (Chyi & Lasorsa, 2002; Chyi, 2006). In other words, even free online offerings failed to contribute substantial local, non-print readers to the overall newspaper readership. The information surplus model provides an explanation for this phenomenon.

The surplus of information has changed not only the "attention share" of news but also how people select, process, and perceive information. Regarding the shrunken attention span, Davenport and Beck (2001) asked if "we are the first society with ADD" (attention deficit disorder) as production of Ritalin, the drug used to treat ADD, is up 9 times since 1990 (p. 7). DeGrandpre (2001), author of *Digitopia: The Look of the New Digital You*, believes that sensory-saturated users in the digital world will only pursue more hypersensitizing media experience:

> The human brain that finds itself submerged in a world of constant stimulation will become a brain that attends to only the most alluring stimuli in the environment . . . Everything in the media world must be bigger, faster, louder, more all-encompassing, and more hyperrealistic than it was only six months ago. (p. 119)

As traditional news media compete with various information sources for attention, research shows that news is not perceived as relevant as it once was, and not as appealing as other types of information is. When author Mindich asked a handful of young adults why they don't read news, they said news is "stressful," "detached," "non-engaging," and "not as much fun" (Mindich, 2005, pp. 47–48).

To address these challenges, newspapers have been trying to provide customized news by emphasizing softer news and local news and redesigning their look to mimic other media (Sylvie & Witherspoon, 2002). The proliferation of TV channels and the production cost associated with hard-news coverage also resulted in softer and personality-driven TV news (Hamilton, 2004).

Having realized that news is now just one of the many information categories competing for users' attention share, the newspaper industry is eager to redefine its role as an information provider. The key question, in economic terms, is: How can newspapers effectively differentiate their products—online and offline—when literally numerous competitors are constantly offering alternatives? In a monopolistically competitive information market, what kind of product differentiation strategies apply?

Disagreement exists as to how newspapers compete with other information sources. Some critics believe that "we need something very close to what a good newspaper is but with a different ideology and ethic: a medium that gives its consumers nearly as much power as its reporters and editors have—a medium that isn't afraid of unfettered discussions, intense passions, and unashamed opinion" (Katz, 1994, p. 5). Along these lines, many U.S. newspapers have been experimenting with these ingredients by offering interactive, multimedia content online while trying to keep the integrity of their news products intact.

Information Wants to Be Desirable?

In East Asia, some mainstream newspapers took a very different approach and, by doing so, achieved economic success. The most salient example is probably Hong Kong, one of the most media-rich markets in the region. With more than a dozen local dailies (two in English and the rest in Chinese) actively serving the market of nearly 7 million residents, newspaper penetration has been high. A random-sample survey conducted in 2002 (Chyi, 2006) shows that 89 percent of respondents read print newspapers, spending on average 57 minutes per day reading newspapers. In comparison, as of 2002, only 41 percent of Americans read a newspaper yesterday; the average time spent on reading newspapers was 15 minutes (Pew Research Center for the People & the Press, 2004; "The State of the News Media," 2007). So what makes newspapers so appealing in Hong Kong?

Hong Kong's popular press is characterized by "absolute market-driven journalism" (So, 1997). It started with *Apple Daily*, launched in 1995 by the maverick media tycoon Jimmy Lai. His "reader-centric" journalism was so successful that most newspapers in Hong Kong followed suit by taking the tabloid approach—a process described as "the apple-ization" of Hong Kong newspapers (So, 1997). To the present day, entertainment-driven, tabloid-style publications featuring sensational content dominate the print market in Hong Kong.

Apple Daily's content strategies are determined by the interests of the reader (e.g., through weekly focus groups), with 40 reporters focusing on political topics, 100 writing about lifestyle issues (such as entertainment, shopping guide, restaurant reviews) and another 90 covering crime (Steinberger, 1996). Among the Top 3 circulated newspapers in Hong Kong, sensory-stimulating content prevails with large (often bloody) photos, eye-catching headlines and colorful graphics. As the newspapers have taken "the lowest common denominator" philosophy to the extreme, it is not uncommon to publish sexually explicit materials such as photos of attractive women and graphical descriptions of sex-related activities and ads (Figure 5.2). Although heavily criticized, Hong Kong newspapers often argue that this is a "freedom of the press" issue.

Because the Apple model turned out to be so successful in Hong Kong, Jimmy Lai replicated the model by launching the Taiwan version of *Apple Daily* in 2003. Before long, several smaller dailies folded and two major elite newspapers

Figure 5.2 Pages of the November 30, 2008 edition of *Apple Daily* (Photograph by Alfred Lee).

have also lost their market share. As of Q2, 2007, *Apple Daily*'s daily circulation reached 523,376 and is currently the No. 2 most read newspaper in Taiwan (The Audit Bureau of Circulations—ROC, 2007).

While newspapers in Hong Kong and Taiwan have demonstrated that "the lowest common denominator" approach does attain readers' attention, would such practices become the norm in western media markets? Nakednews.com, a Canada-based news site, features female anchors who undress while delivering news. If anchors undressing is considered out of line (Mindich, 2005), how about the coverage of Paris Hilton by the mainstream news media? Are we not seeing the same strategies being employed by the U.S. media as they also move toward entertainment-driven journalism?

Journalists, media critics, scholars, and parents in different societies have expressed deep concerns about the social and political consequences of all these changes characterizing today's news environment. Such concerns are legitimate as profit-maximizing news media may do harm to democracy by entertaining but not informing the public (Lung, 2005). When news is redefined and ethics abandoned, society one day will have to pay the price (Woo, 2002).

Consumer Sovereignty: Reasons to be Optimistic

Yet, there are reasons to be more optimistic in larger media markets, especially the U.S., where an exceptionally strong Internet segment exists. Heavily invested media websites, Web 2.0 sites (most are U.S.-based, targeting English-speaking users), and innovative projects created by companies like Google primarily for U.S. users offer a much wider range of content choices to everyday citizens. Despite the decline in news consumption and the not-so-desirable trend toward market-driven journalism, from an average user's perspective, almost unlimited information choices are available to everyone. In that sense, "anyone looking for information has never been better equipped" ("The future of newspapers: Who killed the newspaper," 2006).

Can this be Bad?

In economics, the concept of "consumer sovereignty" states that "the consumer is the best judge of his or her own preferences" (Hoskins, McFadyen & Finn, 2004, p. 78). When people behave on their self interest, more often than not, society as a whole will be better off. Is there a reason not to believe that these economic principles also apply to information consumption? Is there a reason not to believe that people would seek information to keep themselves informed (in their own terms)? Technology actually facilitates the information-seeking process by bringing all the information in front of us and therefore helping us become better-informed citizens. Media analysts believe numerous bloggers and citizen journalists together can hold politicians accountable, and major newspapers probably would survive anyway ("The future of newspapers: Who killed the newspaper," 2006). So there are reasons to be optimistic. As the quality of democracy almost always depends on the quality of people, we may want to shift our attention away from media-centric concerns (e.g., "Will newspapers die?") and focus more on people-centric issues, such as media literacy and education.

New Research Agenda

In the research forefront, media scholars are expected to expand the scope of their research by examining new factors that are redefining today's media environment. Those scholars who rely on existing theories without critically re-examining the historical contexts or assumptions underlying those theories run the risk of ignoring key aspects of this new environment and thus keep communication theories from evolving.

Take studies on the Internet, for example. The Internet revolutionizes our information environment with innovative characteristics such as boundary-transcending capability, two-way information flow, multimedia presentation, real-time data transmission, and information surplus. Each of these traits warrants great opportunities for expanding existing theories and building new ones. One successful example of the former is how the diffusion of innovation theory has evolved to include "interactivity" as a factor differentiating the adoption rates between interactive and non-interactive technologies. The expanded theory states that interactive media require a "critical mass" of adopters before its S-shaped curve accelerates, so the rate of adoption for interactive media is expected to be slower in the early stages, but increases more rapidly than non-interactive innovations (Williams, Rice, & Rogers, 1988).

To effectively study new media—a fast-moving research target—theories must capture the defining factors pertinent to the new information environment so as to stay relevant and to provide insights into the research topic. The "information surplus" phenomenon is such a factor and, if understood properly, may inspire new ways of thinking about theory renovation and expansion. To illustrate the theoretical significance of "information surplus," the following discussion explores new research possibilities associated with this factor from media use, media content, and media effects perspectives. The purpose is not to review theories exhaustively but to provide suggestions for incorporating information surplus when studying the new media landscape.

New Questions on News Media Use

Given the above-mentioned decline in news consumption, one of the first topics on researchers' minds is media use. Research on newspaper readership, displacement effects, and uses and gratifications generally falls into this category. Some general research questions read: Who is using what media? For what purposes? Who is not using what media? Why? Do people spend less time on the traditional media because of new media? These are legitimate questions and some carry practical implications. However, from a theoretical perspective, they are not new. For example, research that examined newspaper readership dates back to the 1960s (McCombs, Mullins & Weaver, 1974; Poindexter, 1979; Westley & Severin, 1964).

Theories can (and should) evolve as the media environment keeps changing. The uses and gratifications approach is a good example. This perspective has been used effectively to address "What are the uses and gratifications of (any new media technology)" since the 1970s. As the Internet emerged as a mass medium in the 1990s, media scholars indicated that the uses and gratifications paradigm held some prospect for understanding the Internet because "it offers a vehicle to lay out a taxonomy of a broad range of communication activities in cyberspace" (Newhagen & Rafaeli, 1996). Morris and Ogan (1996) suggested that the concept of "audience activity"—presumed by the uses and gratifications approach—should be included in the study of Internet communication. In recent years, some media economists have expanded the scope of the uses and gratifications paradigm to examine competition between traditional and digital media outlets. Dimmick (2003) incorporated the concept of gratifications into his theory of the niche and examined the Internet as a functional alternative to traditional news media (Dimmick, Chen, & Li, 2004). Lacy (2004) differentiated different types of utility to analyze user demand for a mix of media products—old and new—in a "fuzzy market structure" (Lacy, 1993, p. 55).

In a media environment characterized by information surplus, numerous information outlets oversupply information to compete for user attention. The theoretical implication is that each user is presented with ever-increasing choices of media products—news and non-news, media- and user-generated, within and outside the traditional market boundaries. At the macro level, media use studies may benefit from a more comprehensive approach—e.g., considering multiple market definitions and differentiating substitutes available (Bates, 1991, 1993; Chyi & Sylvie, 1998; Dimmick, 2006; Lacy & Bauer, 2006) when examining demand and competition. At the individual level, research opportunities exist regarding how users manage information surplus.

From the users' perspective, information-seeking has become an extremely complex decision-making process. Before use, people must first make choices among numerous media products that are imperfect substitutes (Lacy, 2004). To study consumers' media selection process, Wildman (2006) suggested the application of the search models developed in the literature of information economics. Lacy and Bauer (2006) called for a more sophisticated demand theory, the need for which is even more pressing in the context of information surplus.

In terms of information-processing, prior research has examined behavioral variables such as "selective exposure" (Zillmann & Bryant, 1985) and "incidental exposure" (Tewksbury, Weaver, & Maddex, 2001). Other non-conventional strategies for coping with information overabundance, such as "information avoidance" (Case, Andrews, Johnson, & Allard, 2005) and "multitasking" (Jeong et al., 2008), may trigger relevant and intellectually stimulating research questions. Negative consequences of information-processing, such as "information overload" (Bawden, Holtham, & Courtney, 1999; Nordenson, 2008), also deserve scholarly attention.

New Questions on Media Content

Information surplus changes media content in two ways—causing dramatic increases in quantity and in diversity. The excessive information available at the price of zero carries important implications regarding user perception, as recent research in behavioral economics indicates that users tend to perceive products with a higher price tag as more enjoyable (Plassmann, O'Doherty, Shiv, & Rangel, 2008). Methodologically, media output usually is examined through content analysis. Today, with the volume of information available on the Internet, new methodological approaches such as data-mining techniques should supplement content analysis.

In terms of diversity, traditional media research considered content diversity an important issue—the underlying rationale being that traditional communication channels are scarce resources so media should present and promote diverse opinions. Since the 1950s, media researchers have shared such a view (Coulson & Lacy, 1996; Entman, 1985; Lacy, 1987). Yet, in the new media environment, diverse content is almost always accessible and in plentiful supply. Waterman (2006) predicted that higher channel capacity actually would increase program diversity by eliminating least-objectionable program types in electronic media. Future research should re-conceptualize content diversity in light of information surplus.

As old assumptions fade, new assumptions about the information environment surface, and many need to be verified empirically. For example, with so much information available on the Web, some people have come to believe that all knowledge is on the Web. Tankard and Royal (2005) challenge this idea by empirically examining "what's on the Web—and what's not?" They found that the Web contains more material from recent years, more important information (determined by the amount of space assigned to a topic in an encyclopedia), more information about countries with larger populations, and more information about large corporations. Therefore, the World Wide Web "appears to contain all available information, but it does not" (Tankard & Royal, 2005, p. 369). This study illustrates the importance of closely examining a highly complex information environment characterized by information surplus.

New Questions on Media Effects

In the area of media effects research, there are also opportunities for expanding existing theories to incorporate new factors associated with information surplus.

Take the well-established agenda-setting theory as an example. Since the theory was first put to the test by McCombs and Shaw (1972) in 1968, more than 350 empirical studies have been conducted in various settings and under different conditions to examine the agenda-setting function of the news media (Dearing & Rogers, 1996). In recent years, the theory has expanded to include the second level of agenda-setting, where the unit of analysis shifts from an object to the aspects or attributes of the object (McCombs & Reynolds, 2002). During the process, many new variables are introduced into the paradigm, making the theory one of the most robust media effects theories in communication research.

How can agenda-setting theory shed light on the changes brought about by information surplus? I see two possibilities here: first, as media content diversifies, the concept of "agenda" could be expanded to incorporate heterogeneous items, such as news as well as non-news items. This thinking transforms the concept of "news agenda" into a more generally defined "information agenda."

We know the media exert strong agenda-setting effects on the public's news agenda, and it would be interesting to examine such effects on people's "information agenda."

The second direction attempts to answer the question "who sets the media agenda." In the digital world, news content is distributed through a variety of technologies. For example, Google News, a program-based, non-human news agent, aggregates content from more than 4,500 news sources. In the meantime, technologies such as RSS feeds allow for highly personalized news selection, as Negroponte (1995) once envisioned with "the Daily Me" concept. In addition, many news Web sites incorporate user input to determine the salience of specific news items—e.g., NYTimes.com features the "Most Popular" stories on the main page. Social-networking news sites such as Digg.com push the trend further by maximizing peer readers' influence on news selection and thus carry out the "the Daily Us" concept (Gillmor, 2004). So who is setting the media agenda in the Web 2.0 era? The dynamic relationship between multiple agenda-setters and that between the media agenda and the public agenda are of particular interest.

Conclusion

This study defines "information surplus" as the excessive amount of information available to users even at the price of zero. Because nothing can stop the gap between the supply and demand curves from widening as more information is being created and distributed at unprecedented speed, further decline in news consumption is inevitable.

Newspaper industries in different media markets respond to readership decline with varying degrees of market-driven practices, the consequences of which have raised discussions about news media's social responsibility in the digital era. In the US, where an exceptionally strong Internet segment exists, average users are presented with numerous, ever-growing media choices, resulting in a need for reinventing communication theories to capture the defining factors shaping the new media environment. Information surplus as one such factor is often taken for granted in communication research but its theoretical significance lies in the great opportunities for expanding existing theories and building new ones as illustrated in the examples given earlier in this chapter.

As Archimedes suggested, "Give me a place to stand on, and I will move the Earth." Communication researchers may benefit from spending time scrutinizing such "places" to effectively study media use, content, and effects in the digital age.

Acknowledgment

The author would like to thank Amy Zerba, Sonia Huang, Alfred Lee, Jay Chang, and Zichi Kuo for their assistance with this project.

References

Ahlers, D. (2006). News consumption and the new electronic media. *Press/Politics* *11*(1), 29–52.

The Audit Bureau of Circulations—ROC. (2007). *ABC News*. Retrieved September 22, 2008, from http://www.abc.org.tw/.

Avriel, E. (2007, February 8). *NY Times publisher*: Our goal is to manage the transition from print to internet. Retrieved May 10, 2007, from http://www.haaretz.com/hasen/spages/822775.html

Bates, B. J. (1991). Breaking the structural logjam: The impact of cable on local TV market concentration. *The Journal of Media Economics*, *4*(3), 47–58.

Bates, B. J. (1993). Concentration in local television markets. *The Journal of Media Economics*, *6*(3), 3–22.

Bawden, D., Holtham, C., & Courtney, N. (1999). Perspectives on information overload. *Aslib Proceedings*, *51*(8), 249–255.

BBC News. (2006). YouTube hits 100m videos per day. Retrieved May 10, 2007, from http://news.bbc.co.uk/1/hi/technology/5186618.stm.

Boyes, W., & Melvin, M. (1996). *Economics* (3rd ed.). Boston: Houghton Mifflin.

Case, D. O., Andrews, J. E., Johnson, J. D., & Allard, S. L. (2005). Avoiding versus seeking: The relationship of information seeking to avoidance, blunting, coping, dissonance, and related concepts. *Journal of the Medical Library Association 93(3)*, 353–362.

Chyi, H. I. (2006). Re-examining the market relation between online and print Newspapers: The case of Hong Kong. In X. Li (Ed.), *Internet newspapers* (pp. 193–205). Mahwah, NJ: Lawrence Erlbaum Associates.

Chyi, H. I., & Lasorsa, D. L. (2002). An explorative study on the market relation between online and print newspapers. *Journal of Media Economics*, *15*(2), 91–106.

Chyi, H. I., & Sylvie, G. (1998). Competing with whom? Where? And how? A structural analysis of the electronic newspaper market. *Journal of Media Economics*, *11*(2), 1–18.

Coulson, D. C., & Lacy, S. (1996). Journalists' perceptions of how newspaper and broadcast news competition affects newspaper content. *Journalism & Mass Communication Quarterly*, *73*(2), 354–363.

Davenport, T. H., & Beck, J. C. (2001). *The attention economy: Understanding the new currency of business*. Harvard Business School Press.

Dearing, J. W. and Rogers, E. (1996). *Agenda setting*. Thousand Oaks, CA: Sage.

DeGrandpre, R. (2001). *The incredible shrinking attention span. In digitopia: The look of the new digital you*. New York: AtRandom.

Dimmick, J. (2003). *Media competition and coexistence: The theory of the niche*. Mahwah, NJ: Lawrence Erlbaum Associates.

Dimmick, J. (2006). Media competition and levels of analysis. In A. B. Albarran, S. M. Chan-Olmsted, & M. O. Wirth (Eds.), *Handbook of media management and economics* (pp. 345–362). Mahwah: NJ: Lawrence Erlbaum Associates.

Dimmick, J., Chen, Y., & Li, Z. (2004). Competition between the Internet and traditional news media: The gratification-opportunities niche dimension. *Journal of Media Economics*, *17*, 19–33.

Entman, R. E. (1985). Newspaper competition and first amendment ideals: Does monopoly matter? *Journal of Communication*, *35*(3), 147–165.

Farhi, P. (2008). Online salvation? *American Journalism Review*, 2008 (December/January).

Fidler, R. (1997). *Mediamorphosis: Understanding new media*. Thousand Oaks, CA: Pine Forge Press.

The future of newspapers: Who killed the newspaper? (2006, August 24). *The Economist*, Retrieved September 22, 2008, from http://www.economist.com/opinion/displaystory.cfm?story_id=7830218.

Ghosh, R. A. (1998). Cooking pot markets: An economic model for the trade in free goods and services on the Internet. *First Monday*. Retrieved September 22, 2004, from http://www.firstmonday.dk/issues/issue3_3/ghosh/.

Gillmor, D. (2004). *We the media*. Sebastopol, CA: O'Reilly.

Gomes, L. (2006, August 30). Will all of us get our 15 minutes on a YouTube video? *Wall Street Journal Online*. Retrieved September 22, 2008, from http://online.wsj.com/public/article/SB115689298168048904-
5wWyrSwyn6RfVfz9NwLk774VUWc_20070829.html?mod=rss_free.

Hamilton, J. T. (2004). *All the news that's fit to sell: How the market transforms information into news*. Princeton, NJ: Princeton University Press.

Hoskins, C., McFadyen, S., & Finn, A. (2004). *Media economics: Applying economics to new and traditional media*. Thousand Oaks, CA: Sage.

Jarvis, J. (2007). Times deselected. *BuzzMachine*. Retrieved September 20, 2007, from http://www.buzzmachine.com/2007/09/17/times-deselected/.

Jeong, S., Zhang, W., Fishbein, M., Davis, E., Bleakley, A., Jordan, A., & Hennessy, M. (2008). Multiple media use and multitasking with media among high school and college students: A diary method. In M.B. Hinner (Ed.), *Freiberger Beitraege zur Interkulturellen und Wirtschaftskommunikation: A forum for general and intercultural business communication*. Frankfurt am Main, Germany: Peter Lang GmbH.

Katz, J. (1994, September). Online or not, newspapers suck. *Wired Magazine*, 2(09), 50. Retrieved September 22, 2008, from http://www.wired.com/wired/archive/2.09/news.suck.html.

Lacy, S. (1987). The effects of intracity competition on daily newspaper content. *Journalism Quarterly*, 64(2), 281–290.

Lacy, S. (1993). Understanding & serving readers: The problem of fuzzy market structure. *Newspaper Research Journal*, 14(2), 55–67.

Lacy, S. (2004). Fuzzy market structure and differentiation: One size does not fit all. In R. G. Picard (Ed.), *Strategic responses to media market changes* (pp. 83–95). Jönköping, Sweden: Jönköping International Business School, Jönköping University.

Lacy, S., & Bauer, J. M. (2006). Future directions for media economics research. In A. B. Albarran, S. M. Chan-Olmsted, & M. O. Wirth (Eds.), *Handbook of media management and economics* (pp. 655–674). Mahwah, NJ: Lawrence Erlbaum Associates.

Lung, Y. (2005, March 16). Excuse me: where is Athens? [Chinese]. *China Times*. Retrieved September 22, 2008, from http://forums.chinatimes.com.tw/report/lonin/94031610.htm.

McCombs, M. E., Mullins, L. E. & Weaver, D. H. (1974, April 5). Why people subscribe and cancel: A "stop-start" survey of three daily newspapers. *American Newspaper Publishers Association News Research Bulletin*, 3, 12.

McCombs, M. E., & Reynolds, A. (2002). News influence on our pictures of the world. In Jennings Bryant and Dolf Zillmann (Eds.), *Media effects: Advances in theory and research* (2nd ed., pp. 1–18). Mahwah, NJ: Lawrence Erlbaum Associates.

McCombs, M. E. and Shaw, D. L. (1972). The agenda-setting function of mass media. *Public Opinion Quarterly*, *36*, 176–187.

Mindich, D. T. Z. (2005). *Tuned out: Why Americans under 40 don't follow the news*. New York: Oxford University Press.

Morris, M., & Ogan, C. (1996). The Internet as mass medium. *Journal of Communication*, *46*(1), 39–50.

Negroponte, N. (1995). *Being digital*. New York: Alfred A. Knopf.

Newhagen, J. E., & Rafaeli, S. (1996). Why communication researchers should study the Internet: A dialogue. *Journal of Communication*, *46*(1), 4–13.

Newspaper Association of America. (2007). Total paid circulation. Retrieved September 22, 2008, from http://naa.org/TrendsandNumbers/Total-Paid-Circulation. aspx.

Nordenson, B. (2008). Overload! Journalism's battle for relevance in an age of too much information. *Columbia Journalism Review*, *2008*(November/December).

Peiser, W. (2000). Cohort replacement and the downward trend in newspaper readership. *Newspaper Research Journal,21*(2), 11.

Pew Research Center for the People & the Press. (2004, June 8). Online news audience larger, more diverse. Retrieved September 22, 2008, from http://people-press.org/reports/pdf/215.pdf.

Pew Research Center for the People & the Press. (2006, July 30). Online papers modestly boost newspaper readership: maturing Internet news audience broader than deep. Retrieved September 22, 2008, from http://people-press.org/reports/pdf/282.pdf.

Plassmann, H., O'Doherty, J., Shiv, B., & Rangel, A. (2008). Marketing actions can modulate neural representations of experienced pleasantness. *Proceedings of the National Academy of Sciences*, *105*(3), 1050–1054.

Poindexter, P. M. (1979). Daily newspaper non-readers: Why they don't read. *Journalism Quarterly*, *56* (4), 764–770.

Rudd, M. J., & Rudd, J. (1986). The impact of the information explosion on library users: Overload or opportunity? *Journal of Academic Librarianship*, *12*(5), 304.

Schiller, V. (2007). Letter to the readers about TimesSelect. Retrieved September 22, 2008, from http://www.nytimes.com/ref/membercenter/lettertoreaders.html?ref=media

Sifry, D. (2007). The state of the live Web, April 2007. Retrieved September 22, 2008, from http://technorati.com/weblog/2007/04/328.html.

So, C. (1997). Absolute market-driven journalism: The case study of Apple Daily. [Chinese]. In J. Chan, L. Chu, & Z. Pan (Eds.), *Mass communication and market economy* (pp. 215–233). Hong Kong: Lu Feng.

The State of the News Media. (2006). The project for excellence in journalism. Retrieved September 22, 2008, from http://www.stateofthemedia.org/2006/narrative_newspapers_audience.asp?cat=3&media=3.

The State of the News Media. (2007). The project for excellence in journalism. Retrieved September 22, 2008, from http://www.stateofthemedia.org/2007/narrative_overview_audience.asp?cat=3&media=1.

The State of the News Media. (2008). The project for excellence in journalism. Retrieved September 22, 2008, from http://www.stateofthenewsmedia.org/2008/narrative_newspapers_audience.php?cat=2&media=4.

Steinberger, M. (1996). An apple a day: Jimmy Lai's tough tabloid. *Columbia Journalism Review*, 1996 (March/April).

Stepp, C. S. (2008). Maybe it is time to panic. *American Journalism Review, 2008* (April/May).

Sylvie, G., & Witherspoon, P. D. (2002). *Time, change, and the American newspaper.* Mahwah, NJ: Lawrence Erlbaum Associates.

Tankard, J. J. W., & Royal, C. (2005). What's on the Web and what's not. *Social Science Computer Review, 23*(3), 360–370.

Tewksbury, D., Weaver, A., & Maddex, B. (2001). Accidentally informed: Incidental news exposure on the World Wide Web. *Journalism & Mass Communication Quarterly, 78*, 533–554.

Varian, H. R., & Lyman, P. (2003). How much information? 2003. Retrieved September 22, 2008, from http://www2.sims.berkeley.edu/research/projects/how-much-info-2003/execsum.htm.

Waterman, D. (2006). The economics of media programming. In A. B. Albarran, S. M. Chan-Olmsted, & M. O. Wirth (Eds.), *Handbook of media management and economics* (pp. 387–416). Mahwah, NJ: Lawrence Erlbaum Associates.

Westley, B. H., & Severin, W. J. (1964). A profile of the daily newspaper non-reader. *Journalism Quarterly 41* (4), 45–50, 156.

Wildman, S. S. (2006). Paradigms and analytical frameworks in modern economics and media economics. In A. B. Albarran, S. M. Chan-Olmsted, & M. O. Wirth (Eds.), *Handbook of media management and economics* (pp. 67–90). Mahwah, NJ: Lawrence Erlbaum Associates.

Wilkinson, E. J. (2003). Newspaper executives' hopes for academic research: Based on research by the International Newspaper Marketing Association. Retrieved September 22, 2008, from http://www.inma.org/pdf/newspapers-academia.doc.

Williams, F., Rice, R. E., & Rogers, E. M. (1988). *Research methods and the new media.* New York: Free Press.

Woo, M. (2002). *The negative effect of Next Media's success on Hong Kong society.* [Chinese]. Yazhou Zhoukan.

Zillmann, D., & Bryant, J. (1985). *Selective exposure to communication.* Hillsdale, N.J.: Lawrence Erlbaum Associates.

Chapter 6

Blogs, Journalism, and Political Participation

Homero Gil de Zúñiga

These days, much has been discussed about the role of new technologies and their effects on people's daily lives. While academics have long studied such effects, even everyday people seem to marvel over the pace and impact of technological change (Bimber, 2001). Thus, to some extent and as expressed in other chapters of this book, we all hope to better understand how new technologies influence our lives.

Among the myriad new technologies and tools online, one in particular seems to hold a singular place in our media-saturated world, which some social scholars have dubbed the *information society* (Lyon, 1988; Webster, 1995; Castells, 2000). I am referring here to *weblogs,* or blogs. In this chapter, I would like to focus on the role that blogs may have as novelty mechanisms of communication, information and mobilization.

Although still at an early stage, blogs are a singular new media tool because they might represent the ultimate online mechanism by which people communicate, interact, learn, stay informed, discuss issues and, finally, participate or remain engaged in political or civic activities. They are an efficient means of communication in part because practically anyone can set up a blog, often at little to no cost and with only basic computer skills. Moreover, blogs facilitate discussion across time and space because they are asynchronous and accessible to anyone with an Internet connection, and their hyperlinked structure encourages truly interconnected exchange in a many-to-many communication setting.

Since their introduction around 1999 (Herring, Scheidt, Kouper & Wright, 2007), blogs have grown exponentially in popularity, making them one of the most prominent activities on the Internet.[1] As of December 2008, an estimated 133 million blogs have been catalogued since 2002, and at least 900,000 new posts, or blogs entries, are produced every single day (Technorati, 2008a). This vast quantity of information and immense opinion conglomerate is generally known as the *blogosphere* (Quick, 2002). Although it is true that many of these blogs do not strictly cover topics that deal with current events and political information, some of the most widely read blogs discuss public affairs, and in some cases have done so with great impact on the wider media discourse (Wall, 2005). The influence that these blogs—and blogs generally— have on mainstream media and public opinion is a subject matter that deserves consideration.

Therefore, in this chapter I intend to analyze, first, what blogs are and their relationship with journalism as a profession. Second, I will try to shed some light on how blog consumption—that is, reading and contributing in the blogosphere—intervenes in explaining citizens' levels of political participation. In order to do so, I will herewith present analyses based on national U.S. and Colombian data (Puig & Rojas, 2008; Gil de Zúñiga, 2008).[2]

Blogs

As an embryonic tool for information and communication, and given their dynamic nature, blogs are somewhat difficult to define and codify in a universal way. Initially, academics referred to them as mere interactive diaries that facilitated information exchange among their participants, otherwise known as *bloggers* (Bausch, Haughey & Hourihan, 2002). More concretely, I define them as follows (Gil de Zúñiga et al., in press):

> Blogs are interactive, non-synchronous Web pages whose host uploads postings that center around a topic. The topic need not be news, nor need it be written following the standards and practices of traditional media. Although not all blogs allow for writing comments on the postings, blog readers typically are assumed to be able to respond by writing comments to bloggers' postings as well as to other readers' comments.

As previously noted, although not all blogs are related to issues of politics or current events, there is a gradual increase in the number of such blogs, and they are becoming more noticed among Internet users. In 2004, only 9 percent of people who were using blogs said they ever visited blogs about politics or current events, and only a scant 3 percent of the total blogosphere could be classified as political (Rainie, 2005; Blogpulse, 2007). Nevertheless, blogs that deal with public affairs and related issues are today among some of the most frequently visited blogs, as a recent Nielsen Online study found (Ratner, 2008).

Thus, it's becoming increasingly important to see this new interactive media and communication tool as central to understanding the modern political landscape. For instance, among the "A-list" blogs, or the 10 most visited in 2008, there were more than 80 million unique visitors; that roughly corresponds to the entire Internet user population of Italy, Spain, the Netherlands and Romania combined (Internet World Statistics, 2008). New to the top 10 list in 2008 was the HuffingtonPost, which fashions itself as an "Internet newspaper" covering politics and news of public interest (Technorati, 2008b). Also on the list was the Daily Kos, another well-known political blog. In May 2008, the HuffingtonPost was the blog with most inbound hyperlinks from other blogs, while the Daily Kos remained among the top 10 blogs in terms of total hyperlinks (Technorati, 2008c).

With blogs, a new door has been opened for public opinion formation creating a parallel information realm or space—a space that enriches and supplements what traditional media provide both online and offline. It's a space in which mainstream media have ceased to be the unique suppliers of and gatekeepers for news and political information. This development has provoked certain restlessness for many journalists, just as it has piqued the curiosity of media scholars (Tremayne, 2007; Gil de Zúñiga, Lewis, Willard, Valenzuela, Kook Lee & Baresch, 2009). As blogging has grown in popularity and in its influence on politics and media discourse, and as (newspaper) journalism increasingly has adopted an online orientation, the two streams have crossed paths, raising new and interesting questions about the nexus of blogging and journalism. It is precisely this intersection that will be analyzed in the following section. Before that, however, let us consider more closely (1) the most common topics in the blogosphere and (2) the motivations for blogging in general.

There are a number of studies that seek to explain the rise of blogs—how they ought to be classified, and what motivates their use (Dearstyne, 2005; Kerbel & Bloom, 2005; Trammell, Tarkowski, Hofmokl & Sapp, 2006). In terms of topical focus, the most frequent subject in the blogosphere revolves around ordinary issues and life experiences of the bloggers themselves. These personal blogs are closely followed by blogs that talk about hobbies, sports and technology. In third place are blogs that deal with current events, political issues, and news about the government. Last are blogs that usually post about entertainment-related topics, such as videos games, movies or music (see Table 6.1).[3]

As for the motivations to blog, scholars have catalogued that some of the most usual motivations relate to seek information, to provide commentary, to participate in community forums, to document daily life, and to express oneself (Nardi, Diane, Michelle & Luke, 2004; Kaye, 2007; Huang, Yong-Zheng, Hong-Xiang & Shin-Shin, 2007; Li, 2007). And among all of them, one of the categories that continuously gains strength relates to information creation (Kaye, 2005; McKenna & Pole, 2004). In this study, we might envision a three-part typology.[4] A factor analysis found that bloggers are primarily motivated to create and maintain their sites in order to (1) inform and influence the opinion of their readership, (2) express themselves, or (3) forge and reinforce social

Table 6.1 Most Common Subjects in the Blogosphere

My Life Personal Experiences	Hobbies Sports Technology	News & Politics	Entertainment	Other Undisclosed
37.4%	18.7%	16.3%	6.6%	21%

Table 6.2 Factor Analysis of Motivations for Blogging

	Informing influencing	Expressing self	Networking / being in touch
To motivate others to action	**.822**	.009	−.054
To influence the way people think	**.764**	.262	−.183
To share practical knowledge	**.756**	−.020	.337
To express yourself creatively	.207	**.792**	−.145
To entertain people	−.035	**.690**	.218
To document personal experiences and share them with others	.048	**.682**	.278
To stay in touch with friends/family	−.172	.084	**.758**
To network or meet new people	.189	.176	**.651**
Eigenvalues	2.276	1.585	1.053
% Variance	28.5%	19.8%	13.2%

Extraction method: Principal component analysis. Rotation method: Varimax with Kaiser normalization. Primary loading of a variable on a factor is indicated by boldface type. N = 233

connections, staying in touch with family and friends as well as meeting new people (see Table 6.2).

Bloggers and Journalism

The intersection between blogs, also often referred to as *citizen journalism*, the blog that is specifically devoted to inform and comment about issues that matter to public opinion, and a more traditional journalism initiates a set of issues that need attention. These range from one of the more obvious questions, "Are bloggers real journalists?",[5] to more complex challenges, such as whether blogs serve a journalism-like function in creating and promoting a better democratic process and a healthier political landscape. This section intends to address the first of the questions, and the subsequent portion will take up the latter.

Some of the blogs that generate greater traffic and are more widely read have been created by professional journalists, and for some time people have steadily associated the tasks that blogs perform to be similar to those that are taken for granted in the more traditional media—online and offline (Kahn & Kellner, 2004; Lawson-Borders & Kirk, 2005). Nevertheless, this contrasts with the idea that most bloggers do not understand that what they do should be considered a form of journalism. To be more precise, barely 34 percent of bloggers perceive their blog is a form of journalism. Under this circumstance, is blogging a form of journalism or not? Journalism professionals and academics continue to debate this question (Andrews, 2003; Blood, 2003; Robison, 2006; Singer, 2005, 2007). The debate often centers around the extent to which bloggers behave as qualified journalists, abiding by the deontological practices of the profession (Haas, 2005; Lasica, 2003; Matheson, 2004). These practices are bound up in the abiding rules of journalism: check sources and cite them; be objective;

admit and correct published mistakes; and so on (Tremayne, 2007). I contend that bloggers' perception about their blogs being a form of journalism, as well as the motivations they have to publish their blogs, may explain altogether this relationship. The following Pearson's correlations may support this possibility (see Table 6.3).

After controlling for the potential effect of demographic variables—age, gender, ethnicity, income and education—results provide a better understanding of the relationship between the perception of blogs as a form of journalism, the topics bloggers cover, their motivations to engage in blogging and whether they behave as professional journalists. The fact of perceiving one's blog as a form of journalism is not related with the topics he chooses, with one exception: news and political issues. Thus, the more a blogger perceives her blog as a form of journalism, the more likely it is that her blog primarily will cover current events and political information ($r = .238$, $p < .001$). Similarly, the fact of perceiving their blog as a form of journalism is positively correlated with the different motivations bloggers describe to create and maintain their sites. Having such a perception is statistically associated with desiring to keep their readers informed ($r = .242$, $p < .001$) and expressing themselves ($r = .335$, $p < .001$); alternatively, it has nothing to do with the motivation to keep in touch with family and friends and meet new people. But, more importantly, the most interesting point lies in the relationship between bloggers' perception about their blog as journalism and their behavior as journalists. Here I am referring to the most traditional and formal depiction of professional journalists.[6]

Those bloggers who see their blog as a form of journalism usually report behaving in a way that ascribes to a more professional orientation: citing sources, correcting mistakes, including links to source material and verifying facts ($r = .353$, $p < .001$). Furthermore, this journalistic behavior is also associated with the motivations that drive users to create and maintain their blogs, as well as with the topics they choose to cover. For instance, a journalistic behavioral orientation is meaningfully and positively related to showing a preference for influencing and informing one's readers and also with writing about topics that pertain to current events, public affairs and politics. According to these results, there is a positive relationship between bloggers' perception of their blog as a form of journalism and actually behaving as a journalist. Thus, the more they perceive it this way, the more they will be inclined to post about public affairs and current events, and the more they will adopt the behavioral norms of traditional journalists.

Although there is still much to clarify about the intersection between blogs and traditional journalism, this chapter serves as a first step in that direction, with the hope of encouraging more studies to extend and elaborate upon this line of research. On the one hand, these findings may be interpreted as good news for the health of journalism. These results suggest that in certain settings and under the right conditions, blogging and journalism may go hand by hand, mutually engaging in the dissemination of news and information for the public

Table 6.3 Table top diagonal: Zero-order Pearson correlations
Table bottom diagonal: Partial-order Pearson correlations

	Journalistic Behavior	Perception Blog Form Journalism	Inform & Influence	Express Self	Network Be in Touch	News and Politics	My Life Personal Experiences	Hobbies Sports Technology	Entertainment
Journalistic Behavior	—	.350***	.539***	.250***	.001	.378***	-.354***	.087	.116
Perception Blog Form Journalism	.353***	—	.234***	.204***	-.018	.248***	-.147**	-.023	.074
Inform and Influence	.572***	.242***	—	.211***	.040	.181**	-.277***	.166***	-.075
Express Self	.355***	.335***	.222***	—	.275***	-.013	.171**	-.127*	.120*
Network Be in Touch	.128	-.021	.001	.261***	—	.095	.237**	-.125**	.098
News & Politics	.329***	.238***	.160*	.020	.040	—	-.357**	-.220**	-.122**
My Life Personal Experiences	-.273***	-.041	-.324***	.005	.086	-.26***	—	-.388**	-.215**
Hobbies Sports Technology	.011	-.031	.085	-.046	-.034	-.32***	-.299***	—	-.133**
Entertainment	.039	-.053	-.068	.202***	.153*	-.113	-.153*	-.135*	—

*** p <.001 ** p <.01 * p <.05; N = 233; df = 226 (for partial correlations).
Control variables are: age, gender, ethnicity, income and education.

sphere. Nevertheless, even while there are some bloggers who perceive their work as a form of journalism and therefore behave as such, it's true that the great majority of bloggers have nothing to do with traditional journalism.

Blogs and Political Participation

So far I have examined the somewhat pervasive and increasingly influential incursion of citizen journalism into the public and media discourse through blogs. Also, in a brief way, I have presented evidence about the relationship between citizen journalism and traditional journalism, and the conditions under which they might walk in the same direction, governed by a deontological journalistic code of conduct. In this section, I focus on the effects that blogs may have on their readers, and also examine the effects, if any, that this type of media consumption has in the realm of political participation.

The effects of individuals' media use on political engagement has been analyzed by a number of scholars (McLeod et al., 1996; McLeod, Scheufele & Moy, 1999; Shah, Schmierbach, Hawkins, Espino & Donovan, 2002; Wellman, Quan-Haase, Boase & Chen, 2003; Jennings & Zeitner, 2003; Papacharissi, 2004). Generally, a basic axiom has been presented. When citizens use the media to keep up to date, be informed, and increase their knowledge about public affairs and current events, they tend to participate at a higher rate than those who do not use the media in such a manner. Conversely, research indicates that when media use is directed to fulfilling entertainment functions or simply for recreation or amusement, then such media consumption will be associated with lower levels of political interest, general social participation and civic engagement (Shah, McLeod & Yoon, 2001; Shah et al, 2002). These relationships have been empirically proven to remain constant regardless of the media platform, whether traditional or digital (Althaus & Tewksbury, 2000; Kraut et al., 2006; Shah, Cho, Eveland & Kwak, 2005). This association between participation and media use is so consistent that scholars have coined the phrase *virtuous circle*, by which practicing one of them will unobtrusively predict individuals to engage in the other one and vice versa (Norris, 2000; Verba, Schlozman & Brady, 1995; Eveland, Shah & Kwak, 2003). More recently, however, some studies have shed new light on this virtuous circle, stipulating a clearer directionality or causality in the aforementioned relationship. This way, information-seeking behaviors come to predict to a larger degree a future political participation than the opposite direction of the circle (that is, political participation predicting future media use) (Rojas, 2006; Shah et al., 2005; Semetko & Valkeburg, 1998).

Nevertheless, when it comes to blogs, there seems to be a long way in order to elucidate the mechanism of this so-called virtuous circle. An initial effort in this regard showed that general blog use predicts political participation—and it does so beyond the effect of other variables that were included in the model and which also predict political participation (see Table 6.4).[7]

Table 6.4 Hierarchical Regressions Predicting Political Participation

	Online Discussion	Online Campaigning	Online Participation	Offline Participation
Block 1 – Demographics				
Gender (Male = 0)	−.119**	.080**	.114***	.058
Age	−.072	.001	.002	.149***
Education	−.104*	−.026	.004	.029
Income	−.070	−.016	−.045	−.002
Community Type	−.029	−.005	−.039	.018
Incremental R²(%)	**4.6***	**0.8**	**2.3***	**8.1***
Block 2 – Internet				
Internet (years)	−.001	.058	.043	.002
Home connection	.059	.013	.020	.032
Work connection	.043	−.021	−.018	.066
Incremental R²(%)	**0.9**	**2.2***	**1.8***	**0.9#**
Block 3 – Offline Media				
Newspaper	−.041	−.020	.039	.131***
Television	.014	−.052	−.040	.012
Political Books	.135***	.153***	.213***	.203***
Political Documentaries	.026	.098**	.100**	.066*
Public Affairs	.043	.105**	.085*	.177***
Incremental R²(%)	**4.1***	**10.4***	**11.9***	**14.5***
Block 4 – Online Behaviors				
Traditional Media Source	.097*	.149***	.149***	.108**
Blogs	.227***	.197***	.141***	.028
Incremental R²(%)	**6.3***	**6.2***	**4.2***	**1.1***
Total R² (%)	**15.7***	**19.7***	**20.2***	**23.1***

1. Cell entries are standardized regression coefficients (Betas)
2. P-Values with 2-tailed significance: * $p < .05$, ** $p < .01$, *** $p < .001$
3. Online Discussion N = 620; Online Campaigning N = 760; Online Participation N = 774; General Offline Participation = 773.

It is clear, then, that this type of citizen media consumption has positive consequences in the realm of political engagement and participation (ß = .108, p < .01, for participation online and (ß = .028, n.s.; for offline participation). I further content that the fact that blog use predicts online political participation but does not achieve statistical significance when predicting offline participation is likely because of (1) the emergent diffusion of blog use and (2) the fact that it would be more appropriate to discriminate between general use of blogs and a more specific use—that is, a blog use that centers on politics and public affairs. Indeed, as a recent study empirically demonstrated, using blogs to acquire information also predicts offline political participation (Puig & Rojas, 2008).

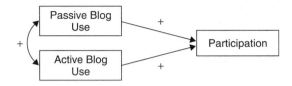

Figure 6.1 Theoretical representation of the relation between passive blog use, active blog use and political participation.

To move beyond this explorative point, the next step I sought to take with regard to informational blog use and political participation is to examine distinct behavior by everyday users in the blogosphere. I tried to determine whether a more passive use of blogs—i.e., reading and browsing blogs but never commenting on others' posts—or a more active use of the blogs—i.e., commenting and publishing entries in blogs that cover information and current events—differently predicts political engagement. Results indicate a subtle difference between a passive behavior and a more active one. Although both are highly statistically correlated (r = .406, p < .001), the latter robustly predicts that citizens engage in political participation (ß non-standardized = 5.90, p < .01; see Table 6.5). It still remains to be seen whether this segregation between these two types of behavior represents a fixed state of blog use; or, conversely, if it may be that individuals who begin to browse and lurk on informational blogs in a moderated way, increasingly begin to post and comment and end up participating more actively. Such active behavior would ultimately increase the level

Table 6.5 Logistic Regression Predicting Political Participation (Voting) and Pearson's Correlations between Active Blog Use and Passive Blog Use

	Political Participation		
Block 1-Demographics			
Gender (Male = 0)	0.3		
Age	12.3***	*Active Blog Use*	*Passive Blog Use*
Education	17.5***		
Income	3.8*	Active Blog Use —	.406***b
Block 2 – Blog Use		Passive Blog Use .471***a	—
Passive	3.35#		
Active	5.90**		

Notes
1 Logisitc Model succesfully predicts 66% of possibilities.
2 * p < .05, ** p < .01, *** p < .001, # p < .1
3 Model Wald 34.9, p <.001, N = 353

1 * p < .05, ** p < .01, *** p < .001. N = 353; df = 347
2 (a) Zero order correlation.
   (b) Partial correlations controlling for gender, age, education and income.

of political contribution. This is, of course, a recommendation for future research in this area.

Similarly, as the types of blogs—news vs. entertainment—and the use individuals make of those blogs—active vs. passive—significantly explain the process of participating in politics, other characteristics may also alter the relationship and the effects that blogs have on participatory behaviors. A suggestion to advance research along these lines may be based on the distinct tones and the different language employed in the comments while discussing or deliberating upon an issue. For instance, there might be variations in the learning process, self-efficacy perception and ultimately political participation depending on whether the discussions took place in a civil or uncivil tone.

Final Remarks

The first conclusion I may draw is that blogs are rapidly diffusing in our *Information Society* and they are probably here to stay. Moreover, blogs are emerging both as an alternative and as a complementary channel for people to be informed about public affairs and current issues and to discuss, reflect and deliberate. Thus, blogs may facilitate the creation of a common public sphere—a space that, albeit virtual, contributes to a better-informed citizenry and a healthier democracy. Perhaps the first stone to this foundation has been established, as there is a clear relationship between using informational blogs and casting votes, donating money to candidates, or simply participating at a higher level in the current political process.

In a recent book, Gillmor (2006) describes blogs as journalism by the people, for the people, in a very optimistic way. Although the situation that I just described in this chapter is promising, it all has to be interpreted with caution. This chain, or virtuous circle, of media use and political participation has been largely established with other traditional media online and offline. Nevertheless, for it to transpire correspondingly to the blogosphere, a number of precepts might be needed. At the outset, not all blogs are of journalistic value and not all them influence positively and meaningfully, the public opinion— and by extension, civic engagement and political participation. I believe there is room for optimism as some citizen journalists who actually perceive their work as a form of journalism end up behaving as traditional journalists. This may just be a first step. However, it is an important first step as it provides the means of useful information—by the citizens, to the citizens and for the citizens—for a healthier democracy.

In theory, then, blogs have the potential to greatly affect society and the way we communicate, get informed and participate in the democratic process. This might occur in at least two ways: (1) by altering the form in which citizens learn and discuss important issues and (2) by extending the work of journalism.

Blogs can provide the essential public space for citizens to learn about and debate issues that matter to them and their communities. Theoretically, such deliberation and discussion in the public sphere could lead to a body politic that is more informed and thus more engaged. In short, blogs may help create a better environment for better politics.

Like political discussion among citizens, journalism is also essential for sustaining a healthy democracy. Journalists have long provided the news and information that a society needs to learn about its leaders and their policies. Likewise, journalistic-oriented blogs contribute to the dissemination of information, both in quantity and in quality—adding to the amount of news and commentary available online, as well as presenting sometimes novel or alternative agendas not represented in the mainstream media. Furthermore, blogs can serve as an additional watchdog for society, not only monitoring the work of politicians, but also scrutinizing the coverage and possible biases of traditional journalists.

Notes

1 Other new media/new technologies that may be also included in this list are, for instance, Social Network Sites as Youtube or MySpace; Voice over Internet Protocols as Skype; and citizen based video websites as Youtube or BlipTV.
2 U.S. data: I am grateful to John B. Horrigan and the Pew Internet and American Project for providing the data used in this research and also would like to acknowledge that the Pew Project bears no responsibility for the interpretations of the findings or the conclusions reached in this study. Further details about the sample can be found at http://www.pewinternet.org/PPF/r/46/dataset_display.asp.

Data for Bloggers and Journalism Section: Data were collected through phone interviews with 233 self-described bloggers, 18 and older, who had been identified in previous PIAL surveys. The interviews were conducted from July 5, 2005, to February 17, 2006; during that period, as many as 10 attempts were made to reach every sampled telephone number. PIAL calculated a response rate of 71% for these callbacks to bloggers; response rates from the original surveys ranged from 28.4% to 34.6%. The margin of error for the complete data set on bloggers is ±6.7% with respect to weighted data. PIAL's results are weighted to compensate for non-response and match national parameters for sex, age, education, and race, all of which are U.S. census definitions.

Data for Blogs and Political Participation Section: this part of the study relies on data collected by the Pew's series between the 4th and 22nd of November, 2004. Survey interviews were conducted with a probability sample of 2,200 subjects 18 years of age or older, of which 1,324 had Internet access. Pew Project calculated a 31% response rate to their survey, with a margin of sampling error for the complete data set of ± 2.3% with respect to weighted data.

Colombian data: I am also grateful to Hernando Rojas (UW Madison) and the Centro para la Investigación en Comunicación Política of Universidad Externado de Colombia for providing the data used in this research and also would like to acknowledge that the Research Center bears no responsibility for the interpretations of the findings or the conclusions reached in this study.

Data for Bloggers and Political Participation Section: data were collected between June 22 and July 10, 2006. It took place after the general presidential elections in Colombia. The sample was designed to represent Colombian adult population, who for the most part live in urban areas (75% of 47 million Colombian citizens live in cities). Participants were selected using multi-level, stratified and random techniques yielding a total of 1,009 faces to faces cases with a response rate of 84%. For greater detail about the data see Puig, E. & Rojas, H. (2008). Internet use as an antecedent of expressive political participation among early Internet adopters in Colombia. *International Journal of Internet Science*; Gil de Zúñiga, H. (2008). The dark side of the blog: analyzing dynamics of blog use and their impact on political participation. *World Association for Public Opinion Research*. New Orleans, May 13–15, 2008.

3 See note 2 for greater details on data.

4 See note 2 for greater details on data.

5 For a complete model on Blogs as a form of Journalism see: Gil de Zúñiga, H., Lewis, S., et al. (2009). Blog as a Form of Journalism. *International Communication Association*. Chicago, Illinois.

6 Journalistic behavior was measured with an additive index of six items measuring respondents' frequency in engaging in the following journalism-like practices: quote other people or media sources directly; post corrections to something you have written; discuss current events or news; include links to original source material you have cited or used in some way; spend extra time trying to verify facts you want to include in your post; and get permission to post copyright material. This new construct was recoded so higher values expressed more frequent engagement in such activities (M = 8.14, SD = 5.09, range: 0–18, Cronbach's α = .83).

7 The table is a re-impression from *New Media & Society* journal. For a complete description of methodology and learn more about blog use and political participation see: Gil de Zuniga, H., Puig, E. and Rojas, H. (in press). "Blogs, traditional media online and political participation: An assessment of how the Internet is changing the political environment," *New Media & Society*.

References

Althaus, S., & Tewksbury, D. (2000). Patterns of internet and traditional news media use in a networked community. *Political Communication, 17*(1), 21–45.

Andrews, P. (2003). Is Blogging Journalism? *Nieman Reports* 57: 63–64.

Bausch, P., Haughey, M., & Hourihan, M. (2002). *We blog: Publishing online with weblogs*. Indianapolis, IN: Wiley.

Bimber, B. (2001). Information and political engagement in America: The search for effects of information technology at the individual level. *Political Research Quarterly, 54*(1), 53.

Blogpulse (2007). URL (consulted March 2007): http://www.blogpulse.com/index.html.

Blood, R. (2003). Weblogs and journalism: Do they connect? *Nieman Reports* 57: 61–63.

Castells, M. (2000). *The rise of the network society*. Cambridge, MA: Blackwell Publishing.

Dearstyne, B. (2005). Blogs: The new information revolution? *Information Management Journal, 39*(5), 38–44.

Eveland, W. P. Jr., Shah D. V., & Kwak, N. (2003). Assessing causality in the cognitive mediation model: A panel study of motivations, information processing and learning during campaign 2000. *Communication Research* 30, 359–386.

Gil de Zuniga, H. (2008). The dark side of the blog: Analyzing dynamics of blog use and their impact on political participation. *World Association for Public Opinion Research*. New Orleans, May 13–15, 2008.

Gil de Zuniga, H., Lewis, S., Willard, A., Valenzuela, S., Kook Lee, J. & Baresch, B. (2009). Blog as a form of journalism: A model linking perception, motivation, and behavior. *International Communication Association*. Chicago, Illinois.

Gil de Zuniga, H., Puig, E. & Rojas, H. (in press). Blogs, traditional media online and political participation: An assessment of how the Internet is changing the political environment. *New Media & Society, 11.*

Gillmor, D. (2006). *We the media: Grassroots journalism by the people, for the people*: O'Reilly Media, Inc.

Haas, T. (2005). From "public journalism" to the "public's journalism"? Rhetoric and Reality in the Discourse on Weblogs. *Journalism Studies, 6,* 387–396.

Herring, S. C., Scheidt, L. A., Kouper, I., & Wright, E. (2007). A longitudinal content analysis of weblogs: 2003–2004. In M. Tremayne (Ed.), *Blogging, citizenship, and the future of the media* (pp. 3–20). New York: Routledge.

Huang, C.Y., Yong-Zheng, S., Hong-Xiang, L, & Shin-Shin, C. (2007). Bloggers' motivations and behaviors: A model. *Journal of Advertising Research* 47, 472–484.

Internet World Stats. (2008). URL (consulted December 2008): http://www.internetworldstats.com/stats4.htm.

Jennings, M.K., & Zeitner, V. (2003). Internet use and civic engagement: A longitudinal analysis. *Public Opinion Quarterly, 67*(3), 311–334.

Kahn, R., & Kellner, D. (2004). New media and internet activism: From the "battle of Seattle" to blogging. *New Media & Society, 6*(1), 87.

Kaye, B. (2005). It's a blog, blog, blog world: Users and uses of weblogs. *Atlantic Journal of Communication, 13,* 73–95.

Kaye, B. (2007). Blog use motivations: An exploratory study. In Mark Tremayne (Ed.), *Blogging, citizenship and the future of media* (pp. 127–148). New York: Routledge.

Kerbel, M. R., & D. Bloom (2005). Blog for American and civic involvement, *Press/Politics, 10*(4), 3–27.

Kraut, R., Kiesler, S., Boneva, B., Cummings, J., Helgeson, V., & Crawford, A. (2002). Internet paradox revisited. *Journal of Social Issues, 58,* 49–74.

Kwak, N., Poor, N., & Skoric, M. M. (2006). Honey, I shrunk the world! The Relation between internet use and international engagement. *Mass Communication and Society, 9*(2), 189–213.

Lasica, J. D. (2003). Blogs and journalism need each other. *Nieman Reports* 57: 70–74.

Lawson-Borders, G., & Kirk, R. (2005). Blogs in campaign communication. *American Behavioral Scientist, 49*(4), 548.

Li, D. (2007). Why do you blog: A uses-and-gratifications inquiry into Bloggers' Motivations. *International Communication Association.* San Francisco.

Lyon, D. (1988). *The information society: Issues and illusions*: Cambridge, UK: Polity Press.

Matheson, D. (2004). Negotiating claims to journalism: Webloggers' orientation to news genres. *Convergence, 10,* 33–54.

McKenna, L., & Pole, A. (2004). Do blogs matter? Weblogs in American politics. American Political Science Association. Chicago, September 2–5.

McLeod, J. M., Scheufele, D. A., & Moy, P. (1999). Community, communication and participation: The role of mass media and interpersonal discussion in local political participation. *Political Communication, 16*(3), 315–336.

McLeod, J. M., Daily, K., Guo, Z., Eveland, W. P., Jr., Bayer, J., Yang, S. & Wang, H. (1996). Community integration, local media use, and democratic processes. *Communication Research, 23*(3), 463–487.

Nardi, B., Diane, J. S., Michelle, G., & Luke, S. (2004). Why we blog. *Communications of the ACM, 47,* 41–46.

Norris, P. (2000). *A virtuous circle: Political communications in post-industrial democracies.* Cambridge, MA: Cambridge University Press.

Papacharissi, Z. (2004). Democracy online: Civility, politeness, and the democratic potential of online political discussion groups. *New Media & Society,* 6(2), 259.

Puig, E., & Rojas, H. (2008). Internet use as an antecedent of expressive political participation among early Internet adopters in Colombia. *International Journal of Internet Science,* 2(1). URL (consulted December 2008): http://ijis.net.

Quick, W. (2002). Blogosphere. URL (consulted May 2006): http://www.iw3p.com/DailyPundit/2001_12_30_dailypundit_archive.php#8315120.

Rainie, L. (2005). The state of blogging. URL (consulted May 2006): http://www.pewinternet.org/pdfs/PIP_blogging_data.pdf.

Ratner, A. (2008, April 6). The 10 biggest blogs are—how's that again? *The Baltimore Sun,* 24A.

Robinson, S. (2006). The mission of the j-blog: Recapturing journalistic authority online. *Journalism* 7, 65–83.

Rojas, H. (2006). Orientations towards political conversation: Testing an asymmetrical reciprocal causation model of political engagement. Paper presented at the Annual Meeting of the International Communication Association (Political Communication Division), June 2006, Dresden, Germany.

Semetko, H. A., & Valkeburg, P. M. (1998). The impact of attentiveness on political efficacy: Evidence from a three-year German panel study. *International Journal of Public Opinion Research* 10, 195–210.

Shah, D., Cho, J., Eveland W.P., & Kwak, N. (2005). Information and expression in a digital age. Modeling Internet effects on civic participation. *Communication Research,* 32(5), 531–565.

Shah, D., McLeod, J., & Yoon, S. H. (2001). Communication, context and community: An axploration of print, broadcast and Internet influences. *Communication Research,* 28, 464–506.

Shah, D., Schmierbach, M., Hawkins, R., Espino, R., & Donovan, J. (2002). Nonrecursive models of Internet use and community engagement: Questioning whether time spent online erodes social capital. *Journalism & Mass Communication Quarterly,* 79, 964–987.

Shah, D. V., Cho, J., Eveland W. P., & Kwak, N. (2005). Information and expression in a digital age. Modeling Internet effects on civic participation. *Communication Research,* 32(5), 531–565.

Singer, J. (2005). The political j-blogger: "Normalizing" a new media form to fit old norms and practices. *Journalism,* 6, 173–198.

Singer, J. (2007). Contested autonomy. *Journalism Studies,* 8, 79–95.

Technorati.com (2008a). URL (consulted December 2008): http://technorati.com/pop/.

Technorati.com (2008b). URL (consulted December 2008): http://technorati.com/pop/.

Technorati.com (2008c). URL (consulted December 2008): http://technorati.com/blogging/state-of-the-blogosphere/.

Trammell, K. D., Tarkowski, A., Hofmokl, J., & Sapp, M. A. (2006). Rzeczpospolita blogów [Republic of blog]: Examining Polish bloggers through content analysis. *Journal of Computer-Mediated Communication,* 11(3), 702–722.

Tremayne, M. (2007). Harnessing the active audience: Synthesizing blog research and lessons for the future of media. In M. Tremayne (Ed.), *Blogging, Citizenship, and the Future of the Media* (pp. 261–272). New York: Routledge.

Verba, S., Schlozman, K.L., & Brady H.E. (1995). *Voice and equality: Civic volunteerism in American politics*. Cambridge, MA: Harvard University Press.

Wall, M. (2005). "Blogs of war": Weblogs as news. *Journalism, 6*(2), 153.

Webster, F. (1995). *Theories of the Information Society*. London: Routledge.

Wellman B., Quan-Haase, A., Boase, J., & Chen, W. (2003). The social affordances of the Internet for networked individualism. *Journal of Computer Mediated Communication* 8(3), URL (consulted May 2006): http://jcmc.indiana.edu/vol8/issue3/wellman.html.

Chapter 7

The Many Faced "You" of Social Media

Sharon Meraz

Internet enthusiasts can all agree that we are facing a fundamental shift in how information technologies support content creation and distribution over the World Wide Web (Anderson, 2006; O'Reilly, 2005; Scoble, 2007). Though the early Web was conceived of as a read-write platform (BBC, 2005), its openness to amateur content contributions was limited to those individuals who knew computer programming languages. The Web's interactive shift was facilitated in the 1960s with the free software movement and the 1990s with the open source revolution (O'Reilly, 1999). These shifts now form the foundation for the growth of blogging software, which diffused in the latter 1990s through such tools as Blogger, Wordpress, and Movable Type. Through using blogging tools, the non-technophile citizen can now post content to the Web through an automated point and click interface as opposed to programming in computer code (Leadbeater & Miller, 2004; Lenhard, Fallows, & Horrigan, 2004).

As a Web activity, blogging continues to be embraced within both the US and on a global scale. As of 2007, there were over 70 million Weblogs, with 120,000 being created each day and 1.4 million being created every second (Sifry, 2007). Due to Web 2.0 technologies such as blogs, the mass media landscape is undergoing a fundamental, disruptive transformation as the average citizen can now create media content (Anderson, 2006; Christensen, 2003a, 2003b; Reynolds, 2006). Traditional mass media's monopoly power over news production tools is no longer a tenable assumption in this new world of abundant news technologies (Shirky, 2008). Citizens can now leverage their Web-based social networks for creating knowledge and meaning outside elite cueing, which is transforming how information is created, interpreted, and diffused in the Internet age (Barabasi, 2002, 2003; Gladwell, 2002; Leadbeater & Miller, 2005; Scoble & Israel, 2005; Weinberger, 2002). This encouragement of collaboration, community, and conversation among citizens through tools like blogs is part of why many claim that media is becoming more social (Hinchcliffe, 2006).

The social, peer-produced trend of media is one that is capable of supporting conversation, repurposing, and redistribution. Individuals are saving and sharing their Web links through such social bookmarking applications as Furl,

Del.icio.us, and Stumble Upon. The choice to network is now easily facilitated online by such social networking applications as Facebook, MySpace, and LinkedIn. Putting multimedia content online for free is made possible by such applications as Flickr, YouTube, UnCut Video, and JumpCut. Sharing music is facilitated through applications such as Last.fm and iLike. And, more of our lives are being moved to the Internet as we now utilize the Web as a platform for data warehousing. Files and folders can now be stored on the Web in such online file storage sites as JungleDisk, AllmyData.com, and iBackup as opposed to the physical desktop. Content is no longer limited by its original container (Curley 2004), and through utilizing Web 2.0 tools, Web content can now flow freely through the acts of syndication, redistribution, and remixing.

This paper assesses one segment of this new social media trend: peer-to-peer news sharing in social media news aggregators. In these social media aggregators, news is said to be determined by the selection and voting decisions of "citizen marketers" (McConnell & Huba, 2007) who find Web content and submit it to these sites for voting by users of the peer community. Through analyzing and comparing the content in four peer-production social aggregator sites, Digg, Reddit, Netscape, and Newsvine, this paper examines the democratic potential of these sites through the lens of user engagement and news sources. It is argued that these peer produced, open systems can support a more egalitarian democracy that is open to the contributions of the average citizen (Ito, 2003; Moore, 2005). This paper analyzes such claims as the phenomenon of social media news sites gain traction among both Web publics and traditional media online news sites.

Web 2.0, Social Media, and Participatory Democracy

Though there has been confusion about the meaning of social media (Coates, 2006), Internet thinkers have suggested several characteristics that underlie social media systems such as blogs, podcasts, vlogs, wikis, social news aggregators, and social bookmarking services (Spannerworks, 2007). The primary idea behind these systems is that they are open to user participation, allowing many-to-many network connections that build value and power beyond the broadcast model of top-down content production (Scoble, 2007). These distributed and decentralized systems enable individuals to participate with media through commenting, creating mashups, syndicating content through RSS or social bookmarks, or hyperlinking to the content (Scoble, 2007). For the majority of these social systems, individuals can participate for free by registering in the system, and these systems gain resilience through distributing power among users in the network as opposed to concentrating power among a cadre of elite individuals (Hinchcliffe, 2006).

This shift in media's interactivity towards a more social platform has impacted traditional media's ability to maintain sole influence in this new Web environment. The social media trend has been supported by technologies that are architected through design to support participation (O'Reilly, 2004). Citizens can not only create content, a phenomenon dubbed user generated content (UGC) or citizen media, but can decide on which content becomes popular in both search engines and peer-driven communities. The ability to select a more personalized form of news is fueled by the "long tail" of media options that now exist on the Internet due to the growth of amateur, citizen media (Anderson, 2006).

Many Internet theorists believe that this move to social media forms could improve civic engagement and political participation among a public made apathetic as a result of uni-directional, one-way media technologies (Putnam, 1995, 1996, 2000). According to Ito (2003), technology can facilitate an emergent democracy through allowing citizens to self-organize and address issues democratically without one citizen being required to know the whole. The Internet can reduce the transactional and organizational costs of communication, coordination, and information sharing among decentralized political groups, thus facilitating networked community among geographically dispersed individuals (Bonchek, 1995; Shirky, 2008). According to Lasica (2003), participatory democracy permits "individuals [to]play . . . an active role in the process of collecting, reporting, sorting, analyzing, and disseminating news and information—a task once reserved exclusively to the news media." Gillmor (2004) sees participatory democracy as a form of decentralized citizen engagement, moving American journalism from a lecture to more of a conversation or seminar.

Not all agree that the Internet can reinvigorate democracy. Many accuse the Internet of facilitating the easy fragmentation of Web publics into homogeneous communities of practice, a phenomenon dubbed the echo chamber effect. Related to groupthink philosophy, Sunstein (2000, 2002) cited that the Internet could be harmful to democracy because of the role it can play in fragmenting, insulating, and encouraging enclave deliberation through filtering both what is produced and what is read. Resulting in daily editions of the "Daily Me" (Sunstein, 2001), Sunstein highlighted the most extreme result of cyberbalkanization—group polarization and the movement to more extreme positions than that held at predeliberation levels due to the effects of limited argument pools and perspectives. This fracture of the public sphere into several "counterpublics or enclaves" is viewed as a threat to democracy because of negative informational cascades, which result when groups remain insulated and homogenous in both perspective and composition.

The echo chamber effect can be exacerbated in social media environments that depend on friendships and social information filtering to determine popularity. In many of these social news aggregators, members can see the stories that their friends have submitted. The ability to boost the ratings of stories by using friendship ties as the criteria for determining relevance has exacerbated the collaborative filtering of news on some of these sites, leading to what is called the "tyranny of the minority" by the popular few (Lerman, 2006). The fear that only a few users control these sites is a harmful prospect for the democratic selection of news and information in these sites.

Social Network Theory

As part of the World Wide Web network, the question could be posed: to what extent do social media networks share similar characteristics to the larger super-structure environment of the World Wide Web network? Networks such as the World Wide Web are often called scale-free networks because they grow over time, but often by a process of preferential attachment. According to Barabasi and Albert (1999), newly added entrants to these scale-free social systems tend to connect to those entrants that already display a high degree or connectivity with the result that the rich get richer. When modeling these scale-free social systems, a power law distribution is often present with a heavy tail that drops off more slowly than the tail of a Gaussian distribution (Barabasi, Albert, & Jeong, 2000).

Several studies have shown that patterns of link structure within networks on the World Wide Web network exhibit a power law distribution. Huberman et al., (1998) found that the amount of Web pages surfed among 107 staff and faculty at the National Center for Supercomputing was inversely proportional to the Web site's depth. Nielsen (1997) found similar trends in Sun Microsystem's Web pages. Power law trends have also been found in the growth of Web sites (Huberman & Adamic, 1999). Web site traffic has also been found to exhibit power law characteristics. Examining market share on the Web through analysis of the AOL usage logs of 120,000 Web sites, the authors found that the distribution of visitors to the sites followed a power law distribution. Rating popularity as the number of unique visitors to a site per month, the authors found that the top 119 sites captured 32.36 of the user volume. Examining Web blog traffic, Kottke (2003) found power law trends in examining the links to the top 100 Weblogs as derived from Technorati data in terms of inbound links. Shirky (2003) found power laws in LiveJournal listings regarding number of friends listed, with a few users having the majority of the friends.

Little to no work to date exists on power law dynamics within social media news communities. What preliminary evidence exists suggests that these social news aggregators also adhere to power law network effects. For example, Digg has often been accused of having a "rock concert" approach to news filtering (Clarke, 2006), with only a few individuals responsible for creating the power dynamics behind stories. The concomitant surge in hits that can be achieved by getting a higher ranked story on Digg and getting the referrer effect, termed the "digg effect" (Cybernet, 2006), can result in a huge hit to the server of the referred site, dubbed the "sugar high" (Bailey, 2007). One study found that the top 100 users were responsible for posting 56 percent of Digg's homepage content (SEOmoz, 2006a). Because of its popularity in terms of user participation,

Digg has faced the most public criticism for rigging, mob rule, and groupthink. For example, in 2006, Netscape offered $1,000 as an incentive to the power users of Digg and Reddit to join their site in the role of "Netscape Navigators" (Calcanis, 2006). According to Calcanis (2006), attracting the attention of the power users or influentials through offering monetary incentives is a sensible business strategy for the future as corporations seek to maximize the advantages of word-of-mouth and viral Internet network effects.

This study provides some preliminary data on the nature of power law effects within social media news aggregators. If these sites are subject to strong power law effects, it would mean that select users get more success at achieving popular stories than the majority of users within the network. Such a finding can directly contradict the notion that these sites are employing a more egalitarian decision-making process to news gatekeeping when compared to the elite power structure of traditional media newsrooms.

Gatekeeping

In their most extreme form, social media news aggregator sites are creating a new form of gatekeeping that is bottom-up as opposed to top-down. The term gatekeeper was coined from the sociologist Lewin (1947) in his study of group dynamics; since then, gatekeeping has been used by communication scholars to explain the news selection process. Shoemaker et al. (2001) defined gatekeeping as "the process by which the vast array of potential news messages are winnowed, shaped, and prodded into these few that are actually transmitted by the news media." Shoemaker and Reese (1996) expanded the theory of gatekeeping in their analysis of the sociology of news, citing the following five factors as impact variables on the news selection process: ideological factors, extramedia factors, organizational factors, media professional routines, and individuality.

Prior gatekeeping studies within World Wide Web environments have examined the role that the hyperlink plays in revealing a site's gatekeeping practices (Dimitrova et al., 2003; Trench & Quinn, 2003). Much work has been done on segmented hyperlink choices within partisan political blog communities (Adamic & Glance, 2005; Meraz, 2005; Tremayne et al., 2006; Welsch, 2005). Through examining hyperlink usage, other studies have examined the potential influence of citizen media on traditional media news stories (Marlow, 2004; Singer, 2004). Some hyperlink studies have focused on the continued, powerful influence of traditional media within citizen media news reports (Reese et al., 2007).

With the advent of social media, traditional media's singular gatekeeping function has been compromised. Digg (founded in 2004), Reddit (founded in 2005), Netscape (repurposed as a social media news site in 2006), and Newsvine (founded in 2005) all use different algorithms for determining popular news on their sites. Among the four sites selected for examination in this study, Netscape is considered to have the most editorial oversight. In terms of how stories make it to the front page of these sites, all four sites utilize some/all of the following factors in their gatekeeping process for popular stories: number of votes over time; domain of the link; profile of the submitter; profile of voters; timing of submission; source of votes; manual review as it hits the homepage; number of comments; number of votes; down votes (reddit); and, source of votes. Some of these sites also allow users to see the stories that their friends have submitted (SEOmoz, 2006b), which could result in collaborative filtering. This social filtering or the boosting of a story's popularity based on strong friendship ties has often been used as a basis for criticizing social media news sites. Yet, for all of the criticism, these sites can be said to be social in the sense that stories make it to the front page through the voting decisions of the many community members that are registered at these sites.

Due to this increased citizen power within social media forms, Bruns (2005, 2008) reshapes gatekeeping to gatewatching, a term which captures the empowered citizens' role to decide what constitutes news through the acts of republishing and refiltering news. Some authors have suggested that gatekeeping is no longer a tenable theory due to the fragmented media universe (Williams & Delli Carpini, 2000, 2004). Within social media news aggregators, a new model of gatekeeping is being actively cultivated through encouraging all registered users to decide what ultimately gets selected as the most important news of the day. This phenomenon, also known as "crowdsourcing" in marketing circles (Howe, 2008), espouses tapping into the wisdom of a distributed crowd to complete big assignments through breaking the task into its constituent, modular parts.

This current study will assess the role that hyperlinks plays in indicating which sources are trusted and valued by these social media news networks. As it relates to citizen media and traditional media, this study will examine how these social media news aggregators position themselves in relation to the long tail of Web media options. This study will also examine the phenomenon of "crowdsourcing" in the selection of popular news stories within these social media news aggregators in order to ascertain whether some users have more success than others in achieving front page success.

Research Questions

Prior research has suggested that Internet communities are subject to power law constraints (Huberman et al., 1998; Huberman & Adamic, 1999; Kottke, 2003; Meraz, 2005; Nielsen, 1997; Tremayne, 2004). As the literature highlights, it is often typical for a small subset of entrants or individuals to have more popularity, visibility, and credibility than the majority of network members. Little to date has been done on the user community dynamics of social media news aggregator sites; however, because these networks are World Wide Web networks, there is reason to believe that these communities should adhere to power law principles. This study advances the following research question.

RQ1: To What Extent is there a Power Law in User Community Dynamics for Popular Stories that Appear on the Home Page of Social Media News Aggregators?

When examining the relationship between traditional media and citizen communities, prior studies have shown that traditional media prefer to link to the most popular and successful independent blogs (Farrell & Drezner, 2008), or to other professional newsrooms (Singer, 2005). No work to date has been conducted on the balance of traditional media to citizen source influence in social media news aggregators. With the knowledge that citizen media sites rarely create original news stories outside the hyperlocal context, there is reason to believe that traditional national media will continue to set the agenda for the most important news of the day on these sites. Alternatively, since many of these citizen media sites are set up to share news and information that might not be of interest to traditional news organizations, it is possible that much of the news that is discussed on these communities might be related to niche, citizen media. This study advances the following research question.

RQ 2: Is there Evidence to Suggest that Social Media News Aggregators Show More of a Preference for either Traditional Media Sources or Citizen Media Sources in the Selection of Popular News Stories?

In relation to democracy, one measure of the effectiveness of these communities resides in their ability to reflect the most important news on a day-to-day basis. To be considered vehicles of democracy, these communities should provide a temperature pulse of significant news and events, enabling readers to become democratic citizens. This point is particularly crucial for those individuals that use these sites as a substitute for traditional media news sources or as a gatekeeping device for being alerted to the most important news of the day. This study advances the following research question.

RQ 3: To What Extent do these Sites Highlight Political News as the Most Popular News Genre on their Home Pages?

Finally, these Internet media sites have often been lauded for their ability to provide access to diverse news in a fast changing and rapidly updated environment. One indicator of widespread community involvement could be indicated by the rapidity of changing news popularity throughout the day. This study advances the following research question:

RQ 4: To What Extent do these Communities Provide Access to a Diversity of News Stories Through Changing the Popular News Stories on the Home Page Throughout the Day?

These research questions were examined in four social media news aggregator sites over a five-day period through three different time points on a daily basis.

Method

In an effort to examine as wide a canvas as possible on social media news aggregation sites, this study examined the community efforts of four outlets: Digg, Reddit, Netscape, and Newsvine. To effectively explore the research questions, it was felt that these outlets would have to be examined through a certain consecutive period of time and during different time points within this set time period. The home page of these sites, which show the most popular stories at any given time, was visited and downloaded for three time points (12 pm, 6 pm, and 10 pm) for a five-day period from June 30, 2007 to July 4, 2007. Hourly time points were chosen to reflect the likely times that people have access to news at home and work (lunch break, evening news, and late night news), while the only consideration in the choice of a consecutive time period was to avoid one major news event dominating news cycle coverage.

The top 10 popular news lists were downloaded across all four sites during the aforementioned time period. Data on the story title, user/submitter of story, and source of the news story was extracted via a Web script and entered into a MS SQL database. Before entering data into the database, data was cleaned on the "story title" variable. With this variable, many of the social media sites enabled the renaming original story titles; hence, a Web script was written to retrieve the actual story title through visiting the URL of the story source. In some cases, the original news story did not have a title (which often occurred if multimedia was voted as the most popular Web content). For these situations, the title bar of the source's news page was chosen as an accurate reflection of the story's title. In cases where there was no substitute for the original story title, the title selected for analysis was that advanced by the social media news aggregator.

Each news story was also tagged by genre from a possible genre pool of the following categories: business/economics, crime, education, entertainment, health, media, politics, religion, science, sports, technology, war and terrorism, and other. Multiple coding of the story into overlapping categories was not permitted, and decisions on the categorization of the story were based on the headline, story lead, and the suggested categorization as advanced by the social media news aggregator. Finally, all sources were tagged based on their broad-based affiliation to traditional or citizen media.

A 10 percent subset of data was retrieved by a random query to the database across all time points. This subset of data was coded to assess inter-coder reliability. Using the Holsti coefficient of reliability, an inter-coder reliability of 97 percent was reached. Upon deriving this acceptable inter-coder reliability level, one coder (the author of this study) completing the coding of all other news stories.

Upon completing the story coding, SQL queries were written against the database and data was derived for answering all of the research questions for the study. Since the study was largely exploratory and did not advance hypotheses, writing queries to the database to yield frequency counts, charts, and graphs provided the necessary data for this first-level exploratory analysis.

Results

User Dynamics and the Power Law

Research question 1 probed the nature of power law dynamics through the four networks. Through the June 30, 2007 to July 4, 2007 time period, there were 255 distinct users in all four social media sites across the entire 60 time points measured in this study (three time points by four sites for a five-day period). Overall, there was a mean of 70 users per day across all of the four sites. Figure 7.1 provides a day-by-day breakdown of the numbers of distinct or unique users from each site for the five-day period under analysis. The

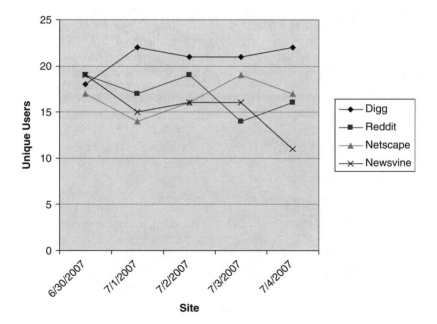

Figure 7.1 Unique users by site between June 20 and July 4.

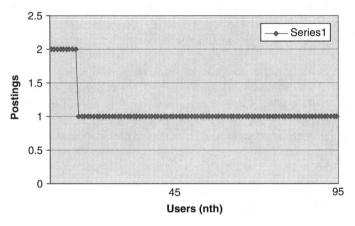

Figure 7.2 Power law in Digg.

breakdown revealed that Digg had the most unique users (95), followed by Reddit (69), Newsvine (47) and Netscape (44). This data yielded some interesting findings. Although Digg is the most publicly criticized for its concentrated user base, Digg provides more of a distinct user population in the top 10 of its story postings when compared with all of the other popular social media news aggregation sites.

But, the question can now be asked: is there a power law? Is there a cadre of top users in each site that is responsible for the majority of stories appearing in the top 10 news stories on the site's home page? Figures 7.2, 7.3, 7.4, and 7.5 illustrate the power law curves for each site's user population based on the tally of unique stories. As the data shows, Digg's top 20 users are responsible for 52 of

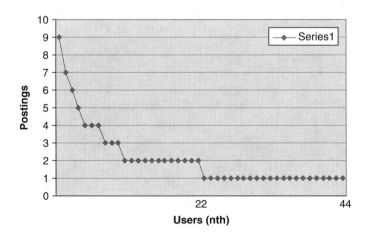

Figure 7.3 Power law for Netscape.

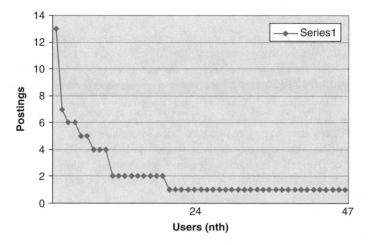

Figure 7.4 Power law in Newsvine.

the 150 stories or 35 percent of the top 10 stories when all stories are considered, and 29 of the 104 stories or 28 percent of all stories when only unique stories are considered. Netscape's top 20 users are responsible for posting 107 of the 150 stories appearing in the top 10 slot over the three time periods, or 71 percent of the content. If only unique stories are considered, Netscape's top 20 users post 68 of the 94 stories or 72 percent of the content. Newsvine's top 20 users are responsible for posting 118 of the 150 stories over the entire time period, or 79 percent of the stories, and 74 of the 101 unique stories or 73 percent of the unique content. Reddit's top 20 users are responsible for posting 76 of the 150 stories over the entire time period, or 51 percent of the content, and 48 of the

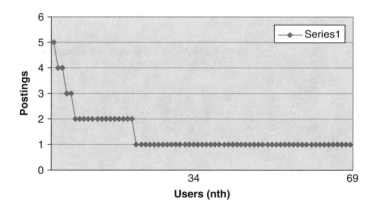

Figure 7.5 Power law in Reddit.

96 unique stories or 50 percent of the unique story content over the time period under analysis.

It can be argued that in all four sites, there are clearly a few users that are able to get an inordinate amount of top stories to appear on the home pages of these sites. Yet, although there is a power law in operation, it does not appear to be as steep for all sites (see Figures 7.2 through 7.5). Digg's top users are often publicly criticized for driving the majority of the content; however, as the data shows, Digg has the flattest power curve. The data reveals that Newsvine and Netscape's top users are more in control of all popular content when compared to Digg and Reddit. Arguably, both Newsvine and Netscape have strong human moderation; yet, this human moderation has created a more unequal power hierarchy between the elite users and the remainder of the site's users when compared to more open systems like Digg and Reddit.

Source Authority

Research question 2 called for an examination of traditional media to citizen media dependence within these said four networks to ascertain whether more authority was given to elite or amateur media sources. Through the five-day period under analysis in all four networks, there were a total of 377 unique news sources for the news stories. Before answering this question, it is important to point out that, similar to the models provided of user data in the previous section, there was also a power law governing source citations. Figure 7.6

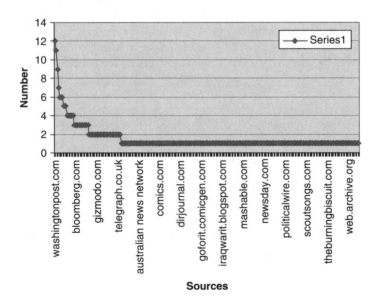

Figure 7.6 Power law for sources.

Table 7.1 Sources by Category Across All Four Sites for the Five-Day Time Period

Source	Frequency (n)
traditional media	134
citizen media	117
community/enthusiast/hobby	62
political other	11
portal news	10
independent media	7
magazine/journal	7
organization/corporate	6
web forum	5
web-only media	4
partisan media democratic	4
education	4
Other	3
partisan media republican	2
Government	1
Total (n)	377

highlights that the most visible media sources in all four sites were traditional media entities. The most popular site was the *Washington Post,* which was cited 12 times in the five-day period under investigation in this study.

Research question 2 can first be examined through aggregating data across all of the four social media news aggregators. Table 7.1 presents data on the breakdown of sources by categories across all of the four different sites. As can be seen from Table 7.1, traditional media barely outnumbers citizen media citations. Traditional media accounts for 36 percent of all unique story mentions when compared with just over 31 percent for citizen media source links. Disaggregating sources from their macro categories reveal that a few sites appear across all four social media news aggregators. Youtube was the only citizen media site to appear in Digg, Reddit, Newsvine, and Netscape; in sharp contrast, traditional media sites the *BBC,* the *Daily Mail,* and the *Washington Post* appear in all four sites. The Yahoo! news portal also appears in all four sites.

A more detailed examination of research question 2 can be achieved by looking at the balance of traditional to citizen media dependence in each of the four social media news aggregators. Table 7.2 presents the breakdown of media sources across all four news aggregator communities. The differences in the sources within these communities provide a good indication of the user publics that visit these news avenues as well as the general ethos of these sites. As can be seen from the data, both Reddit and Digg highlight citizen media sources more than traditional media. Almost 50 percent of Digg's sources point to citizen media in comparison to only 20 percent that point to traditional media. Reddit allocates 43 percent of its links to citizen media in comparison to

Table 7.2 Sources by Category per Site for the Five-Day Time Period

Source	Digg	Reddit	Netscape	Newsvine
traditional media	21	26	33	59
citizen media	51	41	21	11
community/enthusiast/hobby	14	18	22	10
political other	4	1	6	0
portal news	1	1	8	1
independent media	1	0	0	6
magazine/journal	0	0	2	5
organization/corporate	3	3	0	0
web forum	5	0	0	0
web-only media	0	2	1	1
partisan media democratic	1	0	1	2
education	1	2	0	1
Other	2	1	0	1
partisan media republican	0	0	0	2
Government	1	0	0	0
Total (n)	105	95	94	99

27 percent to traditional media. In sharp contrast, both Netscape and Newsvine are more dependent on traditional media sites. Netscape allocates 35 percent of its links to traditional media sites in comparison to 22 percent of its links to citizen media sites. Newsvine shows the most visible bias: 60 percent of its source links point to traditional media in comparison to a paltry 11 percent that point to citizen media.

Themes

Research question 3 probed the extent to which these four social media news aggregators could support democratic conversation and democratic citizenship. This potential was examined through assessing the weight of political news on these sites' popular news listings. Like the former research questions, this current question can be answered in reference to aggregate data for all of the four sites combined as well as on a site-by-site basis. Table 7.3 presents a breakdown of the different genres across the four social news aggregator communities. Across all four news aggregator communities, the genre of politics is the most popular story category, accounting for 191 stories or 32 percent of the 600 unique stories. Further examination of Table 7.3 also reveals some interesting results. The second most popular category of news is the entertainment genre: over 15 percent of news stories that gain popularity in these sites are related to entertainment. A strong, niche area of interest in these communities is technology news. Exactly 15 percent of news is related to the technology genre.

Research question 3 can also be addressed through exploring the genre breakdown on each site. The aggregate level data is also mirrored in individual-level

Table 7.3 Theme Frequency Across All Four Sites for the Five-Day Time Period

Theme	Frequency (n)
Politics	191
entertainment	92
technology	90
war and terrorism	50
Crime	48
Other	39
Health	22
Religion	21
Media	16
Science	15
Business	9
education	5
Sports	2
Total (n)	600

data through three of the four networks (see Table 7.4). Politics accounts for 43 percent of the news on Newsvine, 38 percent of the news on Netscape, and 27 percent of the news on Reddit. The only site that does not reveal politics to be the most dominant genre is Digg. For Digg, technology accounts for approximately 40 percent of news in comparison to politics which accounts for less than 20 percent. Digg's strong focus on technology is not mirrored in the other sites. The technology genre only accounts for 12 percent of the content on Reddit, 5 percent of the content on Netscape, and 5 percent of the content on Newsvine.

Table 7.4 Theme Frequency Per Site For the Five-Day Time Period

Theme	Digg	Reddit	Netscape	Newsvine
Politics	29	41	57	64
entertainment	22	25	34	11
technology	58	18	7	8
war and terrorism	4	12	17	17
Crime	4	18	8	18
Other	13	19	1	6
Health	6	4	9	3
Religion	4	4	7	6
Media	5	1	1	9
Science	3	6	3	3
Business	2	1	7	0
education	0	1	1	3
Sports	0	0	0	2
Total	150	150	150	150

Access to Changing Stories

Research question 4 inquired into the extent to which these communities provide access to a diversity of news stories through changing the popular news stories on the home page throughout the day. Within each of the different sites, it was possible for stories to repeat themselves within the top 10, popular stories through different time periods. With the total potential story base being set at 30 unique stories per day per site (10 new stories for each of the three periods), it is instructive to examine the extent to which stories held traction over time periods. Evidence of story traction or stickiness could provide an outward metric of story importance.

Of the total 600 stories assessed through the June 30 to July 4 time period, 378 stories or 63 percent were unique. With each site contributing a total of 150 stories, the percentage of unique stories for each site were as follows: Digg, 67 percent (104 stories), Newsvine, 67 percent (101 stories), Reddit, 64 percent (96 stories), Netscape, 63 percent (94 stories). Within Digg, 2 percent of the stories occurred through three time periods, 38 percent through two time periods and 60 percent through one time period. In Netscape, 12 percent of the stories occurred through three time periods, 33 percent through two time periods, and 55 percent through one time period. In Newsvine, 14 percent of the stories occurred through three time periods, 18 percent through two time periods, and 68 percent through one. Within Reddit, 7 percent of the stories occurred through three time periods, 41 percent through two time periods, and 52 percent through one time period. As these data highlight, very few stories hold traction across different time periods on a day-by-day basis.

But, the question could be posed. What percentage of stories diffused through the three networks? And, if there was story diffusion, which site was the first one to host the story? Table 7.5 provides data on the common stories through the four sites and on those stories that diffused through more than one network in one day. As the table data highlights, there was no story that occurred in all four sites through the entire five-day period. As can be seen from the data, only two stories were common in all three sites through the five-day period, while 15 stories were common in two or more sites through the study period. Of these 15 stories, 7 were present in the two or more sites at the same date/time. Of those common stories that appeared on one of the four news aggregators first, Reddit was the most popular story originating site with five of the eight stories appearing there first. Interestingly, only two of these stories were submitted to these different sites by someone utilizing the same username. Overall, these findings highlight that these popular social news aggregators seem to have little agreement on a common news agenda on a day-to-day basis. These sites seem to host different content and seem to be supported by different user communities.

Table 7.5 Story Diffusion Among the Four Networks for the Five-Day Period

Story Title	Source	Site A	Site B	Site C	All Sites (No Order)
18 year old offers her virginity for £10,000	maltastar.com	Digg	Newsvine		Reddit
* 7-elevens become simpsons 'kwik-e-marts',	news.yahoo.com	Reddit	Digg		Newsvine, Reddit
a fairly tense moment (photo)	paddlenround.com				
* africans to bono: 'for god's sake please stop!'	american.com	Netscape	Digg		
* blacked out by the corporate media,	smirkingchimp.com				Newsvine, Reddit
impeachment advances					
* bush commutes libby's prison sentence	washingtonpost.com	Digg			Digg, Reddit
bush is told to justify executive privilege	washingtonpost.com	Reddit			Newsvine, Reddit
* did pedophilia hysteria cause child's death?	foxnews.com	Digg			Reddit, Netscape
* google to hmos: pay us and we'll defuse "sicko"	boingboing.net	Reddit			Digg, Netscape
* holocaust survivor leaving us	justicefornone.com	Digg			Newsvine, Reddit
inferior design	nytimes.com	Reddit	Netscape		
july 2nd, 2007	flickr.com				Digg, Reddit
* kiss caught on camera raises issues of big	truthera.com	Reddit	Newsvine		
brother surveillance learning to walk	anthropik.com	Reddit	Digg		
* wikipedian protester	xkcd.com	Reddit	Digg		

* Represents those stories that diffused within the networks within a 1-day period

Discussion and Limitations

With the growth of blogging applications in the 1990s, media has become a more social entity as individuals can join in conversation, engage in collaboration, and attach to community through applications designed to harness the intelligence of the crowd. Traditional media entities, no longer in control of the tools of news production and news dissemination, face an assault on their monopoly power as individuals can now decide what constitutes news and which news items have meaning. This study examines one phenomenon of social media—social media news aggregators. Through social media news aggregators, individuals can bypass the traditional gatekeeping function of the press and determine what news items are the most popular via the process of community collective voting. This study assesses four of the most popular social media news aggregators through the lens of user community dynamics and news characteristics in an effort to learn more about the role and function of these social news communities.

Network theory has revealed that many World Wide Web communities are subject to a power law phenomenon, which creates a disparity between a few popular actors and the majority of other actors who are less popular and less elite (Huberman et al., 1998; Huberman & Adamic, 1999; Kottke, 2003; Meraz, 2005; Nielsen, 1997; Tremayne, 2004). Social media news aggregators are often touted for supporting a new model of news gatekeeping that provides citizens greater access to decision making in terms of what constitutes news (Bruns, 2005, 2008). Unlike this utopian ethic and in keeping with World Wide Web community structures, this study's findings reveal that many of these sites are currently subject to a power law constraint. Within these sites, there are a few, elite individuals that power most of the popular news content on the homepages. Interestingly, though Digg is often criticized for its disproportionate user power structure, this study's findings reveal that Digg has a gentler power law curve and less elite bias when compared with other noted social news sites Reddit, Newsvine, and Netscape. Still, this study has confirmed that all of these social media news aggregators derive a large percentage of their popular news stories from a cadre of elite users who hold disproportionate power in comparison with the majority of the community members.

Such findings suggest some interesting follow-up questions. For example, some can question the utility of social sites that replicate the all-too-familiar traditional media power structure that they were created to supplant or refashion. Others can question whether these sites are really creating an alternative to traditional media if all citizens do not have equal power. Clearly, much of this identified criticism blunts or weakens the democratic potential of these sites if egalitarian citizen power is utilized as the yardstick to measure these sites' capacity to support bottom-up democracy.

In relation to these user community findings, it is clear that the traditional media gatekeeping model has now been reformulated to include the role of the citizen, specifically the Internet power user. Often considered to be a more Web savvy and Web-intense user, these Internet power users have become the new influentials or elite agenda setters in the new media universe of social media applications. Through their actions in suggesting stories to social media sites, these power users garner increased layers of influence through the actions of other users who respect their authority and trust their reputation, and as such, validate their story choice through "up" or "positive" voting. Known as collaborative filtering or social filtering, the impact of recommendations fueled by friendship ties has become a model of social influence in those sites that use voting as a measure of gatekeeping content. This model of social influence, which can be modeled as a two-step flow of influence from these opinion leaders to their followers, resurrects this social influence theory as a useful one for explaining how news diffuses in social media communities.

It is clear that within these communities, traditional media gatekeeping is no longer an applicable model. Though critics can discount these sites for replicating a familiar power structure to traditional media, it is clear that these sites are providing a community-oriented model for news gatekeeping. This study's findings highlight high numbers of daily unique users through all of the sites, suggesting that there is value for those members who frequent this news community. From such a vantage point, these sites provide an invaluable service to democracy through allowing users to interact and participate in the cycle of news production and distribution. Users not only select and filter content but interact with the content through active discussion and commentary.

In this reallocation of power from traditional media to citizen, social media news sites are also rebalancing the power of these traditional media entities' content within these social environments. As the findings reveal, almost 50 percent of Digg's sources point to citizen media in comparison to only 20 percent that point to traditional media; similarly, Reddit allocates 43 percent of its links to citizen media in comparison to 27 percent to traditional media. Unlike Digg and Reddit, Netscape and Newsvine had more links to traditional media; in the case of Newsvine, the company was acquired by CBS and has typically placed greater reliance on traditional media as its trusted news source.

This study's findings suggest that traditional media entities must continue to reshape their news product to make their content portable and distributable across the Internet's many new social media platforms. Currently, sites like the *Washington Post* include widgets to vote for their news articles within these social media news communities. As these findings reveal, we are living in a new media age where traditional media shares power with citizen media sites. Citizens are now being depended upon as authorities on diverse subject matter above the authority of generalist journalist. Traditional media can no longer afford to dismiss the work of citizens, especially given the role of these news aggregators in determining relevancy of news items on the Internet.

This study also sought to examine the types of news that gain popularity in these sites in an effort to examine the role and function of these sites in relation to democratic deliberation. As this study's findings reveal, political content remains the most popular content on an aggregate level through all four sites. On a site-by-site basis, three of the four sites hosted political content as its most popular news type. Due to the immense popularity of political news, it is clear that these sites exist to support civic engagement and political conversation. Yet, the difference in the genre breakdown, site-by-site, also provides a glimpse into the diversity of issue publics on the Web. As Anderson (2006) noted, the growth of citizen media has created an abundance of media supply, which has altered the mass mediated marketplace model to one of a niche-based marketplace. This study's findings suggest that these four communities support different user communities. For example, it is clear that one of Digg's main functions is to be the gatekeeper to technology-related news, a genre that does not gain much front page exposure on traditional news sites.

Another notable finding in this study was the exposure to new news items. All of these communities provide access to a range of diverse, popular stories through different time points on a day-by-day basis. This access to new, changing content can explain why community members are encouraged to participate and why Web publics are drawn to these social media entities. Yet, from a democratic standpoint, one can question the utility of a site that does not provide "stickiness" to important, political news content. If all content is easily disposable, it can be questioned whether these communities support democratic citizenship. As evidenced by the data (see Table 7.5), very few stories repeat themselves across these different communities, and very few stories remain popular across different time points on a daily basis.

A popular genre of news within these communities is entertainment news, a finding which could also fuel strong criticism of these sites' content. Yet, entertainment news remains a strong staple of traditional media news; for example, we can all recall the importance that traditional media placed on actress Paris Hilton's jail time saga or Hollywood actor Tom Cruise's jump on day-time talk show host Oprah Winfrey's sofa when declaring his love for actress Katie Holmes. A significant difference between the entertainment news in these social media news aggregator communities and entertainment news in media realms is the former's focus on the citizen as source or author. Within these social media sites, entertainment news is typically fueled by the citizen media creations, be it in the form of textual or multimedia (audio, photo, or video) media content. Through amassing and then filtering out the best talent on the Web, these social media sites exist to refilter and redistribute the best of entertainment news as developed from citizen media sources.

This study was limited by the five-day time frame. Future studies are encouraged to sample more time points in an effort to produce more generalizable results. With the continued growth of social media news platforms, future studies can also replicate this study by including newer social platforms. Including social news platforms that have been in existence for different periods of time can enable a more in-depth test of how time impacts the dynamics of user community and the popularity of differing news sources within communities.

References

Ad Age. (2007). *Blog readership report*. Retrieved December 3, 2008, from http://answers.vizu.com/pdf/Blog_Readership_Report_March_07.pdf.

Adamic, L.A., & Adar, E. (2003). Friends and neighbors on the Web. *Social Networks*. Retrieved December 3, 2008, from http://www.cs.man.ac.uk/~rizos/web10.pdf .

Adamic, L.A., & Glance, N. (2005). The political blogosphere and the 2004 U.S. election: Divided they blog. *H.P. Labs*. Retrieved December 3, 2008, from http://www.hpl.hp.com/research/idl/papers/politicalblogs/.

Anderson, C. (2006). *The long tail: Why the future of business is selling more of less*. New York: Hyperion.

Bailey, M. (2007). *Social media: Under the microscope*. Retrieved December 3, 2008, from http://www.sitelogicmarketing.com/blog/01-social-media-under-microscope.

Barabasi, A. (2002). *Linked: The new science of networks*. Cambridge, Mass.: Perseus Publications.

Barabasi, A. (2003). *Linked: How everything is connected to everything else and what does it mean*. New York: Plume.

Barabasi, A-L., & Albert, R. (1999). Emergence of scaling in random networks. *Science*, 286 (5439): 509–12, 15 October 1999.

Barabasi, A.L., Albert, R., Jeong, H., & Bianconi, G. (2000). Power law distribution of the World Wide Web. *Science, 287*.

BBC. (2005). *Berners-Lee on the read/write web*. Retrieved December 3, 2008, from http://news.bbc.co.uk/1/hi/technology/4132752.stm.

Benkler, Y. (2006). *The wealth of networks: How social production transforms markets and freedom*. New Haven, CT: Yale University Press.

Bonchek, M. (1995). Grassroots in cyberspace: CMC and collective action. Paper presented at the annual meeting of the Midwest Political Science Association Meeting, Chicago, IL.

Bowman, S., & Willis, C. (2003). *We media: How audiences are shaping the future of news and information*. Retrieved December 3, 2008, from http://www.hypergene.net/wemedia/weblog.php.

Broder, A., Kumar, R., Maghoul, F., Raghaven, P., Rajagopalan, S., Stata, R., Tompkins, A., & Winer, J. (2000). Graph structure in the Web. *Computer Networks*. Retrieved December 3, 2008, from http://www.almaden.ibm.com/webfountain/resources/GraphStructureintheWeb.pdf.

Bruns, A. (2005). *Gatewatching: Collaborative online news production*. New York: Peter Lang Publishing.

Bruns, A. (2008). *Blogs, wikipedia, second life, and beyond: From production to produsage*. New York: Peter Lang Publishing.

Bubblegeneration. (2006). *Edge competencies*. Retrieved December 3, 2008, from http://www.bubblegeneration.com/2006/01/edge-competencies-what-do-googles-use.cfm.

Calcanis, J. (2006). *Paying the top Digg/REDDIT/Flickr/Newsvine users (or "$1000 a* *month for doing what you're doing already"*). Retrieved December 3, 2008, from http://www.calacanis.com/2006/07/18/everyones-gotta-eat-or-1-000-a-month-for-doing-what-youre/.

Christensen, C. (2003a). *The innovator's dilemma: The revolutionary book that will change the way you do business*. New York: Harper Business Essentials.

Christensen, C. (2003b). *The innovator's solution: Creating and sustaining successful growth*. Boston, MA: Harvard Business School Press.

Clarke, J. (2006). *Why Digg is destined for failure*. Retrieved December 3, 2008, from http://www.downloadsquad.com/2006/12/11/why-digg-is-destined-for-failure/.

Coates, T. (2006). *What do we do with "social media"?* Retrieved December 3, 2008, from http://www.plasticbag.org/archives/2006/03/what_do_we_do_with_social_media/.

Copeland, H. (2006). *2006 blog survey reader results*. Retrieved December 3, 2008, from http://weblog.blogads.com/comments/P1246_0_1_0/.

Crumlish, C. (2004). *The power of many: How the living Web is transforming politics, business, and everyday life*. San Francisco: Sybex.

Curley, T. (2004). *Text of opening keynote by Tom Curley*. Retrieved December 3, 2008 from http: conference.journalists.org/2004conference/archives/000079.php.

Cybernet. (2006). *The analysis of a Digg effect 4X in 10 days*. Retrieved December 3, 2008, from http://tech.cybernetnews.com/2006/07/14/cybernotes-the-analysis-of-a-digg-effect-4x-in-10-days/.

Dimitrova, D. V., Connolly-Ahern, C., Williams, A. P., Kaid, L. L., & Reid, A. (2003) Hyperlining as gatekeeping: Online newspaper coverage of the execution of an American terrorist. *Journalism Studies, 4*, 3, 401–404.

Drezner, D.W., & Farrell, H. (2004). *The power and politics of blogs*. Presented at the American Political Science Association.

Eckman, J.P., & Moses, E. (2002). Curvature of colinks uncovers hidden thematic layers in the World Wide Web. *Proceedings of the National Academy of Sciences of the United States of America, 99*(9), 5285–5289.

Enzensberger, H. M. (1970). Constituents of a theory of the media. *New Left Review, 64*, 13–36.

Farrell, H., & Dresner, D. W. (2008). The power and politics of blogs. *Public Choice, 134*, 15–30.

Gillmor, D. (2004). *We the media: Grassroots journalism by the people, for the people*. Sebastopol, CA: O'Reilly.

Gladwell, M. (2002). *The tipping point: How little things can make a big difference*. New York: Back Bay Books/Little, Brown.

Granovetter, M. S. (1973). The strength of weak ties. *American Journal of Sociology, 78*(6), 1360–1380.

Granovetter, M. S. (1983). The strength of weak ties: A network theory revisited. *Sociological Theory, 1*, 201–233.

Grossman, L. (2006). Time's person of the year: You. *Time Magazine*. Retrieved December 3, 2008, from http://www.time.com/time/magazine/article/0,9171,1569514,00.html.

Hacker, K. L., & van Dijk, J. (2000) *Digital democracy: Issues of theory and practice*. London Thousand Oaks, CA: Sage.

Hagen, M. (2000). Digital democracy and political systems. In K.L. Hacker. & J. van Dijk (Eds.), *Digital democracy: Issues of theory and practice* (pp. 55–69). London Thousand Oaks, CA: Sage.

Howe, J. 2008. *Crowdsourcing: Why the power of the crowd is driving the future of business*. New York: Crown Business.

Huberman, B. A., & Adamic, L. A. (1999). Growth dynamics of the World Wide Web. *Nature, 40*, 131.

Huberman, B. A., Pirolli, P. L. T., Pitkow, J. E., & Lukose, R. M. (1998). Strong regularities in World Wide Web surfing. *Science, 280*(3), 95–97.

Ito, J. (2003). *Weblogs and emergent democracy*. Retrieved December 3, 2008, from http://joi.ito.com/static/emergentdemocracy.html.

Johnson, S. (2001). *Emergence: The connected lives of ants, brains, cities, and software*. New York: Scribner.

Kottke, J. (2003). *Weblogs and power laws*. Retrieved December 3, 2008, from http://www.kottke.org/03/02/weblogs-and-power-laws.

Kumar, R., Novak, J., Raghavan, P., & Tompkins, A. (2004). Structure and evolution of blogspace. *Communications of the ACM, 47*(12), 35–39.

Lasica, J. D. (2003).What is participatory journalism? *Online Journalism Review*. Retrieved December 3, 2008, from http://www.ojr.org/ojr/workplace/1060217106.php.

Lazarsfeld, P. F., & Merton, R.K. (1954). Friendship as a social process: A substantive and methodological analysis. In M. Berger (Ed.), *Freedom and control in modern society* (pp. 18–66). New York: Van Norstrand.

Leadbeater, C., & Miller, P. (2005). *The pro-am revolution*. Retrieved December 3, 2008, from http://www.demos.co.uk/publications/proameconomy.

Lenhard, A., Fallows, D., & Horrigan, J. Content creation online. *Pew Internet and American Life Project*. Retrieved December 3, 2008, from http://www.pewinternet.org/PPF/r/113/report_display.asp.

Lerman, K. (2006). *Social networks and social information filtering on Digg*. Retrieved December 3, 2008, from http://www.icwsm.org/papers/4-Lerman.pdf.

Lewin, K. (1947). Frontiers in group dynamics. Channels of group life: Social planning and action research. *Human Relations*, 143–153.

Marlow, C. (2004). *Audience structure in the weblog community*. Presented at the Association for Education in Journalism and Mass Communication, New Orleans.

McConnell, B., & Huba, J. (2006). *Citizen marketers: Where people are the message*. Dearborn Trade.

McPhearson, M., Smith-Lovin, L., & Cook, J. M. (2001). Birds of a feather: Homophily in social networks. *Annual Review of Sociology, 27*, 415–444.

Meraz, S. (2005). *Event blogging the 2004 conventions: Media bloggers, non-media bloggers, and their network connections*. Paper presented to the annual convention of the Association for Education in Journalism and Mass Communication (San Antonio, Texas).

Moore, J. (2003). *The Second Superpower Rears its Beautiful Head*. Retrieved December 3, 2008, from http://cyber.law.harvard.edu/people/jmoore/secondsuperpower.html.

Neuman, M. E. J. (2003). The structure and function of complex networks. *SIAM, 45*(2), 167–256.

Nielsen, J. (1997). Do websites have increasing returns? *Alertbox*. Retrieved December 3, 2008, from http://www.useit.com/alertbox/9704b. html.

O'Reilly, T. (1999). *Open source: Voices from the open source revolution*. Retrieved December 3, 2008, from http://www.oreilly.com/catalog/opensources/book/toc.html.

O'Reilly, T. (2004). *The architecture of participation*. Retrieved December 3, 2008, from http://www.oreillynet.com/pub/a/oreilly/tim/articles/architecture_of_participation.html

O'Reilly, T. (2005). *What is web 2.0?* Retrieved December 3, 2008, from http://www.oreillynet.com/pub/a/oreilly/tim/news/2005/09/30/what-is-web-20.html.

Putnam, R. D. (1995). Bowling alone: America's declining social capital. *Journal of Democracy, 6*(1), 65–78.

Putnam, R. D. (1996). The strange disappearance of civic America. *American Prospect, 24,* 34–38.

Putnam, R. D. (2000). *Bowling alone: The collapse and revival of American community.* New York: Simon & Schuster.

Reese, S., Rutigliano, L., Hyun, K., & Jeong, J. (2007). Mapping the blogosphere: Professional and citizen-based media in the global news arena. *Journalism, 8*(3), 235–261.

Reynolds, G. (2006). *An army of Davids: How markets and technology empower ordinary people to beat big media, big government, and other Goliaths.* Nashville, TN: Thomas Nelson.

Scoble, R. (2007). *What is social media?* Retrieved December 3, 2008, from http://scobleizer.com/2007/02/16/what-is-social-media/.

Scoble, R., & Israel, S. (2005). *Naked conversations: How blogs are changing the way businesses talk with customers.* Hoboken, NJ: John Wiley.

SEOmoz. (2006a). *Top 100 Digg users control 56% of Digg's homepage content.* Retrieved December 3, 2008, from http://www.seomoz.org/blog/top-100-digg-users-control-56-of-diggs-homepage-content.

SEOmoz (2006b). *Everything in the Digg, Reddit, and Netscape algorithms.* Retrieved December 3, 2008, from http://www.seomoz.org/blog/everything-in-the-digg-reddit-netscape-algorithms.

Shirky, C. (2003). *Power laws, weblogs, and inequality.* Retrieved December 3, 2008, from http://www.shirky.com/writings/powerlaw_weblog.html.

Shirky, C. (2008). *Here comes everybody: The power of organizing without organizations.* New York: Penguin Press.

Shoemaker, P. J., Eichholz, M., Kim, E., & Wrigley, B. (2001). Individual and routine sources in gatekeeping. *Journalism Quarterly, 78,* 233–246.

Shoemaker, P. J., & Reese, S. D. (1996). *Mediating the message: Theories of influences on mass media content.* London: Longman Publishers.

Sifry, D. (2007). *State of the live Web.* Retrieved December 3, 2008, from http://www.sifry.com/alerts/archives/000493.html.

Singer, J. B. (2004). *The political j-blogger. Normalizing a new media form to fit old norms and practices.* Presented at the Association for Education in Journalism and Mass Communication Conference, New Orleans, 2004.

Spannerworks. (2007). *What is social media?* Retrieved December 3, 2008, from http://www.spannerworks.com/what-we-think/our-research.

Sunstein, C. (2000). Deliberative trouble? Why groups go to extremes. *Yale Law Journal, 110*(1), 71–119.

Sunstein, C. (2001). *Republic.com.* New Jersey: Princeton University Press.

Sunstein, C. (2002). The law of group polarization. *The Journal of Political Philosophy, 10*(2), 175–195.

Suroweicki, J. (2005). *The wisdom of crowds.* New York: Anchor Books.

Tremayne, M. (2004). The Web of context: Applying network theory to the use of hyperlinks in journalism on the Web. *Journalism & Mass Communication Quarterly, 81*(2), 237–253.

Tremayne, M., Zheng, N., Lee, J., & Jeong, J. (2006). Issue publics on the Web: Applying network theory to the war blogosphere. *Journal of Computer-Mediated Communication, 12*, 1. Retrieved December 3, 2008, from http://jcmc.indiana.edu/

Trench, B., & G. Quinn. (2003). Online news and changing models of journalism. *Irish Communications Review, 9*, 1–11.

Weinberger, D. (2002). *Small pieces loosely joined: A unified theory of the Web*. New York: Basic Books.

Welsch, P. (2005). *Revolutionary vanguard or echo chamber? Political blogs and the mainstream media*. Retrieved December 3, 2008, from http://www.blogninja.com/index.php.

White, D. M.(1950). The gatekeeper: A case study in the selection of news. *Journalism Quarterly, 27*, 383–390.

Williams, B. A., & Deli Carpini, M. X. (2000). Unchained reaction: The collapse of media gatekeeping and the Clinton-Lewinsky scandal. *Journalism: Theory, Practice, and Criticism, 1*(1), 61–85.

Williams, B. A., & Deli Carpini, M. X. (2004). Monica and Bill all the time and everywhere: The collapse of gatekeeping and agenda setting in the new media environment. *American Behavioral Scientist, 47*, 1208–1230.

Von Hippel, E. (2005). *Democratizing innovation*. Retrieved December 3, 2008, from http://web.mit.edu/evhippel/www/books.htm.

Part III

The Impact of the Citizen as Mass Communicator

Chapter 8

What the Blogger Knows

Donald Matheson

In April 2003, Jeff Jarvis of "Buzzmachine" called on fellow bloggers to help Iraqis to start blog newspapers, now that Saddam Hussein had been defeated. He wrote:

> The beauty of weblogging is that it is the world's cheapest—no, history's cheapest—means of publishing. Weblogging brings the power of the press down to the people. And these people need it.
>   Of course, the audience in Iraq would be small at the start: tiny.
>   But the audience who can connect in Iraq and the audience elsewhere in the world who read this would be influential. Thus Iraqis would gain a voice in their country and in the world. And this instant free press would exercise muscles of expression that have atrophied in Iraq. It would teach them how to report and comment and how to find the truth from beyond their borders. (Jarvis, 2003)

As evidence grew of the West's misunderstandings of Iraq, Jarvis might have been a little more cautious in the following years. But the comment misunderstands not only Iraqi politics but also blogging on public affairs, and so forms a useful jumping off point for this chapter. Jarvis's post begins and ends, as blog commentary often does, with the technology and with a liberal emphasis on individual freedom. Important as these are to blogging, they have limited explanatory or predictive power. A theory of blogging's power needs to account for differences in the cultural-political context between the different places in which it is used, as a glance at a few blogs from outside the US shows. "Akaevu.net" in Kyrgyzstan, for example, was used for a month in 2005 much as samizdat publications were in Soviet times to republish others' views and then disappeared (see Sulikova & Perlmutter, 2007). The Syrian poet-intellectual Ammar Abdulhamid was exiled as a result of his writings at his blog "Amarji," becoming something of a stateless peace activist (Abdulhamid, 2006). Yan Wenbo, author of an award-winning Chinese photoblog "18mo," which features images and stories of the maltreatment of dogs in the East, was uncomfortable with any political symbolism attached to his writing: "I encourage different interpretations of my blog" (South China Morning Post, 2005). Blogs do not conjure up an "instant free press," but place their authors in a more complex relationship to the norms and forces of social life. Indeed, the technology-freedom-truth triangle invoked above does not explain U.S. blogging very well either. Many critics (see Ceren, 2006; Wall, 2005) note that political blogs, in the years following the September 2001 attacks, have tended towards narrow and fixed ideological positions much of the time.

Hallin and Mancini (2004, p. 2) argue that much of the literature on the media is ethnocentric, reading local contexts as if the model in one country were universal. Blogs are no different, and need to be theorised in terms of their contexts. The U.S. blogosphere probably reflects and contributes to the polarized politics of the country at present. As Lemann (2006) notes, they are, like the pamphleteers of Tudor London, part of the political, social, and cultural contexts in which they have arisen. In particular, the claim that blogs might enable an "instant free press" suggests that blogs in the West are surrounded not just by social and political forces but also by a set of cultural and political assumptions about matters such as the position of the individual, the nature of authority, the line between public and private, and the like. It is perhaps a little early to write the cultural history of the blog in Anglo-American public affairs, but much can already be said about the wider cultural politics without which Anglo-American blogging would not exist. Blogs need, in other words, to be decentered so we can see them as more than technologies and individual voices. This chapter does not seek to do the comparative work for blogs which Hallin and Mancini do for news journalism. By analysing the cultural-political context of Western blogging, however, it opens up understanding of how blogging emerges in a range of cultures around the world.

The chapter addresses three main aspects of blogging, situating them in relation to some wider cultural changes in Western societies. These three aspects are: an emphasis on immediacy; a valuing of the subjective; and a weakening of hierarchical, centralised institutions. The argument is that the way knowledge is produced and understood in blogging in the US or the UK or other Western societies is a product of particular cultural circumstances that have revalued these things. That is, blogs have emerged in this wider context and therefore reflect it. Various metaphors can be used to discuss these cultural politics. Raymond Williams talked of a culture's "structure of feeling" (Williams, 1977). A number of contemporary critics talk, particularly in relation to digital media, of changing "literacies." Rheingold, for example, writes about digital journalism that:

> Now that access to the means of production and distribution is no longer a barrier, the most important remaining ingredient of a truly democratized electronic newsgathering is neither a kind of hardware nor a variety of

software, but a species of literacy—widespread knowledge of how to use these tools to produce news stories that are attention-getting, non-trivial, and credible. (2003)

The ways in which individuals can read and write to achieve credibility and significance within their society, that is, their "literacy" in that society's forms, underpins a richer understanding of blogging.

This is not to deny that blogging is structured by technology. The easy-to-use blogging software and digital media's removal of the need for printing and distribution infrastructure have made it possible for millions of people to launch blogs. The loosely joined nature of the Internet (Weinberger, 2003) perhaps favors small sites such as blogs which link copiously and rapidly to other sites. The statistics of networks can explain the highly unequal distribution of influence between a few "A-list" bloggers and others (Shirky, 2003). But how people use blogs to achieve things—and therefore the power of the blog to affect people's ideas, values and actions—is largely a cultural matter. Building on arguments in Matheson (2004) and Matheson and Allan (2007), I am assuming that, while bloggers are idiosyncratic in many respects, they are drawing upon a shared set of tools by using the genre of the weblog and that these tools are accorded power in culture. We are in the realm of Schudson's (1995, p. 54) point about the news form: "The power of the media lies not only (and not even primarily) in its power to declare things to be true, but in its power to provide the forms in which the declarations will appear."

Decentering blogging also immediately directs attention away from questions about whether or not weblogs are a form of journalism. Rosen's (2005) argument that "professional journalism has entered a period of *declining sovereignty* in news, politics and the provision of facts to public debate" need not mean that the decline correlates directly to a rise in such power for blogs. There is no zero sum relationship between the two. Rather, both are part of wider changes, and questions of what caused what begin to recede. Our attention is also directed away from the political effects of a technology. Whether or not it was blogging that brought about the resignation of Trent Lott,[1] for example, is a question that only arises if the emphasis is on the technology.

The knowledge practices of the blog will be introduced by an example which exemplifies them. The following excerpt comes from a blog—later closed down by the authorities—written from Falluja, Iraq in late 2004 by U.S. tank officer Neil Prakash:

"Good lord. Where the hell is it coming from?" It was funny as hell as we all looked around bewildered. It's a funny thing about getting sniped. You're probably waiting for me to elaborate, but I can't. That's it. It's just funny. OK . . . so some guy has you in his sights and he's trying to kill you. And he hasn't yet. But the bullets are coming damn close. And you don't know

where he is. So that's funny. And for some reason, any time you come real
close to death, but live . . . that's just absurdly funny.

("Armor Geddon", 28 December 2004)

There are echoes in Prakash's writing of Michael Herr's *Dispatches* (Herr, 1977)
from Vietnam, in its inversion of normal moral standards and states of mind and
its celebration of that abnormality. But "Armor Geddon" differs significantly
from that 1970s text. It is written from the war zone, not from the safety of a
hotel room months later. It therefore relates the experience of a soldier, rather
than recreate it, and does very little to distance the emotions that Prakash experiences in fulfilling his mission to kill the enemy. The blog is personal and subjective, describing Prakash's tooth-brushing (under sniper fire), his fears, his
difficulties in staying awake while on patrol and his sense of responsibility for
those he commands. We get little sense of an overview or analysis of war, but
rather jumbled fragments. It is not quite a battlefield diary, nor a letter home,
although it is at times partly those things, for it addresses a wider readership. Yet
neither is it an army report, military history or journalism. The account, then,
is immediate; it is personal; it is situated outside or on the edge of institutionalized ways of talking. These categories will be the focus of the chapter. While
few blogs are as life and death as "Armor Geddon," and differ in many
respects, I argue that Western blogs on aspects of public life tend to share these
characteristics.

Speed

The blog genre is, first, firmly situated within a contemporary speeding up of
social life, not only in the compression of space and time which the technology
enables, but also in the way that compression is made sense of as something to
be valued. The blog offers thoughts and observations as or soon after they are
formed and so produces a sense of a shared present to reader and writer alike. As
the word immediacy nicely signals, Western culture allows the speed of this
communication to become associated with a sense of the communication
being im-mediate, or unmediated, and therefore vividly and self-evidently
real (see Bolter & Grusin, 1999). Blogs belong, then, to a rhetoric of real-time
reality.

They offer in particular what one reviewer called the "reality of the moment"
(Levy, 2003). Entries are time and date-stamped to signal that they come from
a particular point in time, and their descent down the page as new entries are
posted signals that they are of less value the longer ago they were written. They
tend also to be about the moment they were written, responding to news articles
or other bloggers' posts or to something in the blogger's experiences. Thus the
blog compresses the gap between the writer and the reader or, if read some time
later, takes the reader to the moment that the blog was written. A New Zealand
blogger, David Slack, writes:

> This morning at the gym a man collapsed and they called an ambulance. It occurred to me as I saw them go to work with the defibrillator that I hadn't seen one deployed in real life before. ("Island Life", 24 June 2007)

Unlike narrative, the blog does not recreate a moment, but belongs to that moment. It thus often provides seemingly instant commentary, without the distance of extended reflection or placing the moment within a larger argument or story—no thought goes unsaid, as someone unkindly put it.

Why we have become so literate in these first drafts is a complex question. It is surely associated, though, with a general speeding up of the means of communication which has turned waiting into delay, with television's heavy marketing of live media events as the pre-eminent moments of shared consciousness in society (see Dayan & Katz, 1992; White, 2006), and with the centrality of journalism and its fascination with newness (see Schlesinger, 1987) in wider culture. Such faster and less edited accounts are also associated with a distrust of the normally hidden processes of selecting and editing which characterize the institutions of communication. As one television producer told Seib of her genre:

> The technology has progressed to the point that it allows the viewer to see more of the process of gathering news . . . People are seeing news as it develops. And I'm not sure that's bad. It kind of hits at some of the criticism of the media for slanting the news. You can't say it was slanted when it was live. (cited in Seib, 2001, p. 44)

While such statements are clearly inadequate, they make sense to the extent that they do because of what Virilio (1994) terms the contemporary acceleration of culture. Similarly, the instant rebuttal on a blog (such as Melanie Griffith rebutting gossip in the entertainment media about her marriage at melaniegriffith.com) can claim to be genuine because it stands outside institutions of politics, media or public relations, by virtue of its speed. It promises to be free of the distortions—whether of fact or emphasis or ideology—that the dominant media of television and print are accused of. Speed is linked in our culture to veracity.

At the same time, however, emerging digital forms such as blogging are not wholly explained by this logic. Bolter and Grusin (1999) argue that there is also a competing logic at work in the way digital media "remediate" existing forms. While sometimes drawing on and emphasizing media claims to immediacy, they sometimes also draw attention to themselves as acts of mediation and therefore position author and reader as having a more distanced and sophisticated knowledge of the real. Bolter and Grusin call this reflexive rhetoric of some emerging media "hypermediacy." Fagerjord (2003) details how multimedia texts draw upon these twin logics, claiming to take audiences directly to a shared experience of the real while at the same time highlighting the intervening presence of digital technologies. This double rhetoric is partly about technology—the camcorder, the webcam, the blog and other technologies have all allowed audiences more intimate relations with producers of media at the same time as they have put knowledge about mediation in people's hands. We can all see how real lives can be mediated and how that mediation distorts. But it is also a cultural matter, a matter of literacy. Rushkoff (1994, p. 182) points to the emergence of a "prototypically GenX mixture of cynicism and innocence" in young people's media of the 1990s, such as "Beavis and Butt-head" and MTV's reality programming, as people who had grown up with these technologies started working in the media industry. Media about reality—and about the unreality of reality media—have become popular. Blogs often exhibit just such a doubleness. The Baghdad blogger Salam Pax's description of watching CNN images of bombers take off from England for his home city is one example. While the planes are still six hours away, he sketches in a few words the unreality of seeing one's own possibly imminent death represented on the television. At the same time as Salam's blog takes readers with powerful immediacy to his home, it reminds Western readers of the thinness of both their televisual knowledge of the war and of the language of democracy and freedom which set them loose. Blogs and similar media can provide this combination of presence and distance largely because of a second characteristic I wish to discuss, their emphasis on the person.

Personal

Blogs are, as Cohen (2006) notes, criticized for being both too public and too private. They conflate these categories that were previously kept relatively separate, and so are at once open to the charge of making public things that should be kept private and the charge of dwelling narcissistically on the self. They clearly challenge prevailing norms of talk, as the actions of editors, generals, employers and university authorities to close down or stifle blogs attest. Bloggers do not do so by themselves, because they are part of a wider challenge to norms around matters such as professionalism, rational debate, privacy and selfhood that have enabled the emergence of personal media.

Weblogs are, however, among the most personal of personal media. The words, images and links in a blog tend to build up meaning first and foremost in terms of the selfhood being projected there, rather than in terms of narrative or argument or conversation or some other structure of what discourse analysts call "coherence." Bruce Rolston talks on his blog, "Flit," at one moment about the failure of U.S. security to protect Samarra's sacred mosque, Al-Askari, and the next about how many times he died on the game, "Lord of the Rings Online," last night. The two are not connected, as they would have to be in almost any other genre, but co-exist as parts of the personality Ralston projects. Other blogs may be more narrowly focused on one topic, but need not be, for the blog genre allows a minimal level of coherence, held together largely by the selfhood of the blogger. The coherence of the blog around the blogger is particularly evident when we consider the nature of the blog audience—usually a key aspect of any genre. While television journalism, for example, is placed in quite specific ways in relation to the public which it addresses, entertains and speaks on behalf of (Ekström, 2002), blogging may take on many roles, sometimes in the same post. Bloggers will talk of their posts sometimes as spaces for themselves, to remember or to sort out their thoughts or to experiment, and sometimes as aimed at diffuse audiences. "[I]t's more a question of someone writing a journal in public. It's not addressed to everybody so much as to god knows who," the linguist Geoff Nunberg (2001) comments. Again, the center in terms of which the blog holds is the individual who is expressing him or herself in multiple ways.

Blogging can be used for purposes other than ones involving the projection of personality—sharing information within a company, for example—but can be made sense of in terms of those other purposes only up to a point. Thus while journalists made heavy use of material from text and photo blogs after the London Underground bombings in June 2005, many of the bloggers themselves did not appear to see what they did primarily in those terms. Alfie Dennen of the site "Photoblog" talked of such citizen journalism as "more focused on the idea of communication and using technology to really engage with people than doing the job of journalists" (Holliday, 2006). Photobloggers whom Cohen (2005) interviewed appeared more focused on sharing images with others than with taking them or recording an aspect of the world. As Herring et al. (2004) note of blogging in general, the "common purpose" seems to be to share a subjective response to matters of interest to the self. Recording the world itself tends to be secondary to interpersonal goals in the blog, which, at times when it interrelates with genres such as journalism, may pull them towards such goals.

The extent to which blogs are part of a wider privileging of the subjective is clear from the digital media literature. Media that project versions of the self have been tracked in computer games (Turkle, 1995), home pages (Cheung, 2004), webcams (Turner, 2004), reality television (Dovey, 2000), social software, to mention just some. Attention should be directed, then, as much to the weakening of social norms that have kept the private and public self apart as to the particular genre. Baudrillard (1994) argues that "to be someone" in contemporary culture, particularly young people's culture, entails being in the media. He links this to a collapse of the distinctions between public and private. Certainly, a number of commentators note that, for a range of reasons from the rise of identity politics to the weakening of nation states to media technologies which allow vast audiences to be convened, it is becoming harder for people to imagine the public they are meant to be part of (see Peters, 1995; cited in Fernback, 1997, p. 37). They instead convene their own micro-publics around their selves or their immediate circles, something inconceivable even 20 years ago.

We need to read bloggers' statements of opinion and expression, then, not simply as assertions of individuality, but as a kind of politics which moves in the wake of the cultural political upheavals since the 1960s and the increasing centrality of media as sites of social power. As Kahn and Kellner note, blogs are part of an attempt to reconvene politics in citizen-produced media around everyday life (Kahn & Kellner, 2003). It is in that context that statements such as Salam Pax's below resonate:

> please stop sending emails asking if I were for real, don't belive it? then don't read it. I am not anybody's propaganda ploy, well except my own.
>
> ("Where is Raed?", 23 March 2003)

The blogger participates in defining his own reality, and withdraws to an extent from the claim to have a public reality or to be part of others' politics. Certainly Salam was not reducible to dominant versions of the Iraqi citizen, either White House claims that Iraqis welcomed liberation or Saddam Hussein's claim that his people would resist to the death. Positioning himself partly in Iraqi life and partly in a Western public sphere—he was writing in English—he brought the conflict "down to the level of the rising price of water for families holed up in Baghdad" (Griffiths, 2003, p. 159).

The idea of "being yourself" is only partly sustainable. As critics such as Tolson (2001) and Couldry (2003) show, being "authentic" in media forms lies partly in projecting a version of the self that appears real in media terms and gains validity from its reflection of media representations. But nonetheless the "project of the self," as some cultural studies scholars describe it, appears relevant to how audiences make sense of and value blogs. In research on journalists' blogs from Iraq in 2003 Stuart Allan and I found many instances of bloggers citing the enthusiasm of readers of their personal accounts of war (which were often not intended as public texts but as journals for family and friends) as more credible and thus in some sense more real (Matheson & Allan, 2007). Blogs took readers "behind the scenes" of the public persona into the informal space of descriptions of the everyday. Chris Allbritton, whose reporting from Iraq in 2003–2005 was partly funded by readers of his blog, "Back to Iraq," quoted one of his readers who liked:

> the independence it gave you the reporter. No agendas except your own, which is perfectly acceptable to me. No one is totally objective, but you gave more personal perspectives of 'behind the scenes' of what it takes to do what you do, which was terribly fascinating to me.
>
> (Allbritton, 2003, p. 83)

Many readers of blogs appear comfortable with the subjective version of reality produced there. In information theory's terms, the "provenance" of the information is available for all to see, allowing people to assess it better (Rogerson,

2007). When Riverbend posted accounts on her blog, "Baghdad Burning," of the disappearance of people off the streets of the city in a wave of ethnic cleansing, the fact that her own life was at risk and that she was hearing gossip from neighbors and family (and labeled it as such) and the fact she could move around the city made her version of events more credible for many Western readers than journalistic accounts whose provenance was unclear and possibly the results of propaganda, speculation or cultural ignorance. As Rosen (2005) notes, citing *Newsweek* chief political correspondent Howard Fineman, traditional forms of public information which privilege formal, authoritative and impartial modes are coming under some pressure:

> The notion of a neutral, non-partisan mainstream press was, to me at least, worth holding onto. Now it's pretty much dead, at least as the public sees things.

Subjective voices responding to reality as they see it have steadily risen in value. Thus blogs belong in some sense to a cultural phenomenon of which the rise of Fox News's partisan political news, the popularity of the caustic humor of the "Daily Show," the ballooning of comments pages in newspapers are also part.

De-Institutionalized

The power of these more subjective modes lies only partly in Bill O'Reilly's inability to see past his own politics or in the intimacy of some bloggers' observations. A sociologist would point to their position with respect to institutional power. Blogging's subjective voices are much less dependent than, for example, journalists' on people above them in a hierarchy. The blogger's claim to value does not need to be buttressed by editors, sub-editors or copy editors, fact checkers, other colleagues or the brand of the news organization. Authority lies more in the reader's knowledge of whether the blog was written in the early hours of the morning or mid-afternoon (recorded in the date stamp), where it was written, how the blogger was feeling at the time, how consistent the statement was with other expressions of the blogger, the hyperlinks to other material which the blogger provided, the quality of the argument, the position of the blogger in relation to others, and the like. So Brian Stelter's news industry gossip blog, "Newser," gradually gained authority, although the young man (aged 19 in 2005) had apparently never set foot in a newsroom, as it became known as a place where journalists leaked insider news (McIntosh, 2005, p. 387). Its power lay in its readers' knowledge of its author's position in the circulation of news gossip.

The interpersonal nature of authority evident here constitutes a challenge for forms of publicness where rationality and fact have been central, where, as Habermas puts it, citizens are asked to leave aside their personal interests. Cohen (2006, p. 166) suggests that "the trouble with blogs . . . is not that they are written by ordinary people but that those ordinary people have become too visible, which is to say visible precisely in their ordinariness, precisely in their self-interested individualism." Although not yet legitimate in the eyes of its critics, the blog makes sense in terms of the individual no longer reluctant to speak publicly as an individual. Again, we should be cautious of placing too much emphasis on blogging as having a causative role in this trend. Castells proposes that a long term process of de-institutionalizing can be seen in the networks enabled by communications technology, the globalization of capitalism and the rise of identity politics. He notes the emergence of informational elites who are key players in the networks of knowledge which he sees as increasingly defining both social power and economic productivity. He sees power shifting from the heads of corporations, officials and elected politicians to, as Webster puts it:

> the real movers and shakers, those information workers who operate on the networks, fixing deals here and there, working on a project that finds a market niche, owing more commitment to people like themselves than to the particular company which happens to employ them for the time being.
>
> (Webster, 2006, p. 103)

The impact of such network actors can be seen in many examples, from MoveOn.org, a network founded online by a wealthy couple in San Francisco in disgust at the news media's obsession with Bill Clinton's sex life which then mobilized hundreds of thousands to petition their political representatives, to the book-sharing site, bookcrossing.com, where half a million people are involved in passing books on to each other, at no charge, once they have read them. Networks, as Castells puts it, become a space of considerable power, distinct from modern institutions such as companies, political parties or libraries. Prakash, the milblogger cited earlier, had considerable power (until his blog was closed down) in representing the killing in Falluja as a triumph of American technology and comradeship, as *Wired* magazine, an NPR interview and word of mouth drove readers to his site. Yet he inhabited no official language and spoke from no legitimated position in the military bureaucracy. As a form of knowledge, the blog operates in Castells' "space of flows," and takes some of the power to describe the truth of war into that space.

Again, the actions of individuals in carving out that space, even the strong-willed or the entrepreneurial, should not be over-emphasized. Placing blogging within a wider picture of changing ways of thinking and acting helps account for the millions of blogs that are in existence, and it is illuminated by these parallels. Leadbetter and Miller (2004) investigate the rise of amateurs in British culture, suggesting that a trend for people to invest time and energy in unpaid work to professional standard signals a shift towards bottom-up self-organization. Similarly, Jenkins (2004) argues that a "cultural convergence" is taking place alongside the technological convergence of digital media, in which media consumers expect that they can change and add to media content (see also Deuze 2005; Lessig 2004). The contributors to the *Cluetrain Manifesto* (Levine 1999) express the desire that business structures be recast along the interpersonal—markets should become conversations, in the slogan. The advertising agency Saatchi and Saatchi has sought to recast brands as the more interpersonal category of Lovemarks, which "reach your heart as well as your mind, creating an intimate, emotional connection that you just can't live without" (Saatchi n.d.). A picture emerges of a general weakening of deference towards authority (expressed in stronger form as a distrust of institutions), a strengthening of consumerism as an economic driver and struggle over corporate capitalism's increasing encroachment upon the cultural.

Conclusion

Blogs in Western cultures are not, then, reducible to conventional politics—they cannot be read simply as liberal democracy in action, nor evidence of a renewed public sphere, for they operate partly outside the institutions of politics and outside the values of public debate. Haas (2005) notes that politically oriented blogs—certainly in the US in the period immediately after the September 11 attacks—have tended to be echo chambers for existing elite sources of news and opinion. Warblogging in particular "depends upon the remediation of mainstream media content" (Redden, 2003, p. 162; cited in Haas, 2005, p. 390), and thereby strengthens the dominance of those views. In the light that Jarvis and others cast on blogging, such activity is something of a failure, but in the light of the argument presented here, the direct political impacts of blogging are less important beside the energy of debate unleashed there and the ways relationships are formed. Similarly, the elevation into the elite of A-list bloggers such as Juan Cole, who was one of many unheeded experts before he began to critique U.S. foreign policy on his blog "Informed Comment" and who has since become a major media commentator and spoken to official groups in Washington (Drezner & Farrell, 2004), can be read as evidence of blogging's failure to carve out a space independent of the media or of existing power structures. Or it can be read as evidence for Castells' thesis of informal networks of power.

The point here is not to explain away the emergence of this distinctive form of communication. Nor is it to attempt to enumerate all the antecedents of the genre. It is rather to decenter the blog in order for us to explore the cultural-political context in which it operates and therefore see blogging more clearly. For, to continue Haas's metaphor, the blog's echo of the political and media establishment does not sound the same as that establishment. While often media-centric, staking out much the same territory as journalism, in its practices of selecting, commenting on and to an extent gathering information (Lowrey, 2006, p. 478), the blog does so according to an epistemology which combines immediacy and hypermediacy, which is focused on the subjective and which is not assimilable to institutional ways of thinking. As Glenn Reynolds of "Instapundit" puts it in just the provocative way that blogging understands itself, in blogging "the term 'correspondent' is reverting to its original meaning of 'one who corresponds,' rather than the more recent one of 'well-paid microphone-holder with good hair'" (Reynolds 2003, p. 82). These kinds of challenge to the meaning of cultural categories come into focus in this interpretation.

I would further argue that interpreting blogging in this light is particularly important when considering its potential or actual impact on the practices of journalism. Dennen's observation that most photobloggers were not doing journalism when they published their images of the London Underground bombings signals that it is the categories of public knowledge themselves that are being inflected here. Blogging does not directly destabilise news journalism as the primary arbiter of events in society, for it is doing something slightly different. The parallel with alternative media, which share many of blogging's characteristics, is apposite. A number of alternative media theorists argue that they should be assessed less according to their impact on politics and journalism than the power they give to people to define themselves or contribute to group cohesion (Atton, 2002; Rodríguez, 2001). Decentering the blog, and thus stepping outside the para-ideology of blogging, is important for analysis of its wider significance.

Note

1 Trent Lott was the U.S. Senate majority leader until 2004. Comments he made at a birthday party for the elderly senator Strom Thurmond which suggested the country would have been better off if the then segregationist Thurmond had become U.S. president were largely ignored in national news media until a group of liberal bloggers complained loudly. Lott, perhaps already weakened within the Republican Party, later resigned. See Scott (2004).

References

Abdulhamid, A. (2006, June 14). Just the facts: Truth and the Internet. *Open Democracy*. Retrieved June 27, 2007, from http://www.opendemocracy.net/arts-Literature/pen4_3643.jsp.

Allbritton, C. (2003, Fall). Blogging from Iraq. *Nieman Reports*, 57(3), 82–84. Retrieved July 2, 2004, from http://www.nieman.harvard.edu/reports/03-3NRfall/V57N3.pdf

Atton, C. (2002). *Alternative media*. London: Sage.

Baudrillard, J. (1994). The procession of simulacra. In B. Wallis, & M. Tucker (Eds.), *After modernism: Rethinking representation* (pp. 253–282). Boston: David R. Godine.

Bolter, J. D., & Grusin, R. A. (1999). *Remediation: Understanding new media*. Cambridge, MA: MIT Press.

Ceren, O. (2006). Weblogs: Producers, users and effects on the public sphere. Paper presented at ICA conference, Dresden, June 19–23.

Cheung, C. (2004). *Identity construction and self-presentation on personal homepages: Emancipatory potentials and reality constraints* (2nd ed.). London: Arnold.

Cohen, K. R. (2005). What does the photoblog want? *Media, Culture and Society, 27,* 883–901.

Cohen, K. R. (2006). A welcome for blogs. *Continuum,* 20, 161–173.

Couldry, N. (2003). *Media rituals: A critical approach.* London: Routledge.

Dayan, D., & Katz, E. (1992). *Media events: The live broadcasting of history.* Cambridge, MA: Harvard University Press.

Deuze, M. (2005). Towards professional participatory storytelling in journalism and advertising. *Firstmonday,* 10(7). Retrieved March 15, 2006, from http://www.firstmonday.org/issues/issue10_7/index.html.

Dovey, J. (2000). *Freakshow: First-person media and factual television.* London: Pluto.

Drezner, D.W., & Farrell, H. (2004). Web of influence. *Foreign Policy, 145,* 32–40.

Ekström, M. (2002). Epistemologies of TV journalism. *Journalism,* 3(3), 259–282.

Fagerjord, A. (2003). Rhetorical convergence: Studying web media. In G. Liestøl, A. Morrison, & T. Rasmussen (Eds.), *Digital media revisited: Theoretical and conceptual innovation in digital domains* (pp. 293–326). Cambridge, MA: MIT University Press.

Fernback, J. (1997). The individual within the collective: Virtual ideology and the realization of collective principles. In S. Jones (Ed.), *Virtual culture: Identity and communication in cybersociety* (pp. 36–54). London: Sage.

Griffiths, M. (2003). e-Citizens: Blogging as democratic practice. *Electronic Journal of e-Government,* 2(3). Retrieved 2 September, 2006, from http://www.ejeg.com/volume-2/volume2-issue3/v2-i3-art2.htm.

Haas, T. (2005). From "public journalism" to the "public's journalism"? Rhetoric and reality in the discourse on weblogs. *Journalism Studies,* 6, 387–396.

Hallin, D. C., & Mancini, P. (2004). *Comparing media systems: Three models of media and politics.* Cambridge: Cambridge University Press.

Herr, M. (1977). *Dispatches* (1st ed.). New York: Knopf.

Herring, S. C., Kouper, I., Scheidt, L. A., & Wright, E. L. (2004). Women and children last: The discursive construction of weblogs. In L. Gurak, S. Antonijevic, L. Johnson, C. Ratliff, & J. Reyman (Eds.), *Into the blogosphere: Rhetoric, community, and culture of weblogs.* Retrieved from http://blog.lib.umn.edu/blogosphere/.

Holliday, G. (2006, March 24). Panning for gold in the blogosphere. *Press Gazette,* p. R8.

Jarvis, J. (2003, April 11). The Baghdad blog times. *Buzzmachine.* Retrieved June 30, 2004, from http://www.buzzmachine.com/archives/2003_04_11.html#003480.

Jenkins, H. (2004). The cultural logic of media convergence. *International Journal of Cultural Studies,* 7(1), 33–43.

Kahn, R., & Kellner, D. (2003). *Internet subcultures and political activism.* Retrieved June 1, 2003, from http://www.gseis.ucla.edu/courses/ed253a/oppositionalinternet.htm.

Leadbetter, C., & Miller, P. (2004). *The pro-am revolution: How enthusiasts are changing our economy and society.* London: Demos. Retrieved from http://www.demos.co.uk/files/proamrevolutionfinal.pdf.

Lemann, N. (2006, August 7 & 14). Amateur hour: Journalism without journalists. *New Yorker,* pp. 44–49.

Lessig, L. (2004). *Free culture: How big media uses technology and the law to lock down culture and control creativity.* New York: Penguin.

Levine, R. (1999). *The cluetrain manifesto: The end of business as usual.* Cambridge, MA: Perseus.

Levy, S. (2003, March 28). Blogger's delight. *Newsweek Web Exclusive*. Retrieved September 30, 2005, from http://www.msnbc.com.

Lowrey, W. (2006). Mapping the journalism-blogging relationship. *Journalism, 7*, 477–500.

Matheson, D. (2004). Weblogs and the epistemology of the news: Some trends in online journalism. *New Media and Society, 6*, 443–468.

Matheson, D. & Allan, S. (2007). Truth in a war zone: The role of warblogs in Iraq. In R. Keeble & S. Maltby (Eds.), *Communicating war: Memory, media, military* (pp. 75–89). Cambridge: Cambridge Scholars Press.

McIntosh, S. (2005). Blogs: Has their time finally come—or gone? *Global Media and Communication, 1*, 385–388.

Nunberg, G. (2001, October 12). I have seen the future, and it blogs. *Commentary on Fresh Air*. Retrieved July 1, 2004, from http://www.ischool.berkeley.edu/~nunberg/blog.html.

Peters, J. D. (1995). Historical tensions in the concept of public opinion. In T. L. Glasser & C. T. Salmon (Eds.), *Public opinion and the communication of consent* (pp. 3–32). New York: Guilford Press.

Redden, G. (2003). Read the whole thing: Journalism, weblogs and the remediation of the war in Iraq. *Media International Australia, 109*, 153–166.

Reynolds, G. (2003, Fall). Weblogs and journalism: Back to the future? *Nieman Reports, 57*(3), 81–82.

Rheingold, H. (2003, July 7). Moblogs seen as a crystal ball for a new era in online journalism. *Online Journalism Review*. Retrieved July 11, 2003, from http://www.ojr.org/ojr/technology/1057780670.php

Rodríguez, C. (2001). *Fissures in the mediascape: An international study of citizens' media*. Cresskill, NJ: Hampton Press

Rogerson, S. (2007). Information and integrity in the information age. *Ethical Space, 4* (1–2), 10–12.

Rosen, J. (2005, January 21). Bloggers vs. journalists is over. *PressThink*. Retrieved November 23, 2006, from http://journalism.nyu.edu/pubzone/weblogs/pressthink/2005/01/21/berk_essay.html.

Rushkoff, D. (1994). *The GenX reader*. New York: Ballantine Books.

Schlesinger, P. (1987). *Putting "reality" together: BBC News*. London: Methuen.

Schudson, M. (1995). *The power of news*. London: Harvard University Press.

Scott, E. (2004). *"Big media" meets the "bloggers": Coverage of Trent Lott's remarks at Strom Thurmond's birthday party: Case study* (Joan Shorenstein Center on the Press, Politics and Public Policy). Retrieved September 15, 2006, from http://www.ksg.harvard.edu/presspol/Research_Publications/case_studies.shtml.

Seib, P.M. (2001). *Going live: Getting the news right in a real-time, online world*. Lanham, MD: Rowman & Littlefield.

Shirky, C. (2003). *Power laws, weblogs, and inequality*. Retrieved March 25, 2004, from http://www.shirky.com/writings/powerlaw_weblog.html.

South China Morning Post (2005, January 17). Don't be led astray. *South China Morning Post*, p. 5.

Sulikova, S. V., & Perlmutter, D. D. (2007). Blogging down the dictator? The Kyrgyz revolution and *samizdat* websites. *International Communication Gazette, 69*(1), 29–50.

Tolson, A. (2001). "Being yourself": The pursuit of authentic celebrity. *Discourse Studies, 3*, 443–457.

Turkle, S. (1995). *Life on the screen: Identity in the age of the Internet.* New York: Simon and Schuster.

Turner, G. (2004). *Understanding celebrity.* London: Sage.

Virilio, P. (1994). *The vision machine* (J. Rose, Trans.). Bloomington: Indiana University Press.

Wall, M. (2005). Blogging Gulf War II. *Journalism Studies, 7*(1), 111–126.

Webster, F. (2006). *Theories of the information society* (3rd ed.). London: Routledge.

Weinberger, D. (2003). *Small pieces loosely joined: A unified theory of the web.* Cambridge, MA: Perseus.

White, M. (2006). Television and Internet differences by design. *Convergence, 12,* 341–355.

Williams, R. (1977). *Marxism and literature.* Oxford: Oxford University Press.

Chapter 9

"Searching for My Own Unique Place in the Story"

A Comparison of Journalistic and Citizen-Produced Coverage of Hurricane Katrina's Anniversary

Sue Robinson

It is said that journalism offers America its first draft of history. When anniversaries of historic events arrive, reporters have the task of framing the country's collective memory of the particular incident. In their writings, journalists compose the map to yesterday so that the country can navigate similar situations tomorrow. They recount the event through a lens of hindsight, politicizing it and polishing its memory as they propose agendas for change. Upon the anniversaries of World War II, John F. Kennedy's assassination, Watergate, September 11 and other tragedies, the press attempted to make sense of what was otherwise incomprehensible (Kitch, 2003; Schudson, 1992; Sturken, 1997; Zelizer, 1992). Similarly, when the catastrophic August 2005 event of Hurricane Katrina and the destruction of New Orleans created national rifts in America, the nation looked to the press in the ensuing year to explain the inadequacies and inconsistencies.

During the storm, journalists descended upon the cities and reported about the dying, the missing, the crime, the looting, the rescuing, the despairing, and the blaming. Where government failed in its response, the press stepped in and named itself a savior (Fry, 2006). Reporters told personal stories of fishing people and animals out of the swollen waters. They challenged official reports. They patted themselves on the back. When the anniversary arrived in late 2006, the press set out to retell that story so the nation could process its recovery and prepare for the next one (Kurtz, 2006; Stanley, 2006). However, in this tragedy, the press had help retelling the hurricane story. In thousands of web sites, citizens were remembering in their own way. They offered up their own agenda for moving forward from the catastrophe.

This chapter examines a long-standing tradition of the press to help society form its collective memory of tragedy as that role is evolving for the Internet. The research draws from the literature of the journalistic authority in writing America's history. Medium theory also informs the work, for web scholars have suggested that traditional institutional relationships must give way in an interactive, multimedia environment. The evidence presented in this chapter suggests that online versions of Hurricane Katrina memory differed significantly from the ones found in the mainstream media. Where journalists politicized the event for Americanized community building, the web celebrated the individual account, which was put forward by citizens seeking their own "unique place in the story" (Saizan, 2006). Citizens posed topics for agenda setting, but used the forums to form a unique community around those with an insider's perspective on the hurricane. As a result, the notion of commemoration—in this case, what the anniversary of Hurricane Katrina should mean—was renegotiated in this space, and at the same time, the individual's "self" was situated alongside the journalist as an authoritative memory writer.

The Press: Writing History for a Nation

Considered a political institution, the press has long played a pivotal role as a societal guide directing national discourse. Through journalism, audiences discover a broader meaning that can suggest not only what people should think about (Cohen, 1963), but also affirm who they are and what they believe (Carey, 1989/1992; Hall, 1986; Williams, 1969). This is especially true of crisis coverage. Kitch (2003) argued that the way in which popular magazines write about tragedy reflects the need to find a communal connection with others in the middle of social crisis. Kitch (2005) noted how in the wake of the September 11 terrorist attacks, the press declared firefighters to be heroes— mirroring a trend in American culture at that time to adhere heroic qualities to working-class members. This represented an extension of the American dream analogy. Reporters thus can moralize through such depictions, guiding citizens with lessons to resolve the current crisis and mitigate the ones to come.

In doing this, the press writes the first draft of history, a draft that inevitably reflects the broader, current cultural value systems and national ambiance at the time of the writing (Schudson, 1992). Indeed, often there is a rewriting of what actually happened so that the ultimate historical draft has become politicized (Schudson, 1992; Sturken, 1999) and framed accordingly (Schwartz, 1998). Sense and order can be gained from something that was nonsensical and disorderly. Journalists, in their gatekeeping processes, select certain images and words over others and, thus, present and perpetuate certain collective memories over others (Schwartz, 1998; Zelizer, 1992). Journalists try to imbue credibility into these retellings by offering their own shared experiences as eyewitnesses and official chroniclers (Carlson, 2007; Kitch, 2005; Zelizer, 1992). The tendencies combined with the profession's narrative and documentary styles (Edy, 1999; Zelizer, 1992) position the press as an entertaining yet authoritative teller of the past (Kitch, 2005).

This allows the country to "move forward" (Kitch, 2003), but also to "forget" the transgressions of the past (Zelizer, 1992). Looking backwards to understand the present sets an agenda for the future (Benton & Frazier, 1976; Maher & Chiasson, 1995; Schudson, 1992). Anniversaries of crises offer a chance to solidify or recast that ideological platform put forward by the press at the time of the initial crisis (Frijda, 1997; Schudson, 1992).

For their part, audiences accept the press as an institutional authority by acknowledging the established agenda (McCombs & Shaw, 1972) and participating in the rituals that journalists offer (Carey, 1989/1992; Kitch, 2005; Rothenbhuler, 1998). Of course public memory has always been a constructed thing, something formed "in a realm where the small-and the large-scale structures of society intersected" (Bodnar, 1994, p. 245). For every unified and presented collective explanation of the past, vernacular cultural worlds offer preferred alternative meanings. Indeed, Schudson (1992) noted the variety and complexities involved in all the collective memories of one event, often buried in the "fundamental social processes of social life that are not specifically or self-consciously devoted to memory" (p. 65). However, even the alternative memories that contradict the official past lack the power of dissemination and longevity of a more institutional accounting (Bodnar, 1994).

> Regardless of the number of forums that existed or the complexity of communication over the past, however, the dialogic activity examined here almost always stressed the desirability of maintaining the social order and existing structures, the need to avoid disorder or dramatic change, the dominance of citizen duties over citizen rights, and the need to privilege national over local and personal interests. (Bodnar, 1994, p. 246)

The Internet and History Writing

The choice of medium matters in this process of information control, especially as authorial and consumption power expand and distill with new agency over content (McLuhan, 1994/1998; Meyrowitz, 1985). Holocaust scholar Jonathan Webber wrote that "all too often we ignore the medium of representation and assume that it gives us immediate and unmediated access to the past" (Webber as cited in Zelizer, 1992, p. 239). In fact, though, "the past becomes present only though representation," Webber added. In particular, the Web's combining of media and interactive attributes gives an enhanced manipulative power to audiences over that representative form. For example, bloggers consciously produce content in order to have some control over history, news, and other societal information apart from media (Kaye, 2007).

As a result, first-person accounts of events, audio, photos, and diaries—all the primary-source material used by historians and journalists alike (Davidson & Lytle, 2004)—can be published en mass online. Such unauthorized agency eliminates the (ideological/biased) mediation of a third-party historian or journalist (Carmichael, 2003). Note how Joshua Meyrowitz wrote about the introduction of new technology back in 1985:

> And through electronic "documents," future generations will experience a new sort of past. "History" was once a discursive script written and

acted by the rich, the powerful, and the educated . . . The growing archives of audio and videotape, however, thrust the common person into history. (p. 109)

Calling the digital medium "an eternity service," one scholar noted that the ability to post documentation directly into the public domain "may allow more effective reparations and the reconstruction of civil society structures" (Carmichael, 2003, p. 21). Historians have suggested that when people are allowed to "experience" the past by physically revisiting sites important to the past, for example, they viewed that information with more credibility. Personal accounts of the past have been viewed as more authoritative (Rosenzweig & Thelen, 1998).

Online, people are forming communities where they are virtually revisiting the past of their own selection, creating "meta places of memory," according to Sade-Beck (2004). People can go to the web to find a public-private realm in which co-produced memorialization can occur across media platforms (Geser, 1998; Foot & Schneider, 2002; Foot, Warnick, & Schnedier, 2005; Martini, 2003; Schneider & Dougherty, 2003). Foot, Warnick, and Schneider (2005) found that web sites following September 11 terrorist attacks served as extensions of funerals and personal grieving rituals. The virtual world's multimedia and interactivity provide a convenient site for acts of mourning, in some cases replacing the memorial site pilgrimages to the Vietnam Memorial or Ground Zero (Martini, 2003; Foot et al., 2005). On the web, the personal grief rituals take on more communal qualities, according to Warnick's evaluation of 9/11 sites.

But Sade-Beck (2004) pointed out that in these spaces of remembering often the citizen becomes stuck in a virtual time, always at the time of the crisis. Though the technology does allow a link between past, present, and future, the citizen lingers in the memory. This could mean a stymieing or stifling of any agenda that might otherwise be presented in these spaces. And Meyrowitz pointed out that the individual's production of history tends to be the "every day" experience without context, resulting in a "vacuum in our understanding of the past" (1985, p. 109). It should also be noted that some scholars (most notably McCombs, 2004) dismiss the notion that citizens have any agency to produce any kind of a consistent, cohesive agenda for the country, at least one that is contrary to the journalistic version. Other researchers have found support that there can be a reciprocal exchange of agendas between media (Ku et al., 2003; Lee et al., 2005).

This literature indicates that any collective memory put forward by the press as well as any agenda for change resulting from that memory could potentially be challenged online. Such a challenge might result in a less cohesive story with little direction or blueprint for the future. Scholars have pontificated on the meaning to come out of the hurricane news coverage, including a tendency to show American institutions enduring (Kitch & Hume, 2008), a reliance on the populace in addition to official sourcing (Durham, 2008), and the declaration by journalists that they were the heroes of the crisis (Fry, 2006; Littlefield & Quenette, 2007). The citizen journalism during the event revealed otherwise marginalized voices discussing race, class, community, and national ideology (Allan, 2006). But it is the *anniversary* of Hurricane Katrina that might indicate the more enduring collective memory. Studying how journalists and citizens online covered the tragedy a year later offered an opportunity to explore the possibility that a less cohesive storyline will emerge, as expressed in this news story from August 2006:

> Researchers believe the variety of testimony and individual stories available online could ultimately make history more democratic, Scheinfeldt says. "I think for the history of 9/11 and the history of (Hurricane) Katrina, I think it's much less going to be the history of George Bush's experience of 9/11 and much more the experience of you and me," he says. (Newman, 2006, p. 8D)

How did the citizens' "coverage" of the anniversary differ from the press's reports, if at all? (In other words, how were people remembering the Hurricane Katrina tragedy in these web spaces compared to how the press said they were remembering?) What agenda for change was presented in these forums, and how did that agenda differ from the press coverage, if it did? A third research question nuanced this discussion: How did the citizen coverage of this anniversary challenge the press's institutional authority to tell the ultimate story of Hurricane Katrina? A textual and discourse analysis attempted to answer these research questions.

A Signature Matrix

The first two research questions were explored using a framework adapted from Gamson and Lasch's "signature matrix" (1983), which is essentially a template for analyzing a news story's frames and overall meaning. This concept holds that political, economic, social and cultural ideas hang together in harmonious groupings. In media, news stories offer specific frames and ideologies that shape political and cultural thinking (Bennett, 2003; Goffman, 1974, to name just a few). Gamson and Lasch (1983) suggested a framework for drawing out the connection of specific content to the overall culture. Each cultural artifact represents a "package," which is made up of a series of elements that provide the signature for the particular way of thinking characterizing the overall curriculum of coverage. I have adapted his template for the purposes of looking at memory construction specifically. The analysis documented: Core themes, catchphrases and exemplars, character depictions, and agendas present in the samples. Of course, there were many stories to come out of Hurricane Katrina, and there may be many enduring collective memories as the recovery continues. But this analysis uncovered a version of a particular cultural flashpoint (Schudson, 1992) as presented in the anniversary at the end of summer 2006.

The third research question required a larger discourse analysis, based on the answers to the first two. Discourse analysis examines the flow of information between texts according to a more macro understanding of some paradigm, such as press-citizen constructs of collective memory laid out in the literature review. The resulting signature matrices from this evidence—combined with an understanding of journalist-citizen roles in information control—indicated something significant about the challenges cyberspace activities pose for the press in crafting societal stories with authority.

The sample for this paper comprised both national and local news coverage of the first anniversary of Hurricane Katrina between August 24, 2005 and September 10, 2006: Anniversary articles in CNN, National Public Radio, *The New York Times*, *USAToday*, *The Los-Angeles Times*, *Time Magazine*, *Newsweek*, *U.S. News & World Report*, *The Times-Picayune*, and New Orleans television stations WWLTV, and WDSU—in all, about 200 news articles, video and radio broadcast stories. In addition, the sample included six journalist-generated anniversary publications (CNN, 2006; The Dallas Morning News, 2006; Horne, 2006; McQuaid & Schleifstein, 2006; Time Magazine, 2006; the Times-Picayune, 2006). I then turned to the web to sample the reader forums (CNN, MSNBC, Nola.com) as well as four popular Hurricane Katrina blogs (Tim's Nameless Blog, Thanks Katrina, Beyond Katrina, and Metroblogging New Orleans) as listed on Technorati, the blogging database. The forums and blogs were a mix of local and national authorship. I searched for the words "Hurricane Katrina" and selected those entries during my sampling time period. In all, I analyzed about 300 blog entries and comments.

My unit of analysis was the news article, blog entry, or the individual reader's comments. I conducted a preliminary analysis to categorize the ubiquitous themes and agendas for coding purposes; in all, I identified 25 different themes such as "rebirth" and "politics," and a dozen different agendas such as "federal money" or "remembering." I read through the mainstream news stories first, and then the citizen stories online. I coded each article according to the signature elements identified above. I then performed perfunctory descriptive analyses before textually analyzing the content as recommended by Gamson and Lasch. In the next section, the first two research questions about the overall collective memory and agendas for change will be answered in an examination of the signature matrices produced in the two different samples. Then, the third research question about the specific challenges to journalistic authority will be addressed using the discourse analysis.

Differing Signature Matrices

Table 9.1 shows the different signature matrices, broken down according to theme, agenda, catchphrases/exemplars, and characters. The four components

Table 9.1 Hurricane Katrina Anniversary Signature Matrix

	Mainstream	Citizens
Core themes	Politics	Reality vs illusion
	American identity	Insiders vs outsiders
	Community loss	Personal loss
	Formal ritual	Individual meaning
Agenda for change	Federal dollars	Remember
	Technology	Count Blessings
	Community building	No Agenda
Catchphrases/Exemplars	"Helluva job, Brownie"	"Real story"
	"Mission Accomplished"	"Post Katrina"
	9/11 and Iraq War	"The Thing"
	Past hurricanes	Personal exemplars
Characters	Heroes, victims, villains	Self

together demonstrate the differing collective memories of Hurricane Katrina, as covered by journalists and citizens during the event's anniversary.

Themes

As can be seen in Table 9.1, the majority of the press's stories focused on politics (20 percent of the sample), the loss of New Orleans (20 percent), and the formal anniversary celebrations (20 percent) whereas the citizens wrote about reality vs. illusion (15 percent), insiders/outsiders (25 percent), and personal loss/individual meaning (10 percent). National and local journalists wrote articles during late August 2006 that reaffirmed the dominant structures of America—the government, the press, the Church, American society, etc. In contrast, the citizens wrote about their individual memories, the need to set the record straight, and topics such as human nature.

Much of the journalistic coverage was politicized (Chadwich & Brand, 2006; Jackson, 2006; Kornblut & Nossiter, 2006; Lipton, 2006; Nossiter, 2006a; Rich, 2006).

> When the storm hit the Gulf Coast in the early hours of Aug. 29, Bush was at his Texas vacation home. He didn't visit the area until after he made a speech in San Diego on the 60th anniversary of V-J Day, including a defense of the Iraq war. By the time of an Aug. 31 flight over New Orleans, most of which was under water, much of the public relations damage had been done. (Jackson, 2006)

Even when the citizen sources mentioned their significant personal losses, the press connected those comments to politics (Elias, 2006). On the surface, many of these politicized stories reflected a negativity about the American government, but a closer examination showed that each portrayal is either countered with the good works of another American institution, or the government is depicted as turning itself around. For example, in one CNN story FEMA has learned from its mistakes and is "more prepared this season" (Elias, 2006). The coverage was also noteworthy for what was absent. During the crisis, people predicted that the aftermath would entail in-depth discussions of the race and poverty concerns within the government's inadequate response, for example (Navarrette, 2005). Yet less than 5 percent of the anniversary stories carried race or class issues as their major theme. When these topics were present, they were being used as a descriptor or to show how American community building was more important than ever:

> Despite the mayor's comment that New Orleans will always be a, quote, chocolate city, there are hopeful signs that the black/white divide may be blurring, if only slightly . . . Perhaps it's time to bury the civic sobriquet about the Big Easy. Nothing about rebuilding New Orleans is easy. For the strength to accomplish that, the citizens of the city are turning to each other. (Burnett, 2006)

In this piece, American community could step in where the government failed. In other pieces, it was either the Church (Moran, 2006) or the press (Cooper, 2006; Hoss, 2006; Stanley, 2006) or American ingenuity such as technological advancement (Grissett, 2006) that could save the day.

Online, citizen writings focused on a search for answers about the meaning that could be taken from the destruction of New Orleans. A motivation existed to reveal reality and debunk illusions put forward by both journalists and other citizen writers. "Wise quotes to inspire in crises: 'Crises and deadlocks when they occur have at least this advantage, that they force us to think.' The idea here being that we must remember to take lessons from this tragedy" (Beyond Katrina, 2006b). These lessons could be found within the messages themselves, which were often a form of individualized ritual:

> I made a compilation of videos and photos of my home from before, after and gutted set to "Don't Panic" By Coldplay . . . It helps show my friends the sheer devastation by providing a stark contrast of what was before the hurricane and what was after. (Vu, 2006)

Even those entries that focused on the journalism or the politics of the anniversary did so in relation to the writer's own role in the community (New Orleans, or America) (JoAnn, 2006a; kwakjack, 2006).

> I live in Hope Arkansas, which at that point in time seemed like a pretty long way from New Orleans but as night time of the first day drew near, we

became much closer . . . The first night my wife and I helped with a newly arranged coalition and the first location was the First United Methodist Church . . . I will never forget walking through the middle of the fellowship hall feeling dazed, confused and helpless. The reason for this was seeing the desperation in these people's eyes and realizing how they must feel having lost so much and the uncertainty of it all . . . Though this was such a terrible time in American History, it showed the best aspects of American Humanity in hometown America. (Hays, 2006)

In the above quote, writer John Hays remembered by putting himself in the shoes of the hurricane victims, by including his own story, and by showing his connection to the event. Other posts rejected the notion of a hometown America all together, and instead filled the online space with less nationalistic, more individual-centric viewpoints as in this post: "Leaders should be ashamed for not what has already happened, but for what hasn't happened. I just hope New England never has a hurricane because I wouldn't trust ANYONE to help" (Tam, 2006). Still other writers argued about the dominant themes to come out of the anniversary (Arkgurl, 2006; SirKlaydon2, 2006). Yet taken together, these writings provided random, personalized signposts for readers seeking ways to think about what had happened a year ago.

Agendas

Mainstream news stories suggested that citizens must move forward from the Katrina tragedy by rebuilding using federal dollars (14 percent) and persevering via the community and nation (18 percent). Online stories instead called for new attitudes and remembering (40 percent) or refrained from setting any agenda at all (20 percent).

Nationally, reporters suggested that New Orleans' destruction should serve as a warning for the rest of America. "While the city's situation is in some ways unique, the mistakes made and risks ignored hold lessons for other parts of the nation reliant on levées and vulnerable to floods" (Piecemeal federal response won't protect New Orleans, 2006, p. 14A). The federal government was urged to help with dollars (Kornblut & Nossiter, 2006); citizens were encouraged to prepare themselves (Ripley, 2006); and American science and technology (its ingenuity) would save the day (Elliott, 2006). Locally, the press coverage suggested that people needed to call on their unified community whose missteps during the crisis could be easily justified in the forgiving spotlight of the anniversary (WDSU, 2006). Rebuilding New Orleans was essential for both local and national narratives, for to abandon the city would be akin to abandoning the national notion that American could overcome anything—a key component of the national psyche.

Online, citizens tackled the controversial idea that New Orleans might be doomed as an American city, that it should not be rebuilt (Giesecke, 2006; judyb, 2006a; Message #3, 2006; Message #5, 2006; Message #6, 2006; Message #18, 2006; Message #32, 2006; Message #837, 2006) as in this one from the MSNBC forums:

> I know we never know what is safe and what is not, but when they tell you there is a chance this can happen again, where is the "common sense" that God gave us? I feel that the Lord has tried to wake some people up and if they rebuild, they should be on their on next time, no Goverment help, No one to blame for not getting there fast enough and no tax payer's money to dish out when the nightmare repeats itself . . . Who Agrees?? (Message #837, 2006)

Almost 10 percent of those comments sampled suggested that people abandon the city (compared to about 5 percent in the mainstream coverage). Instead, people were encouraged to rely on one's individual inner strength:

> This is the lesson all the children running at Audubon Park learned today: That good things come with effort. That inner strength can overcome adversity. There is no better lesson for children living, growing and surviving in post-K New Orleans. (Tim, 2006)

Catchphrases/Exemplars

The catchphrases and exemplars helped frame the Katrina stories, presenting the above themes and agendas. Thus, in the mainstream coverage, the catchphrases and exemplars tended to be political in nature. Ubiquitous catchphrases included "Hellava job, Brownie" and "Mission Accomplished" and exemplars were September 11 and the Iraq War (Leibovich, 2006; Lipton, 2006; Rich, 2006). The former referred to the botched performance of FEMA director Michael Brown during the hurricane and the premature declaration by President Bush that the Iraq War had ended; the latter compared the inadequate response to the war on terror and in Iraq.

Online, people peppered the messages with personal exemplars of individual anecdotes, descriptions of survival tales, tributes to loved ones and journal accounts of their struggles in the previous year. "I wonder if this memory is still engraved in my psyche because she reminded me of my own mother or because she epitomized the horror we were seeing. Perhaps it was both" (Jo Ann, 2006). Citizens dubbed the hurricane "The Thing," as if it were a character in a bad horror movie (Giesecke, 2006c; Laurie, 2006). This was one of the major catchphrases in the citizen coverage, along with the terms "The Real Story" and "Post-Katrina."

Characters

Similarly, the sources of information and characters in the stories played specific functions for the memory building in these samples. In the mainstream press coverage, each source played a role in the story, often in contrast to the other character portrayals in the narrative, as in this *Times-Picayune* journalist piece:

> Riggs doesn't think of himself as a hero. But when he heard on his transistor radio that Sheriff Harry Lee was calling for help from boat owners to rescue people on rooftops and balconies in flooded sections of New Orleans, he told his wife that he had no choice but to go. (Bronston, 2006)

The major character depictions in the mainstream press sample also included the journalists themselves as heroes, high government officials as tricksters or villains, and New Orleanians as victims in need of saving.

Online, very few of the posts contained any character at all besides the author's self. That "self" identity in the online posts included the roles of storytellers, journalists, whistleblowers, counselors, journal writers, history drafters, meaning makers, and opinion leaders. The citizens recast themselves as characters performing in this new narrative (Beyond Katrina, 2006d). "I just heard from New Orleans blogger and Rising Tide Conference organizer, Mark Folse reporting on the situation at the 17th Street Canal" (Beyond Katrina, 2006c). And with every writing they attempted to (re)define their "self" as a character, as in this post (Beyond Katrina, 2006e):

> And I especially cringe when I hear folks call those impacted by Katrina, "victims." No victims here as far as I'm concerned...only good, honest, decent, ordinary folks who are going through a major transition. But for the sake of brevity, if we've got to have a label to describe a population of people who've been impacted by the disaster, I prefer to use "survivors."

Citizens produced a story of the "you and me" in Hurricane Katrina, starring the citizen and his or her particular memory.

Challenging Memories According to the "Self"

But what do these differing collective memories mean for journalistic anniversary coverage in light of the interactive functions of citizen writing online? How did citizens challenge the resulting narrative story? This section explores this third research question; the sample sets indicated that citizens countered the press's dominant story of Hurricane Katrina in determining both the purpose of the particular commemoration and the nature of community and group identity.

Purpose of Commemoration

The journalistic coverage of tragic events' commemorations becomes part of a societal grief processing; the stories themselves represent an essential part of the mourning ritual (Kitch, 2003). Both national and local journalists wrote extensively on the formal commemorative ceremonies for Hurricane Katrina on August 29, 2006. Local press recounted names of those lost; the national press joined those people they had interviewed the year prior. Both local and national reporters republished 2005 photos and anecdotes from their initial coverage. The aim here was to reconstruct the narrative of Hurricane Katrina to present a story of redemption, or at least to point the way toward a potential rebirth. Journalists revisited the scene of destruction with "then and now" comparisons to demonstrate the theme of rebirth.

> "The hurt is incredible," he said. "You cannot help but reflect on a day like this." School officials planned a Mass in conjunction with the abbey community to recognize the anniversary. But Serio also stressed the need for students to move forward and celebrate the beginning of a new year and a new chapter in Hannan's 20-year history. "We're not basking in hurt," he said. "We're basking in joy, rebirth and the future." (Hurwitz, 2006)

Here the reporters reminded people of the formal reasoning behind the anniversary. The journalist connects the anniversary to intact and functioning structural institutions like the education system and the government. The writer also advances the narrative of "rebirth." This particular narrative could be found throughout the mainstream coverage:

> UNIDENTIFIED FEMALE: I don't think the real story is finished yet. This is only part one. Part two is where we are right now, dealing with all of this . . . Part three, that's the story that isn't finished yet . . . We're going to rebuild. . . . We will survive. I know that, but we need to do more than that. We need to go back to living with faith, and with hope . . . (Cooper, 2006)

This evidence seemed to indicate that the national recovery process—described by anthropologists, sociologists and media scholars—had begun in this anniversary coverage.

Online, citizens were explicitly bypassing media accounts of the anniversary, even actively dismissing them. People sought the "real story"—as in these MSNBC messages: "Alot of the truth of what is going on down here is not getting out" (Message #471) and "I wonder which mansion on St. Charles [President Bush] will look at to determine that the rebuilding effort is coming along well. How come the City welcome wagon doesn't show him what's really up?" (Untitled, 2006) and many others (Carol, 2006; mominem, 2006). The writers spent much time ensuring that the "real" facts were disseminated.

> Today on Inside Jefferson Parish, I asked Council Chairman Capella specifically about the 17th Street Canal floodwalls. He stated that he was comfortable with the pump stations operational and the fact that water will not be allowed to rise against the floodwalls. (wbennetti, 2006)

The online authors called out for new angles, facts, and attitudes, assuming the role of vigilant meaning-maker. "STOP!!! stop the number manipulation! my head hurts!" cried one blog writer on Thanks Katrina (Judyb, 2006b). Over on Nola.com, another reader begged people to "stop blaming everyone else for your decision—and stop exagerating" (Yosistakate, 2006). Sometimes these diatribes were directed at the institutions of America, particularly the government and the press. Some writers wanted people to use the anniversary to remember not the hurricane, but the inadequate response of the government (Tracy, 2006), including this one: "Bush fiddled while losing an American city and its people!" (Lynn, 2006). Some citizens connected what happened, their memories of that event, with the loss of American values: "It was the only time in my life when I was embarassed to be an American" (Cheraso, 2006).

The "real story" was highly anecdotal, intensely personal. Citizens used the space as a counseling session: "Stacy, thank you dawlin', your words are like liquid gold. But, on the other hand i undersand your confusion" (termite, 2006). Cyberspace offered a vessel of expression for anger, frustration, pride, hope, sadness and sarcasm, such as "There are some great people here, but the leaches of the city will drown them all" (Message #53) and many others (Message #60). They wrote poems, composed song lyrics, and published personal photos (3000 Katrina Pictures, 2006; Cott, 2006; Johnson, 2006; Tobin, 2006). They shared rebuilding tips and gave thank yous (Martel, 2006; TBK, 2006). They empathized.

These survivors used the forums to "take back" the anniversary, and put forward their own versions of the tragedy.

> Today's Katrina anniversary is being overdramatized, inflated and overanguished to the point that most of the country has already tuned out. We appreciate the attention, since there needs to be continued focus on our generation-long recovery down here. But for most of us who are here daily and plan to remain, it'll be a day largely like any other—just trying to keep things operational. We'll mark the anniversary in our own ways, thank you. (Giesecke, 2006a)

This post was followed by this comment:

> I've just decided that I will commemorate August 29 by doing the same thing I did last year, namely not going to work . . . The earth has gone

around the sun exactly once since Katrina, so what? What does that even signify? (Gerry, 2006)

And, this one: "Well, I'm going out to get drunk after work. I have had enough of this shit" (Chris M., 2006). These posts do not reaffirm the traditional institutions, as the mainstream press stories did. While recognizing the role of the media in formally commemorating the event, these writers dismissed the notion that journalists' coverage reflected the purpose of the day—at least for them. In rejecting the journalistic version, citizens were also questioning the collective memory, and thus, undermining it.

Community/Group Identity

Researcher Josh Meyrowitz noted that people use media to form individual as well as group identities, creating "insiders" and "outsiders" (1986, p. 54). The mainstream journalists wrote stories according to an American-insider perspective as in the *Time Magazine Hurricane Katrina: The Storm that Changed America* (2006). Journalists considered themselves insiders, and suggested that they were the only ones who could reveal to people outside the event what was really happening (CNN, 2006; Kurtz, 2006; Leibovich, 2006; Lukas, 2006; Stanley, 2006). Their authority to form this collective memory emerged from their insider knowledge. It was only by reading these official accounts that outsiders could feel as if they were an insider. Once everyone could collect in the same memory, community could triumph adversity.

But in the online forums, some writers demonstrated strong desires to keep separate those who survived Hurricane Katrina from those who merely watched the destruction on television (Beyond Katrina, 2006a, Laurie, 2006).

> Specifics are going to vary by neighborhood, but one thing's for sure these days—those of us who are living here now are the hardcores. We have worlds of patience with each other, but very, very little for those who aren't in the trench with us—or at least trying to be.(Giesecke, 2006b)

The sharing of experience and of social information according to those who were "in the trench" connected these people in a virtual space as a substitute for the loss of their physical place (i.e., New Orleans). This allowed bloggers like Giesecke to assume a certain authority in relating his memory of New Orleans. Cyberspace was a place for those in the know. Instead of revealing information as a way to include people, some writers published to privilege their own memories as the truth, assuring that their selves achieved a certain authoritative ranking inside this cyber-community and this story.

Of course, dissension existed among these groups, and a battle over memory was also being fought in this space:

I am a college graduate born and raised in New Orleans. I have been reading this forum since April 2006. This forum has almost single-handedly
helped me to decide to leave this area. I would not raise a puppy here much
less a family. I marvel at how divided this area is. Katrina exposed the deep
seated hatred and ignorance of some of OUR people in this area. I hope
those people change, but . . . my grandchildren will probably be retiring
then. (Arizonabound, 2006)

The above post showed how ephemeral and fickle these groupings could be
in these blogs and forums, and reflected real divisions and disagreements
among citizens that were not reported by the press on this anniversary. Of
course this could mean that the online writers were not yet ready to produce
a collective accounting of the event in the same way that the mainstream
press was.

Ultimately, very little in the way of a cohesive narrative for Hurricane
Katrina could be discerned on this first anniversary in cyberspace—at least not
in the same way one could be determined for both national and local coverage.
Rather, the citizens sought meaning in raw, seemingly unedited posts that
reflected confusion and despair. "The truth is, though, I've been searching for
my own unique place in the story. I haven't been able to find it" (Saizan, 2006).
In this Beyond Katrina blog entry, Saizan shared her sense of disconnection.
Such emotion was found in the mainstream coverage, but the sense of loss
tended to be countered by upbeat notes about rebirth or politicized tidbits about
President Bush and the Iraq War. Saizan's post continued:

So this is my unique piece, my offering to the anniversary, if you will. The
muse is nudging, I am linked up, and something really powerful and deep is
attempting to come across the wires. I'll ride that while it's here, because
every writer knows the muse is subject to disappear on a whim. Hopefully
something wise will come through . . . something larger than little ole' me.
I'll surrender to that something larger and I'll write, perhaps even all
through the night. I'll record my thoughts about recovery, about change,
about vision. All along this has been and will continue to be my contribution to the cause . . . (Saizan, 2006)

In this intimacy, Saizan helps write her own unique story. In doing so, Saizan
hashes out the meaning of this anniversary for her, and thus, completes her
grief ritual. In this post, she offers up a new agenda for the country: to be
"linked up," to be get connected, to be heard. The authority of the individual
ruled in this space, even if that individual had not yet learned to narratize and
simplify.

Conclusion

Both sample sets reflected a personal grieving process that is somewhat similar to how researcher Carolyn Kitch discussed commemoration in American journalism as part of societal mourning rituals (2003). In her research, Kitch suggested that journalism represents a site of ongoing meaning negotiation for tragic events, whose significance changes with every cultural, political, economic, circumstantial shift. In this sample, the mainstream reporters rediscovered heroes, villains, and victims in the narratives they recast for the anniversary, and thus, the journalists produced an account that revealed the "truth" of Hurricane Katrina and its aftermath according to the American realities of August 2006. They sought to tell the story of "the storm that changed America" (*Time Magazine*, 2006). In these stories, the only "insider" was the journalist, whose presence brought people the real story and whose wisdom authorized him to suggest a national agenda for change (prepare ourselves, spend federal money, call on American ingenuity).

But online, people made a point of trying to "take back" the anniversary and Hurricane Katrina memories, reclaiming content in part by discounting or contradicting media accounts of what "really" happened. The very notion of commemoration (and perhaps also of collective memory) is renegotiated here: what are anniversaries for? How should we be remembering? For citizens, the answers to these questions seemed to be: anniversaries are to count one's blessings and to connect interpersonally; and the only right way to "remember" is to insert the "self" into the story. They sought a refocusing of attention onto the individual as a part of something larger. They used the Internet's interactivity and multimedia, as well as its vast temporal and spatial capacity, reflecting Sade-Beck's meta memory space (2004) and Carmichael's eternity service (2003). In these meta-memory spaces, citizens compiled photo slideshows, composed poems, collected stories, posted audio of songs, interactively argued over the right way to remember, formed new memorial rituals, and generally employed a huge number of memory vehicles within the one channel. In this eternity service, publishers of information sought to record recollections for posterity, so that a citizen-produced first draft of history would endure alongside (indeed, sometimes in opposition to) journalistic versions.

The result was an individualizing of the Hurricane Katrina story in which each person must discover his or her own enduring memory according to personal experience, but then feel confident enough in its accuracy and validity to disseminate it. However, taken as a whole, these messages represented a patchwork of authoritative collective thought. The messages may have been stream of conscience, political, personal, emotional, sarcastic, and/or mean, but they were always communal. Authors always wrote with the aim of sharing some aspect of the self in relation to Hurricane Katrina and New Orleans, always with the aim of seeking connections by their very participation, always with the aim of asserting one's right to be an "insider."

Bodnar (1994) argued that despite the opportunities for individual remembering, traditional structures and established societal values would continue to dominate discussions. While journalists upheld American institutions and values in the mainstream press, citizens in this online sample criticized or discounted traditional societal structures. A much more self-driven, self-absorbed remembering occurred. These cyberspaces offered a chance to renegotiate what it means to be an American when an un-American situation occurs—but on a much more micro level: who is worthy of *my* attention and scrutiny? What does it mean to *me* if the parade does not include Bush? Why did *I* cry at last week's diner re-opening? These messages and blog posts presented themes and agendas not considered (or at least, not fully explored) in the mainstream coverage of the anniversary. Journalists wrote much about government accountability, American ingenuity, and technological salvation, while citizens memorialized and counseled, often presenting no agenda for change at all. Cyberspace represented a new realm, perhaps not for agenda setting in the nation but for agenda *posing* according to the individual.

This evidence suggests that the collective memory put forward by the press must at the very least make room for new individual memory disseminated in cyberspace. This does not necessarily mean that the press's authority to tell the story of past crises like the hurricane has been jeopardized because of the citizen's new agency online to produce content. On the contrary, perhaps that function of the press becomes even more important in light of this evidence. Certainly this research does suggest that new players must be included in the role of *formal* history making (emphasis on formal because of course citizens have always been a major part of informal history making). Indeed, as one writer in this sample described, these citizens are only "searching for their own unique place in the story"—and telling their own stories with authority. Journalists, historians and history/collective memory must incorporate these new stories of America's crises, but in such a way that they augment a collective understanding of the past rather than separate Americans into insiders and outsiders with contrary suggestions for societal improvement.

References

3000 Katrina Pictures [reader forum] (2006, August 30). Nola.com. Accessed June 3, 2006 from http://www.nola.com/forums/jefftownhall/index.ssf.

Allan, S. (2006). *Online news*. New York: Open University Press.

Arizonabound (2006, August 28). No fighting [reader forum]. Nola.com. Accessed June 3, 2006 from http://www.nola.com/forums/jefftownhall/index.ssf.

Arkgurl (2006, September 1). Untitled [reader forum]. Nola.com. Accessed June 3, 2006 from http://www.nola.com/forums/jefftownhall/index.ssf.

Bennett, L. (2003). *News: The politics of illusion*. New York: Longman.

Benton, M., & Frazier, P. J. (1976). The agenda-setting function of mass media at three levels of information-holding. *Communication Research* , 3, 261–274.

Beyond Katrina (2006a, August 29). New Orleans Homeland Security, residents preparing for Ernesto [Blog]. Beyond Katrina.com. Accessed June 4, 2006 from www.beyondkatrina.com.

Beyond Katrina (2006b, August 30). Crisis as opportunity [Blog]. Beyond Katrina.com. Accessed June 4, 2006 from www.beyondkatrina.com.

Beyond Katrina (2006c, August 29). Tension In NOLA today—17th Street Canal [Blog]. Beyond Katrina.com. Accessed June 4, 2006 from www.beyondkatrina.com.

Beyond Katrina (2006d, August 28). Breaking news—residents are being confronted by the New Orleans police for not leaving their property [Blog]. Beyond Katrina.com. Accessed June 4, 2006 from www.beyondkatrina.com.

Beyond Katrina (2006e). The quest continues. Beyond Katrina.com. Accessed June 4, 2006 from www.beyondkatrina.com.

Bodnar, J. (1994). *Remaking America: Public memory, commemoration and patriotism in the twentieth century*. Princeton: Princeton University Press.

Bronston, B. (2006, August 29). Metairie boater heeded call to help the stranded. *The Times-Picayune*, A1.

Burnett, J. (2006, August 26). Imagining a new city in New Orleans [Transcript]. National Public Radio.

Carey, J. (1989/1992). *Communication as culture*. New York: Routledge.

Carlson, M. (2007). Making memories matter: Journalistic authority and the memorializing discourse around Mary McGrory and David Brinkley. *Journalism, 8(2)*, 165–183.

Carmichael, P. (2003, January). The Internet, information architecture and community memory. *Journal of Computer-Mediated Communication*, 8(2).

Carol (2006, August 24). Untitled [Blog]. Metroblogging New Orleans. Accessed June 5, 2006 from http://neworleans.metblogs.com/archives/2006/08/.

Chadwick, A., & Brand, M. (2006, August 24). New Orleans readies for a somber anniversary [Transcript]. Day to Day. National Public Radio.

Cheraso, D. (2006, August 28). Untitled [Blog]. Anderson Cooper's 360 Blog. CNN.com. Accessed June 1, 2006 from http://www.cnn.com/CNN/Programs/anderson.cooper.360/blog/2006/08/trying-to-prevent-next-katrina.html.

Chris M. (2006, August 29). Untitled [Blog]. Metroblogging New Orleans. Accessed June 5, 2006 from http://neworleans.metblogs.com/archives/2006/08/.

CNN (2006). *Katrina: State of emergency*. Kansas City: Andrews McMeel Publishing.

Cohen, B. C. (1963). *The press and foreign policy*. Princeton, NJ: Princeton University Press.

Cooper, A. (2006, August 28). One year later: Dispatches from Katrina [Broadcast transcript]. CNN.

Cott, D. L. V. (2006, August 27). Untitled [Blog]. Anderson Cooper's 360 Blog. CNN.com. Accessed June 3, 2003 from http://www.cnn.com/CNN/Programs/anderson.cooper.360/blog/2006/08/trying-to-prevent-next-katrina.html.

The Dallas Morning News (2006). *Eyes of the storm: Hurricanes Katrina and Rita: The photographic story*. Lanham, MD: Taylor Trade Publishing.

Davidson, James W., & Lytle, Mark (2004). *After the fact: The art of historical detection*. New York: McGraw-Hill, Inc.

Durham, F. (2008). Media ritual in catastrophic time: The populist turn in television coverage of Hurricane Katrina. *Journalism*, 9(1), 95–116.

Edy, J. A. (1999). Journalistic uses of collective memory. *Journal of Communication*, 49(2), 71–85.

Elias, D. (2006, August 29). Special edition: Remembering Hurricane Katrina [Broadcast Transcript]. CNN.

Elliott, D. (2006, August 27). Katrina victims still struggling to find way home [Transcript]. National Public Radio.

Foot, K. A., & Schneider, S. M. (2002). Online action in Campaign 2000: An exploratory analysis of the U.S. political Web sphere. *Journal of Broadcasting & Electronic Media, 46* (2), 222–244.

Foot, K., Warnick, B., & Schneider, S. M. (2005). Web-based memorializing after September 11: Toward a conceptual framework. *Journal of Computer-Mediated Communication, 11*(1). Accessed July 8, 2007 from http://jcmc.indiana.edu/vol11/issue1/foot.html.

Frijda, N. H. (1997). Commemorating. In J. Pennebaker, D. Paez, & B. Rime (Eds.), *Collective memory of political events* (pp. 103–130). Mahwah, NJ: Lawrence Erlbaum Publishers.

Fry, K. (2006, February). Hero for New Orleans, Hero for the nation. *Space and Culture, 9*(1), 83–85.

Gamson, W. A., & Lasch, K. (1983). The political culture of social welfare policy. In S. E. Spiro, & E. Yuchtman-Yaar (Eds.), *Evaluating the welfare state*, (pp. 397–415). New York: Academic Press.

Gerry (2006, August 29). Untitled [Blog]. Metroblogging New Orleans. Accessed June 5, 2006 from http://neworleans.metblogs.com/archives/2006/08/.

Geser, H. (1998). *Yours virtually forever: Death memorials and remembrance sites in the WWW*. Sociology in Switzerland Online Publications. Retrieved September 23, 2005 from http://socio.ch/intcom/t_hgeser07.htm.

Giesecke, C. (2006, August 25). The road back [blog]. Metroblogging New Orleans. Accessed June 3, 2006 from http://neworleans.metblogs.com/archives/2006/08/.

Giesecke, C. (2006a, August 29). A year later [blog]. Metroblogging New Orleans. Accessed June 3, 2006 from http://neworleans.metblogs.com/archives/2006/08/.

Giesecke, C. (2006b, August 24). From the ground up [blog]. Metroblogging New Orleans. Accessed June 3, 2006 from http://neworleans.metblogs.com/archives/2006/08/.

Giesecke, C. (2006c, August 25). Untitled [Blog]. Metroblogging New Orleans. Accessed June 3, 2006 from http://neworleans.metblogs.com/archives/2006/08/.

Goffman, E. (1974). *Frame analysis*. Philadelphia: University of Pennsylvania Press.

Grissett, S. (2006, August 26). Safety must come first, panel urges: Levees "urgent call to action" presents. *The Times Picayune*, A1.

Hall, S. (1986). *Media power and class power*. In S. Cohen, & J. Young (Eds.), *Bending reality: The state of the media* (pp. 5–14). London: Pluto Press.

Hays, J. (2006, August 27). Untitled [Blog]. Anderson Cooper's 360 blog. CNN.com. Accessed June 1, 2006 from http://www.cnn.com/CNN/Programs/anderson.cooper.360/blog/2006/08/trying-to-prevent-next-katrina.html.

Horne, J. (2006). *Breach of faith: Hurricane Katrina and the near death of a great American city*. New York: Random House.

Hoss, M. (2006, August 27). Hoss: Moments of bravery, courage [Broadcast Transcript]. WWLTV.

Hurwitz, J. (2006, August 30). Hannan High School emerges from ruin: School marks its first day at temporary location on the north shore. *Times-Picayune, 1A.*

Jackson, D. (2006, August 28). Katrina plan enacted on some fronts, not on others. *USAToday, 8A.*

Jo Ann (2006, August 29). Untitled [blog]. Anderson Cooper's 360 blog. CNN.com. Accessed June 1, 2006 from http://www.cnn.com/CNN/Programs/anderson.cooper. 360/blog/2006/08/trying-to-prevent-next-katrina.html.

JoAnn (2006a, September 1). Untitled [Blog]. Anderson Cooper's 360 blog. CNN.com. Accessed June 1, 2006 from http://www.cnn.com/CNN/Programs/anderson.cooper. 360/blog/2006/08/trying-to-prevent-next-katrina.html.

Johnson, C. (2006, August 29). Message #141: Homeless hearts [reader forum]. MSNBC.com. Accessed June 1, 2006 from http://www.msnbc.msn.com/id/ 14394865/.

Judyb (2006a, August 25). Rockey you asskisser [blog]. Thanks Katrina. Accessed June 5 from http://thanks-katrina.blogspot.com/2006_08_01_archive.html.Judyb (2006b, August 26). PTSD and it's children [blog]. Thanks Katrina. Accessed June 5 from http://thanks-katrina.blogspot.com/2006_08_01_archive.html.

Kaye, B. (2007). Blog use motivations: An exploratory study. In Mark Tremayne (Ed.), *Blogging, citizenship, and the future of media* (pp. 127–148). New York: Routledge.

Kitch, C. (2003). "Mourning in America": Ritual, redemption, and recovery in news narrative after September 11. *Journalism Studies, 4(2),* 213–224.

Kitch, C. (2005). *Pages from the past: History and memory in American magazines.* Chapel Hill: The University of North Carolina.

Kitch, C., & Hume, J. (2008). *Journalism in a culture of grief.* New York: Routledge.

Kornblut, A., & Nossiter, A. (2006, August 29). Gulf coast marks a year since Katrina. *The New York Times, A1.*

Ku, G., Kaid, L. L., & Pfau, M. (2003). The impact of Web site campaigning on traditional news media and public information processing. *Journalism and Mass Communication Quarterly, 80(3),* 528–547.

Kurtz, H. (2006, September 3). Media returns to New Orleans [broadcast transcript]. CNN.

Kwakjack (2006, August 24). Parade schedule [reader forum]. Nola.com. Accessed June 3, 2006 from http://www.nola.com/forums/jefftownhall/index.ssf.

Laurie (2006, August 25). Untitled [blog]. Metroblogging New Orleans. Accessed June 3, 2006 from http://neworleans.metblogs.com/archives/2006/08/.

Lee, B., Lancendorfer, K., & Lee, K.J. (2005). Agenda-Setting and the Internet: The Intermedia Influence of Internet Bulletin Boards on Newspaper Coverage of the 2000 General Election in South Korea. *Asian Journal of Communication, 15(1),* 57–71.

Leibovich, M. (2006, August 25). A punch line who refuses to fade away. *The New York Times, A11.*

Lipton, E. (2006, August 25). Despite steps, disaster planning still shows gaps. *The New York Times, A1.*

Littlefield, R. S., & Quenette, A.M. (2007). Crisis leadership and hurricane Katrina: The portrayal of authority by the media in natural disasters. *Journal of Applied Communication Research, 35(1),* 26–47.

Lukas, B. (2006, August 29). Lukas: Katrina though the eyes of a photojournalist [broadcast transcript]. WWL-TV.

Lynn (2006, September 1). Untitled [blog]. Anderson Cooper's 360 blog. CNN.com.

Accessed June 1, 2006 from http://www.cnn.com/CNN/Programs/anderson.cooper.
360/blog/2006/08/trying-to-prevent-next-katrina.html.

Maher, M., & Chiasson, L. Jr. (1995). The press and crisis: what have we learned? In L.
Chiasson Jr. (Ed.), *The press in times of crisis* (pp. 219–224). London: Greenwood Press.

Martel, C. (2006, August 30). Thank yous [blog]. Metroblogging New Orleans.
Accessed June 5, 2006 from http://neworleans.metblogs.com/archives/2006/08/.

Martini, E. (2003). Public histories, private memories?: Cybermemorials and the future
of public history (Unpublished manuscript, University of Maryland, 2003).

McCombs, M. (2004). *Setting the agenda: The mass media and public opinion.* Malden,
MA: Blackwell Publishing.

McCombs, M. E., & Shaw, D. L. (1972). The agenda setting function of the mass media.
Public Opinion Quarterly, 36(2), 176–187.

McLuhan, M. (1994/1998). *Understanding media: The extensions of man.* Cambridge,
MA: The MIT Press.

McQuaid, J., & Schleifstein, M. (2006). *Path of destruction: The devastation of New
Orleans and the coming age of superstorms.* New York: Little Brown and Company.

Message #3 (2006, August 28). Over Taxed [reader forum]. MSNBC.com. Accessed
June 1, 2006 from http://www.msnbc.msn.com/id/14394865/.

Message #5 (2006, August 28). H. Stice [reader forum]. MSNBC.com. Accessed June 1,
2006 from http://www.msnbc.msn.com/id/14394865/.

Message #6 (2006, August 28). Faith-Walker-87. [reader forum]. MSNBC.com.
Accessed June 1, 2006 from http://www.msnbc.msn.com/id/14394865/.

Message #18 (2006, August 28). teacherman [reader forum]. MSNBC.com. Accessed
June 1, 2006 from http://www.msnbc.msn.com/id/14394865/.

Message #32 (2006, August 28). kirchezeile [reader forum]. MSNBC.com. Accessed
June 1, 2006 from http://www.msnbc.msn.com/id/14394865/.

Message #53 (2006, August 28). Daisy70458 [reader forum]. MSNBC.com. Accessed
June 1, 2006 from http://www.msnbc.msn.com/id/14394865/.

Message #60 (2006, August 28). Fed up in Houston [reader forum]. MSNBC.com.
Accessed June 1, 2006 from http://www.msnbc.msn.com/id/14394865/.

Message #471 (2006, August 29). MGSwenson [reader forum]. MSNBC. Accessed June
1, 2006 from http://www.msnbc.msn.com/id/14394865/.

Message #837 (2006, September 4). Ginger35010 [reader forum] MSNBC.com.
Accessed June 1, 2006 from http://www.msnbc.msn.com/id/14394865/.

Meyrowitz, J. (1985). *No sense of place: The impact of electronic media on social behavior.*
New York: Oxford University Press.

Mominem (2006, August 27). PTSD and it's children [blog]. Thanks Katrina.

Moran, K. (2006, August 30). Hats off: Ceremony pays tribute to storm's first responders.
The Times Picayune, A1.

Navarrette, R. Jr. (2005, September 18). Seeing the race problem differently. *San Diego
Union-Tribune,* G-3.

Newman, A. (2006, September 5). A digital snapshot of 9/11 takes shape on the
Internet; Online archive holds 150,000 e-mails, photos, much more. *USAToday, 8D.*

Nossiter, A. (2006a, August 26). Bit by bit, some outlines emerge for a shaken New
Orleans. *The New York Times, A1.*

Piecemeal federal response won't protect New Orleans (2006, August 28). *USA Today,*
14A.

Rich, F. (2006, August 27). Return to the scene of the crime. *The New York Times,* A10.

Ripley, A. (2006, August 26). Floods, tornadoes, hurricanes, wildfires, earthquakes . . .: Why we don't prepare. *Time Magazine*, pp. 55–58.

Rosenzweig, R., & Thelen, D. (1998). *The presence of the past: Popular uses of history in American life*. New York: Columbia University Press.

Rothenbuhler, E. W. (1998). *Ritual communication: From everyday conversation to mediated ceremony*. Thousand Oaks, CA: Sage Publications.

Sade-Beck, L. (2004). Mourning and memorial culture on the Internet: The Israeli case. *American Communication Journal, 7*.

Saizan, M. (2006, August 28). Deep space and Katrina recovery [blog]. Beyond Katrina.com. Accessed June 1, 2006 from www.beyondkatrina.com.

Schneider, S. M., & Dougherty, M. (2003, May). Strategic co-production and content appropriation: Press materials on candidate web sites in the 2002 U.S. Election. Paper presented at the International Communication Association, San Diego.

Schudson, M. (1992). *Watergate in American memory: How we remember, forget and reconstruct the past*. New York: Basic Books.

Schwartz, B. (1998). Frame images: towards a semiotics of collective memory. *Semiotica, 121(1/2)*, 1–40.

Sirklaydon2 (2006, September 1). Untitled [reader forum]. Nola.com. Accessed June 3, 2006 from http://www.nola.com/forums/jefftownhall/index.ssf.

Stanley, A. (2006, August 30). An anniversary with strong images, sorrow, self-congratulation and blame. *The New York Times*, A19.

Sturken, M. (1997). *Tangled memories: The Vietnam War, the AIDS epidemic, and the politics of remembering*. Berkeley: University of California Press.

Tam (2006, August 29). Untitled [blog]. Anderson Cooper's 360 blog. Accessed June 14, 2006 from http://www.cnn.com/CNN/Programs/anderson.cooper.360/blog/2006/08/trying-to-prevent-next-katrina.html.

TBK (2006, August 30). Untitled [blog]. Metroblogging New Orleans. Accessed June 5, 2006 from http://neworleans.metblogs.com/archives/2006/08/.

Termite (2006, August 27). Untitled [blog]. Metroblogging New Orleans. Accessed June 5, 2006 from http://neworleans.metblogs.com/archives/2006/08/.

Tim (2006, September 23). On the right path [blog]. Tim's nameless blog. Accessed June 2, 2006 from http://timsnamelessblog.blogspot.com/2006_08_01_archive.html.

TIME Magazine (2006). *Hurricane Katrina: The storm that changed America*. New York: TIME Books.

The Times-Picayune staff (2006). *Katrina: The ruin and recovery of New Orleans*. New Orleans: The Times-Picayune.

Tobin, D. (2006, April 9). Entering Vanessa's House [blog]. Nola.com. Accessed June 3, 2006 from http://www.nola.com/weblogs/bourbon/.

Tracy (2006, August 28). Untitled [blog]. Anderson Cooper's 360 blog. CNN.com. Accessed June 1, 2006 from http://www.cnn.com/CNN/Programs/anderson.cooper.360/blog/2006/08/trying-to-prevent-next-katrina.html.

Untitled [blog] (2006, August 24). Metroblogging New Orleans. Accessed June 5, 2006 from http://neworleans.metblogs.com/archives/2006/08/.

Vu, S. (2006, September 2). Video compilation [reader forum]. Nola.com. Accessed June 3, 2006 from http://www.nola.com/forums/jefftownhall/index.ssf.

Wbennetti (2006, August 24). 17th Street Canal [reader forum]. Nola.com. Accessed June 3, 2006 from http://www.nola.com/forums/jefftownhall/index.ssf.

WDSU (2006, August 25). Song for New Orleans [video]. WDSU.

Williams, R. (1969). *Communications*. London: Chatto and Windus.

yosistakate (2006, September 1). A valid issue [reader forum]. Nola.com. Accessed June 3, 2006 from http://www.nola.com/forums/jefftownhall/index.ssf.

Zelizer, B. (1992). *Covering the body: The Kennedy assassination, the media, and the shaping of collective memory*. Chicago: University of Chicago Press.

Chapter 10

Mapping Citizen Coverage of the Dual City

Lou Rutigliano

As news organizations rely more on the public to cover local news through user-generated content, questions emerge about the gap in such audience participation along socioeconomic lines. The digital divides of access, technical literacy, time, and other resources can lead to a participation divide, and potential gaps in local coverage. If this is the case, which areas then are not covered by citizen media?

Advocates and practitioners of the various online experiments blending professional and amateur reporters have begun calling this work "networked journalism"[1] rather than citizen journalism to focus on the method of journalism rather than the participants. The network metaphor is accurate, for today journalism is a combination of highly-trafficked hubs and millions of disparate nodes, connected by links of varying strength and interaction. Sub-groups form within these media networks to scrutinize information, with the network's boundaries and centers of attention shifting constantly in response to the latest dispatches from full-time reporters, part-time bloggers, and everything in between.

Yet amid the hopes that this new wave of experimentation will lead to better journalism—more inclusive of a broader range of public voices, more willing to challenge power, better able to engage the public and spur political action—is the need to consider the social trends that are shaping journalism and the cities that newspapers cover. Here again the network metaphor is useful, for it connects journalism to Castells' broader concept of the network society. Of particular interest is Castells' predictions of the network society's impact on major cities, specifically the increasing of inequality, the formation of a dual city within the city with extremes of upper and lower classes, and the fragmenting and strengthening of cultural identity in response to these changes. Where the newspaper might once have been the place to attempt to bridge such divides and gather these fragments into some semblance of a community, now such interaction and communication must occur within the network.

It is the characteristics of this broader network that therefore need more attention. Prior research has already begun to question blogging in practice versus its promise. Despite the growth of such citizen media and anecdotal

evidence to the contrary, traditional gatekeepers and elites continue to dominate news discourse as a result of their network position (Harp & Tremayne,
2006; Reese, Rutigliano, Hyun, & Jeong, 2007), while the majority of new
voices tend towards more individualized and personal accounts of reality, rather
than local reporting (Herring, Scheidt, Kouper, & Wright 2007; Papacharissi,
2007). As was the case in pre-blog community networks, participants also come
from middle-class and educated backgrounds (Rainie, 2005). Considering this,
what areas of the offline city might a networked journalism cover?

This study raises this question in the context of Castells's concerns. It examines some hubs of the online citizen media network in Austin, Texas, where
15 percent of adults are bloggers, making it the top blogging market in the US
as of 2007.[2] Although relatively large, this figure suggests again that the citizens
behind citizen-generated content are an elite non-representative slice of the
general population. But does this automatically lead to a limited picture of the
city? To find out, the focus here is not so much on what the bloggers talk about,
but where they talk about. By comparing this map of coverage to economic and
racial demographic patterns in the city, we can begin to see which parts of a city
are within the network and which are on the margins or excluded altogether,
and whether there is some truth to Castells' vision of a dual city, one covered
and one unknown.

The Haves and Have-Nots of Networks

In Castells' (1997) network society, the rapid diffusion of information technology and government deregulation create greater interdependence between
the economies and societies of different nations. This leads to examples of
global cooperation but also greater global competition, individualism, and
inequality between countries and within countries. At the same time that those
actors in favorable network positions use networks to increase their power,
those who are marginal actors in the network, or not connected at all to the network, are rendered invisible and irrelevant. Such divisions are not always the
result of direct action by those in power, but rather the product of the "micro-
physics of power" (Castells, 1997, p. 15)—informal rules and methods that
control and exclude. This "network logic" (Urry, 2003, p. 9) replaces the traditional force of power in a more structured and less fluid society—the central-
ized, concentrated, hierarchical, and formal power found in institutions. Rather
than command the actors within a network to do something, network logic provides a guide that the actors subconsciously follow (Urry, 2003). While the
form of the networks and the logic that they generate is not final in Castells' or
Urry's framework, they fear that the divide between those inside and outside
networks can become irreversible over time.

The laws of how networks function justifies this fear of their rigidity and
resistance to change. Network theory can help determine how hubs form in a
network (Harp & Tremayne 2006; Tremayne, 2006), and network analysis can

reveal the hubs and marginal actors within a journalism network (Reese et al., 2007; Tremayne, Zheng, Lee, & Jeong, 2006). Such research has shown that despite the image of a non-hierarchical network of blogs where power is more evenly distributed than in the traditional mainstream media-audience relationship, there are indeed power relationships and inequalities that remain and distinguish between who is heard and who is not. Because of such forces as preferential attachment and the benefit of early entry into a network, the shape of a network can be determined early on. This dynamic creates an interesting phenomenon, where actors have agency within the network and are not forced to behave in one way or another, but the structure created by that agency can determine future activity.

Critical geography has also questioned the equality of the expanded mobility created by the network society and place-less flows of capital, be it financial or human. Castells (1998) expanded his initial thesis by noting the creation of the dual city, where an elite minority well positioned to benefit from the growth of global networks further distanced itself from an increasingly more remote underclass which was mostly disconnected from the operation and shaping of these global networks, but nonetheless directly affected by them. These different groups relate to the changes wrought by globalization and the spread of information technology in a "power geometry" that finds some groups creating and controlling changes and using it to their benefit to increase their power, while other groups merely receive the impact of these changes that lie beyond their control (Massey, 1994). In Massey's view, the imbalance of power allows further weakening of those on the losing end, as relative mobility and power reinforces the lack of mobility and power of others. Massey uses public transit as an example. The use of cars and private transit erodes the demand and financial base for public transportation—the default form of mobility for the poor. Such differences, when considered in terms of the digital divide, beg the question of who will benefit from and shape the future of journalism as it moves online.

This raises new ethical questions for journalism. The news media's use of blogging, with its interactive relationship between blog author and blog audience, reflects broader changes in media habits. These are a result of the increased diversity and expansion of voices through increased online opportunities, new cultural norms that value participation, openness, sharing, collaboration, and reciprocity, a decreased dependence on experts, and a greater sense of community among media users (Jenkins, 2006). This has led to a change in political institutions, cultural institutions, and now journalism institutions. The same characteristics Jenkins highlights are leading to changes in newsrooms (Singer, 2006) and the professional culture of journalism (Deuze, 2005). Singer's study of the 2004 presidential campaign found that editors of newspaper websites were more willing to engage users and encourage their participation in content creation, leading to changes in journalists' traditional role as gatekeepers. In the spring of 2007, the Gannett newspaper chain added an "Information Center" at each of its 86 local daily newspapers as part of its new online strategy. In addition to constant website updating and journalists roaming the city with laptops that turn them into mobile bureaus, Gannett's plans called for a "Community Conversation Desk" created at each paper that would allow readers to submit content—whether commenting directly on an article or posting their own. The editor of Gannett's paper in Greenville, South Carolina said the paper "utilizes more reader-generated photos and news than ever" while it and other papers increasingly turn to online readers for story ideas (Strupp, 2007).

As the news media continues to rely on citizens to provide news and cover their cities through the news organizations' websites, the digital divide becomes more relevant to journalism. The black holes of information that Castells (1997) warned of, whether the product of a lack of access, media literacy, or even the time required to be an active participant in participatory culture, could lead to gaps in coverage, particularly of traditionally undercovered areas of a city. Citizens on the margins economically, who arguably are most in need of journalism to document their reality, would be least able to cover themselves in a shift to a citizen-driven online journalism. Papacharissi (2002) argues that the characteristics of the virtual public sphere online will be determined by a wide range of forces beyond the technology, as she notes the need to pay attention to inequality of access to the Internet, more nuanced digital divides caused by new media illiteracy, the fragmentation of publics and public discourse, and the potential for the Internet to become merely an extension of the dominant market-driven public sphere that Habermas denounced. Research into the relationship between class and traditional news formats has found that local newspapers (Ettema & Peer, 2004) and local television news (Heider & Fuse, 2004) cover wealthier neighborhoods far more extensively than poor ones. Will the same be true for citizen journalism?

The most visible creators of citizen media online so far have been bloggers, and research has focused on them as a window into the characteristics of citizen media, and its potential to produce journalism. Distinguishing among types of blogs is important, for there are so many different ways that people use blogs that the term is quickly losing any inherent meaning (Schmidt, 2007). However the two most prominent types of blogs are those that deal with personal issues and do not generate news about anything but themselves (Herring et al. 2007; Papacharissi, 2007). Whereas bloggers who do discuss events typically use the reporting of other sources for their raw material, often to dispute it or cite it as support for an argument, generating more commentary than information (Reese et al., 2007). The mainstream media has incorporated blogs into its work, but primarily as an enhancement of traditional reporting routines with little change in the reporter's gatekeeping function (Singer, 2005), despite blogs' technical potential for more conversational and collaborative approaches. This engagement of the blogosphere by the mainstream media has created contested journalistic terrain between the traditional reporting sensibilities of professional staff bloggers, and the more opinionated independent bloggers (Carlson, 2007; Robinson, 2006; Wall, 2005). This creates a spectrum of media ranging from professionals and amateurs discussing a news agenda primarily dictated by the mass media, to individuals free to discuss whatever they wish with no need to follow any code of conduct other than that dictated by law or the desire to have an audience.

Nevertheless the blending of private and public spheres on blogs (Papacharissi, 2007) makes a bloggers' location on this spectrum fluid. The diarist of today could produce journalism tomorrow, whether by circumstance or inspiration. They are within the network, if on the margins of it by choice, making them far more likely to participate in the various venues for citizen journalism than those who are outside the network. The latter category is often the result of persistent digital divides. The digital divide concept is shifting from a binary divide to a continuum that more accurately reflects the different degrees to which people use the Internet (Livingstone & Helsper, 2007). In their study of 9 to 19-year-olds' Internet usage, Livingstone and Helsper (2007) found that while there are few young people who do not use the Internet at all, there are still divides along socioeconomic, gender, and other lines that affect how young people use the Internet, with working class young people more likely to be occasional users and middle class young people more likely to be daily users and have such advantages as Internet access in their bedroom. In what could be a vicious circle, those who don't use the Internet might not see a benefit in doing so (Selwyn, 2003), since existing content and services are geared towards existing audiences. Brock's (2007) analysis of the ideological aspects of online content concludes that it discourages use by African-Americans, and that support for citizen-generated content creation perpetuates such cultural digital divides in contrast to digital citizen media's reputation for democratization.

A geographical focus on the content of blogs can help determine the coordinates of these new private/public spheres, and the areas that these potential citizen journalists might cover. It can also help reveal whether digital culture is creating a divide that could enable the marginalization or outright exclusion—voluntary or involuntary—of some publics from digital media networks, a central aspect of Castells' dual city.

Research Questions/Methodology

This study compares two specific types of online citizen media to see what areas of a city they typically cover. Analyzing references in citizen-created content to specific locations in a city is one way to test how the digital divide is affecting citizen coverage, and to see how effectively a citizen-driven journalism might cover a city.

This study focuses on the city of Austin, Texas, which has a long tradition of citizen media experimentation and Internet activism. Creative industries, including advertising, video game development, film and music have earned Austin a reputation as a top city for the "creative class." The South by

Southwest (SXSW) festival draws tens of thousands of attendees from around the world every March for week-long conferences on technology, film, and music. Austin hosted the World Congress on Information Technology in the summer of 2006, and expanded its free wireless networks throughout downtown to enhance the abundant free wi-fi available in coffeehouses, parks, and buildings throughout the central city—including the University of Texas, whose more than 50,000 students are found gathering with their laptops around wi-fi hotspots on and off campus. The city government has received recognition for its online services, which it relies heavily on—in 2006 the city made its job application process online only. All this activity earns Austin frequent acclaim as one of the most "wired" cities in the country.

Meanwhile there has been much work to try preventing low-income neighborhoods and their residents from being left behind. Although Austin has witnessed a recent boom in growth, there remain drastic economic disparities that adhere to specific geographic boundaries and mirror differences in the racial composition of the city. City demographic maps that use 2000 federal census data to compare concentrations of low-income families show that those neighborhoods with the highest percentage of low-income families are found east of the main north-south highway (I-35), to the north of the 183 highway, and to the south of Ben White Boulevard.[3] The first road cuts directly through central Austin, while the other two roads provide its north and south boundaries. The area to the west of I-35 and between these two roads has substantially lower rates of low-income households. These areas are similarly different in their racial makeup. While the low-income areas have populations of African-Americans or Hispanics that range from 40 percent to 80 percent or higher, the central area of Austin bounded by these main roads generally has populations that are 0 percent to 20 percent African-American or Hispanic.

Several initiatives have been launched in response to these patterns and with the recognition of the need to bring the residents of low-income areas online. The city partnered with the local non-profit Austin Free-Net to develop and maintain public computer labs in about a dozen underserved locations throughout the city. The Austin Wireless City Project non-profit has helped set up 81 (as of November 2007) free wireless hot-spots in libraries, bars, coffee shops, and other locations around the city. Area nonprofits have also formed the 501Tech group, which shares information about free and low-cost hardware, software, and computer training, such as a July 2007 meeting on how nonprofits can install and run their own Drupal-based content management systems.

Meanwhile, Austin's mainstream media have attempted to capture some of the independent energy found online, with the daily newspaper the *Austin-American Statesman* adding dozens of staff blogs, reader forums, and reader blogs to its website in 2006. The alternative weekly the *Austin Chronicle* followed suit with an updated website that emphasized reader forums and comment sections for each article, as well as staff blogs. However what this study focuses on is the online content that is independent from these two more established news organizations. In Austin there are a variety of citizen media types which have gained an audience and sustained production. This study looks at two types—individual weblogs and group weblogs. The Austinbloggers.org website launched in January 2003 and has hundreds of members who continue to actively post, several of whom have received recognition from the mainstream press on a local and state level. Although there is not a purely citizen-driven community network in Austin, the Austin branch of the Gothamist.com chain of city blogs, Austinist.com, has become widely popular and influential, with debate on its site occasionally spilling over into mainstream coverage (such as a controversy surrounding accusations of favoritism in regulation of unofficial parties during the SXSW festival) and former staff moving on to work for the Statesman's website. The national Metroblogging.com chain also has an Austin website, Austin.Metblogs.com.

There are many other citizen media outlets in Austin, such as Craigslist, a Livejournal community, endless Myspace and Facebook members, and message board/review sites such as Yelp and Chowhound. While important and highly popular, these and other websites have some distinct differences from the standard blog format that warrant a separate study. For now, individual weblogs and group weblogs are considered because they are the most similar to the new wave of participatory journalism features on news organization websites. Journalism outlets have become more comfortable with the blog format and have incorporated its more informal nature into their news product. The weblogs reviewed here are closer in terms of producer/audience relationship to the more controlled participatory journalism found on news sites, where a news organization hosts citizen feedback and occasional citizen contributions—much as the Statesman and the Chronicle.

It is rare for an individual blogger to gain a wide audience for their coverage of their city. Although there are some well-known "place blogs" that provide hyperlocal coverage of a specific city or neighborhood, such as BaristaNet.com and H2OTown.info, the majority of individual blogs write about their personal lives rather than news about the places and events surrounding them (Papacharissi, 2007). Yet in theory it is the individual bloggers who seem most likely to join the corps of a news organization's citizen reporter staff. They have the initiative and interest in becoming media producers. They have familiarity and expertise with the software and format, and they have the writing and information-gathering skills needed to produce content for an audience. Most importantly, individual bloggers are likely to be the most consistent producers of content, because they need to meet frequent deadlines to gain and keep an audience. While their posts might not specifically discuss places in the city, it seems possible that they would at least mention places around them or that they visit—even if the place is merely a backdrop to a more personal discussion. Recording and mapping where these places are can provide an idea of where individual bloggers spend their lives. Therefore the first research question is:

RQ1: Where do the Most Popular Individual Weblogs in Austin Talk About?

To measure this, the author did a content analysis of all the posts in the month of April by the most popular individual weblogs in Austin, 416 posts total. The month of April 2007 was the most recent complete month at the point of data collection, which ensured that this would be the most accurate snapshot of the state of blogging in Austin. Selecting the most recent month also made it more likely that links in posts would still be active. The list was drawn from AustinBloggers.org, which has a section that ranks its member blogs based on their Technorati ranking. The first 20 blogs were selected, and ranged in number of inbound blog links from 438 for the most popular—Greek Tragedy[4]—to 22 for Perilocity,[5] the 20th most popular blog on the list. The Technorati ranking counts how many other blogs link to the blog in question and is a standard measure of a blog's popularity. The posts were coded for one of four options: national topic, state topic, local topic, and personal topic. If there were any references in any of the posts to a location in Austin, the place was noted and marked on a map of the city.

There was a high potential that the data from the individual blogs would not include many local places, but there are two group weblogs in Austin—each a member of a national (and now international) chain of similar city-based weblogs with a staff of part-time editors and reporters and reader contributions in the comments—the aforementioned Austinist and Austin Metroblogging. Since these two websites make a point of providing local coverage, the second research question seeks to find what "local" means to them:

RQ2: Where do Locally Focused Group Weblogs in Austin Talk About?

This question was also answered using a content analysis of the two weblogs' posts in the month of April (a total of 265 posts). However the coding scheme was slightly different. Although it was also coded for national, state, and local topics, the author split local coverage into location specific and non-location specific. The places mentioned in the location specific posts were also noted and marked on a second map of the city.

Results/Discussion

The first research question sought to find out what parts of the city the most popular individual bloggers covered. But before reviewing those results, it's important to note that for the most part these bloggers did not discuss local places, events, or people. Several of the blogs that were ranked among the top 20 locally-based blogs were no longer based in Austin. Because of the absence of biographical data or "about me" sections, and the lack of "local" posts, this usually became clear about halfway through reading the month's posts, when the blogger would mention such things as day trips in Northern California or other offhand remarks about their location that made it clear they no longer lived in Austin. It is possible that some other blogs that were counted are not based in Austin anymore either, because they did not provide any clues to their whereabouts, and the content of their posts were not specific to any location. But in the absence of a clear sign that the author did not live in Austin, these blogs were counted as Austin because they were still signed up for the Austinbloggers aggregator website.

The variability in production among the top Austin blogs also complicated RQ1. Although the question sought to find out where these bloggers were writing about, the analysis coded the total number of posts generated by the 20 blogs—416 posts, which was lower than expected, if one assumes that blogs are updated once a day, seven days per week, which for 20 blogs would equal 600 posts. Many of the most popular national bloggers post multiple times per day. Yet the majority of bloggers studied here did not post every day, and some posted just once per week. Therefore a highly productive blogger such as Grits for Breakfast,[6] which writes about criminal justice issues statewide and focused on activity in the state legislature (which was in session when the analysis was done in April 2007), could skew the data. Grits wrote 117 posts in April, compared to the second highest, Don't Mess with Taxes,[7] which wrote 52. Furthermore almost all of Grits posts were coded as "state." Therefore the results are provided both with and without Grits' data.

For many of the posts it was clear which category they belonged in. National posts discussed such dominant news events as the Don Imus firing and the Virginia Tech shootings (both of which happened in April 2007), reviews of nationally-released movies and music, federal tax policy, President George W.

Table 10.1 Individual Bloggers' Coverage Focus (w/Grits)

National	44.9% (n = 187)
State	29.8% (n = 124)
Local	8.1% (n = 34)
Personal	14.1% (n = 59)
Other	2.8% (n = 12)

Table 10.2 Individual Bloggers' Coverage Focus (w/o Grits)

National	60.8% (n = 182)
State	5.3% (n = 16)
Local	11.3% (n = 34)
Personal	19.7% (n = 59)
Other	3.0% (n = 9)

Bush, and businesses or issues that would be commonly known in most parts of the country. In these posts the author would typically link to a mainstream news source and offer their opinion, but they would not connect the national to the local. This only happened a few times and was placed in the "other" category, such as when Don't Mess with Taxes talked about long waits at post offices to file returns and added a description of activity at their local post office. The same was true for state-level posts, which were the lowest type of post in the adjusted percentages. These posts would talk about new laws proposed by the state legislature, or events happening in other Texas cities.

Where there was the most potential for overlap, and the finest distinction, was between the personal and the local. This often required a more qualitative analysis of the specific post to determine how to code it. Strictly personal posts included stories about relationships, dreams, children, hobbies, and homes. At no time did the blogger mention a specific location in recounting these stories, even if the story involved a date or a trip. The post would be focused on the people involved, and again could have taken place anywhere. Locations played no role. However, there were several times that a personal story did involve locations, such as when Greek Tragedy described a visit by friends from New York City, and the various places the blogger took them to show them around Austin. Many times the places served as backdrops to events (i.e., "the meeting is at Brentwood Tavern, which is family-friendly"), or were mentioned offhand (i.e., "after lunch at Whole Foods we went to Seattle's Best"). There were more detailed descriptions of place at times, such as a comparison of experiences at two local live music venues and one blogger's thoughts on several specific streets in East Austin as they shopped around for a house. If a coder defined local in more narrow terms, there would have been a much higher percentage of personal-focused posts. But the intent here was to see which places in town were mentioned at all, to find which places the bloggers frequent and which parts of the city are in their orbit.

These locations were then noted on a map[8] (see Appendix A, and available online in more detail) to show the parts of town that bloggers discussed, to get a better sense of the areas they frequent, the places they are familiar with, and what parts of the city they are able to write about with some authority. Although of course this does not provide a comprehensive look at what sides of Austin the bloggers know, some patterns emerged. The first map shows that almost all of the local posts occurred at places west of I-35, in either the downtown business/entertainment district, central neighborhoods that are white/middle-class, and neighborhoods that are a mixture of retail and residential. There were only six posts that dealt with places located east of I-35 (of 43 total), with none in the southeast or northeast of the city, both areas with higher lower income populations and a higher percentage of minorities. Of those six, five dealt with new real estate developments, a sign of the widespread development east of the highway and the changing population of East Austin, as more professional white singles and families move east in search of more affordable housing. The sixth location is a boutique coffeeshop that opened in 2001. The places that were mentioned from the other areas of town were a mixture of clubs to see live music, stores, restaurants, new shopping malls, the University of Texas' law school and performing arts center, the state capitol, technology-based businesses (such as an incubator for clean energy start-ups), parks, and kitsch such as Austin's "Cathedral of Junk." These were the sites of meetings, dates, lectures, and performances, and the subjects of reviews, recommendations, and reminiscences.

Since previous research has noted the propensity for individual blogs to focus on either microscopic personal trivia or overcovered national topics, RQ2 looked at what areas of town are covered by two group weblogs specifically focused on the local. The posts were first separated into national, state, local (not location specific) and local (place specific), to see how much of their coverage accomplished this, what portion of that coverage discussed places in town, and finally where those places were in comparison to the economic and racial patterns of the city. The two group weblogs analyzed here—Austinist and Metroblogging Austin—which were launched in 2003 and 2004 respectively, have the traditional weblog structure of reverse chronological posts with reader comments, and have staffs (how many hours a week they work and whether they are all paid is not clear) of multiple bloggers. They also live up to their billing as providers of local content, as shown in Table 10.3.

The bulk of the posts were from Austinist, which had 224 "full-length" posts of at least 100-200 words. There were also several posts not included in this analysis because they were either posts with links to other blogs in the "-ist" family of city weblogs, or calender listings. As with the individual bloggers, the national posts included reviews of new music and films, as well as interviews with national cultural figures (bands, writers), and the state coverage primarily dealt with potential state legislation and news from other Texas cities. Posts that were local but non-place specific mentioned citywide trends (i.e., Austin's ranking in national lifestyle polls), news about Austin residents (i.e., writer Lawrence Wright won a Pulitzer Prize in 2007), the weather, traffic, and other general topics.

As with the individual blogs, the local place-specific posts, which were the majority of the content on these two sites, were dominated by the middle to upper class, primarily Caucasian areas of Austin (see Appendix A, and online for more detail[9]). There were more posts that mentioned places east of I-35 than

Table 10.3 Group Blogs' Coverage Focus (total posts = 265)

National	10.5% (n = 28)
State	7.5% (n = 20)
Local	24.1% (n = 64)
Local (place specific)	57.7% (n = 153)

Table 10.4 Locations of Local Posts

Neighborhood	Mid/High Income/Low Minority	Low Income/High Minority
Individual Weblogs	86%	14%
Group Weblogs	77%	23%

on the individual blogs, but these were still relatively rare. Of the 100 places mentioned in the two blogs in April, 18 were in East Austin, three were in Northeast Austin, and two were in Southeast Austin. There were no places mentioned in the low-income Hispanic neighborhoods in North Austin and South Austin. These numbers do not account for the multiple times several places in central Austin were mentioned, such as UT-Austin's 13 mentions, the downtown Alamo Drafthouse movie theater's 12 mentions, and the downtown rock club Emo's 12 mentions (these and other repeats account for the difference between the 153 local place-specific posts and the 100 places mentioned). A closer look at which places were mentioned is also revealing. In East Austin, four of the places were community/cooperative gardens mentioned in a single post about a tour of Austin's community gardens, playhouses and theater companies accounted for four more places, art galleries comprised two places, and two more places were old businesses that were bought and reopened by new management in 2007. But for both the individual and group blogs, the percentage of locations that were in mid-to-high income, low-percent minority areas was far higher than the percentage in low income, high-percent minority areas, as shown in Table 10.4.

Although reader comments were not included in this analysis, differing reactions to two posts on Austinist that occurred within a day of each other underscores this split in city coverage. One of the Northeast Austin posts was about the fatal shooting of a Mexican teenager in front of his father during an armed robbery in a parking lot, and there were no comments on the story. A subsequent post about the ongoing controversy over the impending construction of a Wal-Mart in a Northwest Austin neighborhood drew the most active comment thread of any post reviewed. This is not to say that the readers of Austinist don't care about the shooting. It just appears to be outside their frame of reference for the city. In comparison the Wal-Mart thread attracted many readers who identified themselves as residents of the surrounding neighborhoods. References to lower-income Austinites who would likely shop at the Wal-Mart were all in the third person.

Conclusion

These Austin-based examples of online citizen media's most prevalent forms—the individual weblog and the group weblog—barely, if at all, cover low-income, Hispanic, and African-American areas of Austin. Prior research has found that mainstream print and television news provides far more extensive coverage to wealthier neighborhoods, and it seems that this is the case for the most prominent examples of citizen media in Austin today.

This disparity seems perilously close to Castells' dual city. Part of Austin's population is adept at using digital flows of information to communicate with each other, while the poor and other communities marginalized offline are marginalized online. But the situation is fortunately more complex than that. Residents of low-income neighborhoods do surface in these media networks, but for now only as objects of discussion rather than participants. Also some locations in the neighborhoods themselves, particularly the rapidly gentrifying neighborhoods of East Austin, were mentioned. Although these locations were not indigenous to East Austin, they are a sign of intersections between networks, between Castells' space of flows and space of places. This is closer to Livingstone and Helsper's gradations of inclusion, where working class Internet users have a minimal online presence. The question now is what can trigger communication between the margins and the hubs, and what potential there is to increase the presence of those on the margins in online media networks.

It would be easy to dismiss the marginalization of the poor in citizen media as merely a result of another new innovation that has yet to expand beyond its initial adopters, but there are other obstacles to participation that go beyond access to technology and skills. Maintaining an individual blog in the style and to the degree that it can build an audience at the level of the individual blogs studied here seems to influence its content. Those bloggers who do their own reporting obviously dedicate a great deal of time to their work. A prior study found that those who go online more frequently are more likely to be immersed in digital culture, starting weblogs and contributing comments to weblogs (Rutigliano, 2006). Maintaining a weblog to the degree required to build and maintain an audience—staying abreast of events, interacting with an audience, reading other weblogs and either commenting or linking to their posts to build a rapport, and not coincidentally increase one's Google PageRank—all take time, or at least frequent if not constant access to the Internet. Adding original information gathering to that workload is prohibitive for most.

Therefore beyond these exceptions, most individual bloggers who have built an audience and influence beyond their circle of friends post regularly and on topics that rely more on opinion and the actions of major social institutions than on first-hand reporting. Their content, when it is not personal, is reactive. It uses either news generated by mainstream outlets or the actions of government and corporations that those mainstream outlets generally cover, and then adds its perspective. Even these early adopters, who already have the technology and skills needed to run a blog, appear confined to certain types of coverage. Furthermore these blogs benefit from the availability of an audience that has something in common with them. For a blogger from a low-income neighborhood to gain a following, it would either need a similar audience of peers online to interact with, or the sustained attention of residents from other neighborhoods. Both would be a major challenge.

Since a home-grown blog from a person living in a poor area of Austin faces such obstacles, those who have the resources to run a blog would have to document these areas themselves. But this seems unlikely. There were rare local posts on low-income neighborhoods that were the result of the blogger gathering news during the course of their own daily lives, such as the blogger who described different neighborhoods while looking for an affordable home and found themselves in one of Austin's low-income areas. But such exceptions are a result of people venturing into unfamiliar territory, an occasion that is as rare offline as it is online. Judging by the general coverage areas of the individual bloggers, their lives are relegated to areas of Austin that are relatively poverty-free.

Since the work it takes to sustain an individual blog almost demands dependence on institutions for post fodder, group weblogs that collaboratively cover a city would seem to have potential for providing more inclusive coverage. But this was not the case in Austin. The two examples studied here provided a great deal of first-hand local coverage, but barely covered places outside the central areas of the city that are bounded to the north, south, and east by the highways that separate them from Austin's low-income neighborhoods. When the blogs did venture out to these areas, it was to cover places that are similar to the types found in the central area—rock clubs, art galleries, and playhouses. Most of these were close to the downtown area in regions of East Austin that are steadily gentrifying. Of course it is the prerogative of a commercial website to cover what its audience cares about, and group weblogs focused on culture and targeted at a young professional demographic have sprouted up throughout the US Metroblogging and Austinist were selected because of the fact that they are members of national chains with similar websites in most major American cities. But this illustrates an important point—for all of its potential, and the freedom that citizen media might provide from the influences of corporations and government on the mainstream news media, its reality today is limited by socioeconomic, cultural, and commercial factors that can be just as stubborn.

It is possible that alternatives will arise to this commercialized catering to the dominant online audience, but network logic makes that especially difficult. For one, the law of preferential attachment, which favors those who have early entry into the network, predicts that the patterns found here will intensify over time. Websites with content created for the early adopters gain attention, audience, capital, and influence, in time becoming the hubs of the network and increasing their strength as new websites enter the network. It becomes difficult, though not impossible, to compete with these hubs for shares of attention, audience, capital, and influence and thereby change the structure of the network. Therefore a focus on these citizen media hubs is valid, although they represent a small percentage of the entire network. There are possibly blogs and listservs that focus on life in Austin's low-income neighborhoods—in fact the author has come across a blog produced by a woman living in a trailer park—but their marginal location in the media network echoes their marginalization offline. It is also true that other forms of media, particularly community newspapers, cover these areas. Whether these analog forms of media can intersect with online media networks is the question. Or they might instead provide evidence of an ironic corollary of Castells' globally integrated networks—the fragmentation of the disconnected public into isolated islands of identity.

The mainstream media is now actively engaged in these online media networks, as it tries to harness the rampant activity occurring beyond its control. Yet as this unfolds, it is critical to realize the problematic nature of that activity and respond to it, lest the same pattern recur on news websites. Journalists and journalism's traditional role as a bridge between communities is perhaps in greater demand in the age of online media. Various digital divides are creating gaps in coverage that raise new ethical questions for journalists, whether they work for the mainstream or independently of it. If the digital divide influences which citizens can participate in online spaces for debate and which neighborhoods can be covered by their residents, then journalists should recognize that they need to take a proactive approach to covering these neighborhoods and their residents—the lower half of Castells' dual city. Here technology reinforces an old ethical concern—the need for journalists to reach out beyond powerful and elite sources to those on the margins of society.

Perhaps relying on the citizen journalist to counter the logic of the network is unfair. Perhaps the most important distinction between the professional journalist and the citizen journalist is the professional's ethical responsibility to record these unheard voices and document life in these unknown parts of the city, to force the intersection of the network's centers and margins, and to introduce information to the network that it would otherwise ignore.

Notes

1 Jeff Jarvis and CUNY hosted the first Networked Journalism conference in October 2007, with more than 150 attendees including representatives from several mainstream news organizations, including The New York Times, the Washington Post, Reuters, and the BBC.
2 http://www.editorandpublisher.com/eandp/departments/online/article_display.jsp?vnu_content_id=1003662280.
3 Demographic maps available online as pdf files at: (low-income families) http://www.ci.austin.tx.us/census/downloads/fams50below.pdf (racial composition) http://www.ci.austin.tx.us/census/images/mixed.pdf.
4 http://stephanieklein.blogs.com/.
5 http://riskman.typepad.com/perilocity/
6 http://gritsforbreakfast.blogspot.com/.
7 http://dontmesswithtaxes.typepad.com/.
8 http://tinyurl.com/3cvj6z.
9 http://tinyurl.com/2n68yh.

References

Brock, A. (2005). "A belief in humanity is a belief in colored men:" Using culture to span the digital divide. *Journal of Computer-Mediated Communication*, *11*(1), article 17. http://jcmc.indiana.edu/vol11/issue1/brock.html.

Carlson, M. (2007). Blogs and journalistic authority. *Journalism Studies*, 8(2), 264–279.

Castells, M. (1997) *The power of identity*. Oxford, UK: Blackwell Publishers.

Castells, M. (1998) *End of millennium*. Oxford, UK: Blackwell Publishers.

Deuze, M. (2005). What is journalism? Professional identity and ideology of journalists reconsidered. *Journalism*, 6(4), 442–464.

Ettema, J. S., & Peer, L. (2004). Good news from a bad neighborhood: Urban journalism and community assets. In D. Heider (Ed.), *Class and news*. Lanham, MD: Rowman & Littlefield.

Harp, D., & Tremayne, M. (2006). The gendered blogosphere: Examining inequality using network and feminist theory. *Journalism & Mass Communication Quarterly*, 83(2), 246–264.

Heider, D., & Fuse, K. (2004). Class and local TV news. In D. Heider (Ed.), *Class and news*. Lanham, MD: Rowman & Littlefield.

Herring, S. C., Scheidt, L. A., Kouper, I., & Wright, E. (2007). Longitudinal content analysis of blogs: 2003–2004. In M. Tremayne (Ed.), *Blogging, citizenship, and the future of media*. New York: Routledge.

Hodkinson, P. (2007). Interactive online journals and individualization. *New Media & Society*, 9(4), 625–650.

Jenkins, H. (2006). *Convergence culture*. New York, NY: New York University Press.

Livingstone, S., & Helsper, E. (2007). Gradations in digital inclusion: Children, young people and the digital divide. *New Media & Society*, 9(4), 651–669.

Massey, D. (1994). *Space, place and gender*. Minneapolis, MN: University of Minnesota Press.

Papacharissi, Z. (2002). The virtual public sphere: the internet as a public sphere. *New Media and Society*, 4(1), 9–27.

Papacharissi, Z. (2007). Audiences as media producers: Content analysis of 260 blogs. In M. Tremayne (Ed.), *Blogging, citizenship, and the future of media*. New York: Routledge.

Rainie, L. (2005). The state of blogging. www.pewinternet.org/pdfs/PIP_blogging_data.pdf.

Reese, S. D., Rutigliano, L., Hyun, K., & Jeong, J. (2007). Mapping the blogosphere. Professional and citizen-based media in the global news arena. *Journalism: Theory, practice and criticism*, 8(3): 235–261

Robinson, S. (2006). The mission of the j-blog: Recapturing journalistic authority online. *Journalism*, 7(1), 65–83.

Rutigliano, L. (2006). The internet immersion divide: A barrier to inclusive online communities. Paper presented at annual meeting of the Association for Education in Journalism and Mass Communication, San Francisco, August 2006.

Schmidt, J. (2007). Blogging practices: An analytical framework. *Journal of Computer-Mediated Communication*, *12*(4), article 13. http://jcmc.indiana.edu/vol12/issue4/schmidt.html

Selwyn, N. (2003). Apart from technology: Understanding people's non–use of information and communication technologies in everyday life. *Technology in Society*, 25 (1), 99–116.

Singer, J. B. (2005). The political j-blogger: "Normalizing" a new media form to fit old norms and practices. *Journalism, 6(2)*, 173–198.

Singer, J. B. (2006). Stepping back from the gate: Online newspaper editors and the co-production of content in campaign 2004. *Journalism and Mass Communication Quarterly, 83(2)*, 265–280.

Strupp, J. (2007). Inside Gannett's "Information centers". Editor & publisher, accessed online at http://www.mediainfo.com/eandp/news/article_display.jsp?vnu_content_id=1003605881, last accessed July 11, 2007.

Tremayne, M. (2006). Applying network theory to the use of external links on news web sites. In X. Li (2006), *Internet newspapers: The making of a mainstream medium.* Mahwah, NJ: Lawrence Erlbaum.

Tremayne, M., Zheng, N., Lee, J. K., & Jeong, J. (2006). Issue publics on the web: Applying network theory to the war blogosphere. *Journal of Computer-Mediated Communication, 12(1)*, article 15. http://jcmc.indiana.edu/vol12/issue1/tremayne.html

Urry, J. (2003). *Global complexity.* Cambridge: Polity Press.

Wall, M. (2005). "Blogs of war": Weblogs as News. *Journalism, 6(2)*, 131–152.

Index

Abbott, Andrew 61n2
Abdulhamid, Ammar 151
access to information 34–35
accuracy 10
advertising 2, 20; audiences 48; blogs
   60; interactivity 78; public sphere 31
African-Americans 193, 194, 200
Aftonbladet 7
agency ix, 26, 191; agenda setting 169;
   change 60–61; online customization
   78
agenda setting 102–103; citizen
   journalism 169; Hurricane Katrina
   167, 174–175, 182; Internet power
   users 141; traditional media 129
"Akaevu.net" (blog) 151
Albert, R. 126
Aldrich, H.E. 49
Alford, R.R. 58
Allan, Stuart 153, 158
Allbritton, Chris 158
Allen, George 38
AllmyData.com 124
Altheide, D.L. 51
"Amarji" (blog) 151
American Civil Liberties Union 5
Anderson, C. 142
Anderson, R.B. 80
animation 83–84
Apple 9
Apple Daily 97–98
Archibugi, Daniela 19
Asian tsunami (2004) 4
association vii
attention economy 95–96
audiences x, 44–67; blogs 157, 201–202;
   decline in 2, 92; environmental
   approaches in news sociology 51–52;

fragmentation 23, 57; mass
   communicators' conceptions of
   46–48; metric data 53–54, 57; new
   institutional theory 45–46, 48–50;
   online 45, 47, 52–59; typifications
   48, 60, 61
Austin, Texas 190, 193–203
autonomy 34, 47

"Back to Iraq" (blog) 158
"Baghdad Burning" (blog) 159
Ball-Rokeach, S.J. 52
Balnaves, M. 24
Barabasi, A.-L. 126
Barnhurst, Kevin 51
Baudrillard, J. 157
Bauer, J.M. 101
Bauman, Zygmunt 17, 19, 20, 22
BBC 135
Beam, R.A. 59
Beck, J.C. 96
Beck, Ulrich 19, 20, 23
Benson, R. 59
Bimber, B. 29, 37
Blip.TV 3
Blog Africa 3
BlogHer.com 8
blogosphere 36–37, 108, 152, 192–193
blogs x, 2, 5, 36–37, 108–122, 151–165;
   adopted as "reporting tools" 56;
   "A-list" 36–37, 109, 153, 161;
   bloggers as volunteers 55;
   commercialization 60, 202; cultural
   context 151–152, 153, 161; definition
   of 109; de-institutionalization
   159–161; "displaced citizen psyche"
   xi; as form of journalism 111–114,
   153; geographical coverage 190,

193–203; group 3, 195, 196, 199–200, 202; history writing 168; Hurricane Katrina xi, 171, 179; hyperlinks 127, 129; increase in 44, 93, 123; Kenya 5; motivations for 110–111, 112; personal nature of 156–159; political participation 114–117; power law distribution 126; power relationships 191; private dissent 39; reference groups 47; right to respond 6; shift to conservatism 60; software 123; speed 154–156; subjects 110; successes 8; survey of news managers 53; types of 192–193; *see also* citizen journalism
Boczkowski, P. 55
Bodnar, J. 168, 182
Bolter, J.D. 80, 155
bookcrossing.com 160
Bressers, B. 55
Brock, A. 193
Bronston, B. 176
Bruns, A. 128
Burnett, J. 173
Bush, George W. 172, 178
"Buzzmachine" (blog) 151

Calcanis, J. 127
capitalism 20, 31, 161
Carey, J. viii, 21, 31, 51
Carmichael, P. 181
Cassidy, William P. 53
Castells, M. 160, 161, 189–190, 191, 192, 201, 203
catchphrases 172, 175
change ix, 22, 25, 56, 58, 59, 60–61
children 10
Chowhound 195
Chyi, Hsiang Iris x, xii, 91–107
citizen journalism 24, 55, 58, 60, 71; geographical coverage 193–203; Hurricane Katrina xi, 166, 170, 171, 172–176, 177–180, 181–182; networked journalism distinction 189; rhetoric of 54; social media news aggregators 127, 129, 134–136, 141, 142; YouTube 38; *see also* blogs; participatory journalism; user-generated content
"citizen marketers" 124
citizenship 17–19; citizen-consumers 25; global 20
civic engagement ix, 21, 25, 29–43;

blogging 36–37; decline in 29; digital technologies 34–36; modes of 30; private sphere 39–40; public sphere 30–32, 39–40; Riesman's work 33–34; social media forms 125; YouTube 37–39
class 189, 192, 193, 199–200
Cluetrain Manifesto 161
CNN 9, 36, 38, 173
cognitive load 81–82
Cohen, K.R. 156, 157, 159–160
Cole, Juan 161
Coleman, S. 29, 35
collaborative communication 2, 24
collaborative filtering 125–126, 128, 141
collective intelligence 23, 25
collective memory xi, 166, 167–168, 169–170, 179, 181–182
commemoration 167, 169, 176, 177–179, 181
commercialization viii, 31, 32, 35, 202; *see also* profit
communities 3, 18
competition 2, 55–56
consumer sovereignty 99
consumerism 161
consumers 18, 20–21, 25, 26
content analysis 101–102
content management 79
contiguity 73, 79–82, 84
convergence x, 24, 54, 160–161
conversation 5–6, 123
Cook, T.E. 52
Cooper, A. 177
cosmopolitanism 19–20
Couldry, N. 158
counterpublics 31–32
Craigslist 3–4, 195
credibility 9, 52, 58–59, 153, 167, 169
crisis coverage *see* Hurricane Katrina
crowdsourcing 128
"cultural convergence" 160–161
customization 75, 78, 96
cyberbalkanization 125
cyberspace *see* Internet
cynicism 31

Daily Kos 2, 109–110
Daily Mail 135
The Daily Show with Jon Stewart 38, 159
The DailyMe 84, 103
data warehousing 124
databases 6

Davenport, T.H. 96
De Jong, Alex 18
De Santos, M. 55
Deal, T.E. 49–50
DeGrandpre, R. 96
Del.icio.us 124
DeLong, Brad 5
democracy vii, viii, ix, 25; blogs x, xi,
    117, 118; civic engagement 30, 33–34;
    cosmopolitan 19; ethical
    responsibility xii–xiii; global citizens
    20; informed citizenship 17–18;
    journalism and 21; online media 35;
    participatory 125; public sphere
    30–32; publicizing representative xii;
    quality of 99; social media news
    aggregators 129, 136, 140; see also
    politics
Dennen, Alfie 157, 162
Deuze, Mark ix, xii, 15–28, 50, 53
Dewey, J. vii–viii
dialogue 58
Digg x, 103, 124, 126–128, 130–139,
    140–141, 142
digital divide 189, 191, 192, 193–194,
    203
"digital natives" 72, 84
Dillon, A. 71–72
Dimmick, J. 101
disimplementation 54–55
"displaced citizen psyche" xi
diversity of content 102
Donohue, G.A. 52
dual city 189, 190, 191, 193, 201, 203
"dumbing down" viii
Dunwoody, S. 77

echo chamber effect 125–126, 161
"18mo" (blog) 151–152
Emulex 9
entertainment news 97, 98, 136–137,
    142
environmental approaches in news
    sociology 51–52
ethical responsibility xi, xii–xiii, 203
ethnocentrism 23, 152
Ettema, J.S. 47, 58
Eveland, W.P. 77
Everyblock.com 3, 6
exemplars 172, 175
expert knowledge 51–52, 74

Facebook 2, 124, 195

Fagerjord, A. 155–156
fairness 10
"field of social forces" model 59
Fineman, Howard 159
Flickr 3, 7, 124
"Flit" (blog) 156
Foot, K. 169
forums 54
Fox News 159
Fraser, N. 31–32
Friedland, R. 58
Furl 123

Gamson, W.A. 170
Gannett newspaper chain 191–192
Gans, Herbert 23, 47
gatekeeping: civic engagement 29;
    journalists 16, 23, 167; mainstream
    media 91, 110; online personalization
    75; social media news aggregators
    127–128, 129, 140, 141
gatewatching 128
Giddens, Anthony 16, 19
Giesecke, C. 178, 179
GigaOm 3
Gil de Zúñiga, Homero x, xii, 108–122
Gillmor, Dan ix, xii, 1–11, 117, 125
Glasser, T.L. 58
"global village" 19
Global Voices Online 8
globalization 19, 22, 23, 160, 191
Google 84, 99
Google News 103
graphics 80–81, 82
Griffith, Melanie 155
group blogs 3, 195, 196, 199–200, 202
Grusin, R.A. 155

Haas, T. 161
Habermas, Jürgen 30, 31, 159, 192
Hallin, D. 21, 22, 152
"hard" news 16
Hart, R.P. 31
Hartley, John 16, 23–24
Hays, John 173–174
headlines 77–78
Held, David 19
Helsper, E. 193, 201
Herbst, S. 31
Herr, Michael 154
Herring, S.C. 157
Hirsch, P.M. 57
Hispanics 194, 200

Holovaty, Adrian 6
Hong Kong 97
Huberman, B.A. 126
Huffington Post 109–110
Human Rights Watch 5
Hurricane Katrina xi, 16, 166–188;
    agenda for change 172, 174–175, 182;
    catchphrases/exemplars 172, 175;
    characters 172, 176;
    community/group identity 179–180;
    purpose of commemoration 177–179;
    signature matrix 170–172; themes
    172–174, 182
Hurwitz, J. 177
hyperlinks: blogs 109–110;
    comprehension of text 72, 81;
    gatekeeping 127; importance of 7;
    social media 124, 128, 129
hyperlocality 16, 25
hypermediacy 155, 161
hypertext 71–72, 79–80, 81

iBackup 124
iBrattleboro 3
identity 21, 25, 179–180
identity politics 157, 160
iLike 124
images 80–81, 82
independence 10
Indifferents 33
individual interest 76–77
individualism 18–19, 25, 160, 190
inequality 26, 35, 189, 190, 192
information: access to 34–35; blogs 118;
    "information agenda" 102–103;
    information explosion 93;
    information overload 93, 101;
    presentation of 74–75; see also
    information surplus; knowledge
information seeking: complex decision-
    making 101; consumer sovereignty
    99; motivation for 77; political
    participation 114, 115
information society 108
information surplus x, 91–107; attention
    economy 95–96; consumer
    sovereignty 99; new research 99–103
information theory 158
"Informed Comment" (blog) 161
infotainment viii, x–xi
Inglehart, Ronald 20
innovation viii, 8–9, 54
Inside-Dopesters 33

"Instapundit" (blog) 162
institutionalism 45–46, 48–51, 53–55,
    59–60, 61n1
interactivity 77–79, 84, 100, 124
interest 76–77, 81; "kick-outs" 82–84
Internet viii, 2–3, 6, 22–23; access to
    information 34–35; agenda setting
    103; audiences 47, 48, 52–59; civic
    engagement 29; commercialization
    35; content creation 123; contiguity
    79–82; digital divide 189, 191, 192,
    193–194, 203; enhanced learning
    71–72; geographical coverage
    193–203; history writing 168–170;
    Hurricane Katrina 166–167, 171,
    173–176, 177–180, 181–182;
    information surplus 91–107;
    innovation 8–9; interactivity 77–79;
    interest 76–77; "kick-outs" 82–84;
    links 7, 72, 127; loose coupling 50;
    media logic thesis 51; mimicry 48, 55;
    new mixed media ecology 24; new
    research 99–100; personalization 75;
    PICK model 74–85; power users 127,
    140–141; presentation of information
    74–75; as primary news source 71;
    private sphere 39–40; as read-write
    medium 1–2, 123; reciprocity 35;
    social media 123–147; social network
    theory 126–127; worldwide
    proliferation 18; see also blogs; citizen
    journalism; Web 2.0
involvement 73, 76–79, 84
Iraq 151, 153–154, 158, 159, 175
iReport 9
"Island Life" (blog) 155
Ito, Mitzuko 21, 125

Jackson, D. 172
Jarvis, Jeff 95–96, 151, 161
Jenkins, H. 24, 160–161, 191
Jobs, Steve 9
journalism schools 11
JumpCut 124
JungleDisk 124

Kahn, R. 158
Kaplan, R.L. 52
Katz, J. 96–97
Keller, Bill 56
Kellner, D. 158
Kenya 5
"kick-outs" 73, 82–84

Kintsch, W. 73
Kitch, Carolyn 167, 181
knowledge: expert 51–52, 74; Hurricane
    Katrina 179; literacy 152–153; *see*
    also information
Korea 8
Kottke, J. 126
Kovach, Bill 16
Kubik 15, 17

Lacy, S. 101
Lai, Jimmy 97–98
Lasch, K. 170
Lasica, J.D. 125
Last.fm 124
Leadbetter, C. 160
learning 71–72, 76; blogs 117–118;
    contiguity 80; interactivity 78;
    "kick-outs" 83
legitimacy 45, 48, 49, 50, 51–52, 58–59,
    60
Lemann, N. 152
Levy, P. 23
Lewin, K. 127
LinkedIn 124
links *see* hyperlinks
Lippmann, W. vii–viii
liquid journalism ix, 17, 24–26
liquid modernity 17, 22, 23
literacy 152–153, 156; electronic
    environments 80; new media xii,
    9–11; scientific 71
Livejournal 195
Livingstone, S. 193, 201
London bombings (2005) 4, 157, 162
loose coupling 45, 49–50, 54, 55, 56
Lott, Trent 153, 162n1
low-income neighborhoods 194,
    198–200, 201–203
Lowrey, Wilson ix, xii, 44–67
Luhmann, Niklas 24

MacGregor, P. 54, 57
Mackay, J. 56
Malik, Om 8
Mancini, P. 152
maps 3
Marathe, S.S. 75
marginality xi, 190, 192, 201, 203
Marshall, Joshua Micah 4
mashups 7, 124
Massey, D. 191
Matheson, Don xi, xii, 151–165

Mayer, R.E. 80
Mayrhofer, D. 24
McCombs, M.E. 102
McQuail, D. 59
media 1–2; blogs 192–193; effects
    102–103; mainstream 21, 58–59,
    110, 192, 203; media logic thesis 51;
    media system dependency theory 52;
    new media literacy 9–11; new mixed
    media ecology 18, 24, 25, 26; new
    research 100–103; online 34–36;
    public sphere 31; watchdogs 37;
    see also newspapers; social media;
    television
"mediapolis" 18
medium theory 166
Meraz, Sharon x–xi, xii, 123–147
meta-memory spaces 181
Meyer, John 49–50, 51, 54
Meyrowitz, Joshua 168–169, 179
Miller, J.D. 85
Miller, Paul 160
Miller, Peter V. 48
mimicry 48, 55
Mindich, David 92, 96
modernity 16–17, 21, 22, 24
monitorial citizen 18, 29, 35–36;
    blogging 37; civic engagement 34;
    consumerism 25; YouTube 38–39
Moralizers 33, 36
Morris, M. 100
mourning rituals 169, 177, 181
MoveOn.org 160
multimedia 80, 84, 85
MySpace 16, 124, 195

Nakednews.com 98
Nass, C. 75
Negroponte, N. 103
Nerone, John 51
Netscape 124, 127–128, 130–139,
    140–141
network society 23, 189, 190, 191
networked journalism 189–190
networks 1, 189, 190–193; hubs
    190–191, 202; individualized 18–19,
    25; marginality 203; power 160,
    161, 190; social 16, 79, 123–124,
    126–127
"new humanism" 24
new institutionalism 45–46, 48–50, 52,
    61n1; *see also* institutionalism
new media literacy 9–11

New York Times 4, 6–7, 9, 93; blogs 36; NYTimes.com 103; TimesSelect 95–96; transparency 56
Newhagen, J.E. 100
Newman, A. 170
news: audience ratings 56; collaborative manufacture of 25; decline in consumption 51, 92, 94, 95; environmental approaches in news sociology 51–52; information surplus 91, 95–97; interactivity 78; live nature of 155; mainstream media 58–59; online audiences 53–55; public discontent 21–22; selection of stories 127–128, 129; social media 130–139; tabloidization 97–98; understanding complex 72, 73–74
news aggregators x–xi, 124, 125–143
news values 16–17, 22
"Newser" (blog) 159
newspapers: audiences 44, 53, 56–57; competition 2; customized and softer news 96; decline in readership 92, 103; Gannett newspaper chain 191–192; homogeneity 55; Hong Kong 97; layout structures 79; product differentiation 96–97; reference groups 47; Taiwan 97–98
Newsvine x, 124, 127–128, 130–139, 140–141
Nielsen, J. 126
nightclubs 15
norms 48, 61, 157
Norris, Pippa 20
nostalgia 32
Nunberg, Geoff 157

Obama, Barack 38
Ogan, C. 100
OhmyNews.com 8, 24
Okolloh, Ory 5
Olien, C.N. 52
openness 58
opinion leaders 37
O'Reilly, Bill 159
Orientalism 23
Outing, Steve 55

Palfrey, John 72
Palser, Barb 56
Pambazuka 3
Papacharissi, Zizi vii–xiii, 29–43, 192
Parr, Barry 8

participatory democracy 125
participatory journalism 4–5, 6–7, 59, 60; new cultural logic 58; news websites 195; YouTube 38; *see also* citizen journalism
pastoralism 23
peer-to-peer news sharing *see* social media
personalization 39–40, 73, 75, 84, 125
Peterson, R.A. 47
Pew Research Center for the People and the Press 21–22, 92, 118n2
photobloggers 157, 162
PICK model x, 73, 74–85; contiguity 79–82; involvement 76–79; "kick-outs" 82–84; personalization 75
podcasting 3, 6
politics: blogs 36–37, 109, 112, 114–118, 158, 161; citizenship 17–19; global 20; Hurricane Katrina 172–173; individual 32–33; new forms of civic engagement 29; online media 35–36; Riesman's work 33–34; simplification of complex issues 31; social media news aggregators 129, 136–137, 142; YouTube 37–39; *see also* democracy
"pop-up" leisure facilities 15
Poster, Mark 21
post-industrial society 23, 30, 31, 32
postmodernity 22, 31, 58
power: blogs 191; dual city 191; networks of 160, 161, 190; news media 52; social media news aggregators 141
power law dynamics 126–127, 128–129, 131–134, 140
Prakash, Neil 153–154, 160
private sphere: blogs 37, 157, 193; civic engagement ix, 32, 39–40
product differentiation 96–97
profit 45, 57, 59, 60, 98; *see also* commercialization
public opinion 30, 31, 110
public relations 31, 56
public service 59
public sphere 30–32, 39–40; blogs 37, 117, 157, 161, 193; cyberbalkanization 125; digital divide 192
Putnam, Robert 19, 31

Quinn, G. 57

race 173, 194
Rafaeli, S. 100

Rangel, Charles 6
reciprocity 35
Reddit x, 124, 127–128, 130–139,
    140–141
Reese, S.D. 127
reference group perspective 46–47
relational organizations 49, 53, 56, 57,
    59, 60
reporting 9–10
Reynolds, Glen 162
Rheingold, H. 152–153
Riesman, D. 33–34, 36, 39
Riverbend 159
Robinson, Sue xi, xii, 166–188
Rolston, Bruce 156
Rosen, Jay 53, 153, 159
Rosenstiel, Tom 16
Rowan, Brian 49, 50, 51, 54
Royal, C. 102
RSS 103, 124
Rushkoff, D. 156
Rutigliano, Lou xi, xii, 189–205
Ryan, J. 47
Ryfe, D. 52

Sade-Beck, L. 169, 181
Said, Edward 23
Salam Pax 156, 158
satire 38
Scammell, Margaret 25, 36
Schiller, Vivian 95
Schneider, S.M. 169
schools 49–50
Schudson, Michael: citizenship 17;
    collective memory 168; democracy
    vii, viii, xii, 32; journalists 52; media
    power 153; monitorial citizen 18, 25,
    29, 34
Schuilenburg, Marc 18
Schwartz, Jonathan 5
scientific literacy 71
Scott, W.R. 49–50, 53
Second Life 3, 16
Seesmic 8
"self, project of the" 157, 158
Sennett, R. 39
September 11th 2001 terrorist attacks
    161, 166, 167, 169, 175
SFist 3
Shaw, D.L. 102
Shirky, Clay 8, 126
Shoemaker, P.J. 127
Shoesmith, B. 24

signature matrix 170, 171–172
Silverstone, Roger 18
Singer, J.B. 191
situational interest 76–77, 81
situational understanding 73–74, 78,
    81–82
Slack, David 154–155
Slashdot 3
Smolkin, Rachel 56
Snow, R.P. 51
social influence theory 141
social institutions 19, 22, 23
social media x–xi, 123–147; changing
    stories 129–130, 138–139, 142; echo
    chamber effect 125–126; gatekeeping
    127–128, 140, 141; participatory
    democracy 125; power law dynamics
    126–127, 128–129, 131–134, 140;
    source authority 129, 134–136, 141;
    themes 129, 136–137, 142
social networks 16, 79, 103, 123–124,
    126–127
SoCo Cargo Experiment 15, 17
"soft" news 96
stability ix, 45
stasis ix, 56, 60, 61
Stelter, Brian 159
Stoli Hotel 15
Stone, Lisa 8
storytelling xi, 26
structure ix, 60, 191
Stumble Upon 124
Sumpter, R. 56–57
Sun Microsystems 5, 126
Sundar, S.S. 75, 77
Sunstein, C. 125

tabloidization viii, 97–98
Taiwan 97–98
Talking Points Memo 4
Tankard, J.J.W. 102
teachers 11
technology: civic engagement 34–36;
    democratizing 5; media-creation tools
    1; new forms of civic engagement 29;
    online viii; participatory journalism
    7; resistance to 45; see also Internet
technology news 136–137, 142
television: audience ratings 56; decline
    in audiences 92; impact on civic
    involvement 31; mimicry 55;
    reference groups 47; relational
    organizations 53

text-based understanding 74
Thompson, John 18
Thompson, T.A. 57
thoroughness 10
Tichenor, P.J. 52
TimesSelect 95–96
Tocqueville, Alexis de vii
Tolson, A. 158
translocalism 20
transparency 10, 56
"transumerism" 15, 17
Trench, B. 57
Tunisia 7
Twitter 8, 79, 84

uncertainty 17, 22, 25, 26, 55, 60
UnCut Video 124
Urry, J. 190
user-generated content 71, 125;
    digital divide 193; Gannett
    newspaper chain 192; information
    surplus 93; *see also* blogs; citizen
    journalism
uses and gratification paradigm 100–101

Veblen, Thorstein 48
Venue VBOX 15
Virilio, P. 155
Vu, S. 173

Warnick, B. 169
Wartella, E.A. 47
Washington Post 6, 135, 141
Waterman, D. 102
Weaver, D.H. 50, 53–54
Web 2.0: consumer sovereignty 99;
    information surplus 93, 94;
    interactivity 78; social media 123,
    124
Webber, Jonathan 168
Weber, Max 48, 60
weblogs *see* blogs
Webster, F. 160
Wellman, Barry 18
"Where is Raed?" (blog) 158
Whitney, D.C. 47
Wikipedia 3
Wildman, S.S. 101
Wilhoit, G.C. 50
Williams, Raymond 152
World of Warcraft 3
World Wide Web *see* Internet

Yahoo! 135
Yan Wenbo 151–152
Yaros, Ron x, 71–90
Yelp 195
young people 10, 71, 84, 92, 96, 193
YouTube 3, 4, 29, 37–39, 93, 124, 135

25